The Ex-Offender's Job Hunting Guide

10 Steps to a *New* Life in the Work World

Ron and Caryl Krannich, Ph.Ds

Foreword by Joyce Lain Kennedy

IMPACT PUBLICATIONS
Manassas Park, VA

ISBN: 1-57023-236-9

Library of Congress: 2005923860

Publisher: For information on Impact Publications, including current and forthcoming publications, authors, press kits, online bookstore, and submission requirements, visit the left navigation bar on the front page of our main company website: www.impactpublica tions.com.

Publicity/Rights: For information on publicity, author interviews, and subsidiary rights, contact the Media Relations Department: Tel. 703-361-7300, Fax 703-335-9486, or email: info@impactpublications.com.

Sales/Distribution: All bookstore sales are handled through Impact's trade distributor: National Book Network, 15200 NBN Way, Blue Ridge Summit, PA 17214, Tel. 1-800-462-6420. All special sales and distribution inquiries should be directed to the publisher: Sales Department, IMPACT PUBLICATIONS, 9104 Manassas Drive, Suite N, Manassas Park, VA 20111-5211, Tel. 703-361-7300, Fax 703-335-9486, or e-mail: info@impactpub lications.com.

Contents

Foreword

Joyce Lain Kennedy

AT FIRST GLANCE, SOME MAY ASSUME this book is another in a long list of job search guides. I am not one of them.

To my eye, *The Ex-Offender's Job Hunting Guide* holds the potential of becoming one of the decade's most significant books. Ace authors Ron and Caryl Krannich introduce in these pages authentic and painstakingly researched answers to a huge question that's hard to get helping-hands around:

Exactly what must ex-offenders do to avoid being shut out of life-changing employment?

Good question. As a nation, we are locking up more people for longer periods than at any time in our history. A quarter-century ago we had a total prison population of 500,000. That number has quadrupled to more than 2 million men and women behind bars today. Add to these numbers another 5 million on parole or probation.

Talk about consequences to society – the lockup and monitoring tab runs billions of dollars, which means cuts in other essential needs like education and health care.

Despite the calamitous correctional costs, the prison system isn't adequately rehabilitating offenders who have paid their debt to society and who now need to take care of themselves on the outside. The stats are jaw-dropping:

Nearly 700,000 men and women are released each year from prisons, jails, and detention centers. But within three years, seven out of 10 ex-offenders are returned to prison.

Many factors – from drugs and indolence, to education and skills – are responsible for the cycle of reincarceration plaguing us. But I think that most observers would agree that a root cause of the dysfunctional prison system is joblessness.

Ex-offenders must rock-climb higher cliffs to reach rewards of good employment than do seekers who are free of criminal records. Moreover, most ex-offenders don't have a clue about how to find decent jobs that give them good reasons to stay clean on the outside, supporting themselves, paying taxes, raising families, and contributing to the economy.

I speak from personal knowledge about ex-inmates being babes in the job woods. Over the years I've heard from countless offenders and ex-offenders, as well as their mothers, wives, and other loved ones:

How can I (or my loved one) start a new life with a good job with a future? How do I find people who will consider hiring me? How do I explain my background? Do I have to admit I've been in prison? Can you recommend groups that help ex-offenders? Can you recommend books about the job search?

I've always wished that I had better resources to recommend to those soulful questioners. Not that other authors haven't addressed ex-offender employment issues. Some have done admirable work. But most focus on the need to clean up bad attitudes and only incidentally explain the infrastructure and finer points of smart job search.

The latter body of knowledge is where Ron and Caryl Krannich shine. With solid credentials as two of the nation's top employment experts, they use these pages to pair a powerful grasp of effective job search principles with the special needs of released felons.

Far from being "just another job search manual," *The Ex-Offender's Job Hunting Guide* is a force for good in changing lives and conserving public resources.

To ex-offenders, here is a blueprint for The Good Life.

Joyce Lain Kennedy is a syndicated careers columnist whose work appears in newspapers and on websites across the country.

1

Getting a New and Improved Life

S O YOU'VE PAID YOUR DEBT to society. Now it's time to focus on your future and move ahead with your life. Just how forgiving is society of your background? How well will family members, friends, and strangers accept you? Are you mentally prepared for what may come next, especially rejections from prospective employers because of your background? Will your criminal record accompany you throughout your life? Who will you initially hang out with? Will they help or hinder your re-entry? Are you essentially on your own, or will you seek assistance from individuals and community groups that are familiar with the challenges facing someone with your background? Will you become a story of successful re-entry, or will you return to prison within the coming months?

What comes next as you enter the free world and start to shape the next stage of your life? How do you plan to "make it" on the outside? Have you had an attitude, motivation, and self-esteem check-up recently? Do you have goals and dreams? How realistic are you about your future? Do you know what you do well and enjoy doing? Can you locate employers who need your skills and share your goals? Will you be truthful when asked if you've ever been convicted of a crime? How will you explain your criminal record? Whom will you approach for assistance? How will you go about landing a decent job? Will you keep that new job and turn it into a long-term and rewarding career that could well change your life and the lives of those around you?

One final question for the weeks and months ahead: Do you have the necessary attitudes, skills, abilities, and values to land a good job that could turn your life around?

There's No Place to Hide These Days

These and many other questions are central to the following pages. As you will quickly discover, ex-offenders and others with red flags in their backgrounds have no place to hide these days. Indeed, in today's increasingly high-tech and litigious society, more and more employers conduct thorough background checks, contact references, and administer a variety of revealing aptitude, psychological, and polygraph tests. If you have a felony conviction, you are most likely marked for life. That conviction will follow you everywhere, from looking for a job and establishing credit to getting a visa to enter other countries. If you think you can make that conviction disappear, except in your mind, forget it. Therefore, it's best that you be prepared to explain your conviction in the most positive, yet honest, way possible. That involves dealing with potential objections to your background and demonstrating that you are a **person of value** to others. To do otherwise is to engage in wishful thinking – that you try to can escape your background as you create a whole new you.

A Sometimes Unforgiving World

You'll also discover a very forgiving world for those who demonstrate sincere efforts to change their lives for the better.

Re-entry is all about picking yourself up and running in the right direction. Despite sincere efforts to change their lives, ex-offenders often face an unforgiving world. Let's face it: ex-offenders are not welcome in many places. If you've done the crime and feel you've completed your time, think again. You are viewed by many people as a risky person to do business with. Depending on your crime, many people may not want you as a neighbor, employee, or customer. Sex offenders, for example, are often viewed as the lowest of criminals. Just start filling out a job application when you encounter that red flag question on the first page –

Have you ever been convicted of a crime? If yes, give details.

How will you answer that potentially job-stopper question? Will you tell the truth, the whole truth, or let this incriminating question pass you by with a lie? Minor vehicular, drug, and petty larceny convictions, for example, are more acceptable to the community, and ostensibly more rehabilitative, than violent assault, homicide, and sex offenses. Indeed, many past offenders continue to pay for their earlier indiscretions, as individuals and institutions discriminate against them in the housing, financial, and job markets. You may, for example, have difficulty renting an apartment or getting a loan to purchase a home, establishing credit, opening a checking account, applying for a credit card, and finding a good paying and secure job. In addition, depending on your crime, you may be restricted from entering certain professions, traveling outside the United States, and voting in elections. At the same time, you may also discover a very forgiving world for those who demonstrate sincere efforts to change their lives for the better. You'll want to get to know these people better as you re-enter and progress in the free world.

Psychological Challenges and Freedom

The psychological adjustments of post-release can be especially challenging. Few people really understand what you've gone through and the problems you now face. Nor should you expect them to empathize and lend you a helping hand. Your future lies in your own hands, assisted by a set of supportive relationships you develop in the coming weeks and months. Indeed, over the last several months or years you've been in a controlled environment where survival and acceptance meant following the rules and taking orders rather than expressing your independence and initiative. You lost your independence, and many of your friends and family may have abandoned you. Worst of all, you may have lost one of your most valuable inner assets – your self-esteem. Experiencing failure, feeling abandoned, and lacking meaningful work, you may become angry, confused, and negative. You find it difficult to get motivated, keep focused, and remain positive about your future and your relationships.

Focus on Your Future

But that's the past, and it will soon be in the distance as you move ahead in your life. It's now time to seriously focus on your future as you prepare for the many psychological challenges as well as the practical day-to-day aspects of living a new and more productive life. While you will always carry some baggage (your past conviction and incarceration) that can at times weigh you down, you **must** focus on the future with renewed optimism and a "can do" attitude that reflects independence, initiative, and entrepreneurship. Most important of all, you will need to build a new set of relationships and skills that will result in job and career success.

Experience Job Search Success

One of the best ways to deal with the challenges of post-release is to **experience success**. You can do this by becoming a successful job seeker who lands a good job that will give you a renewed sense of self-esteem and help you rebuild your life financially and socially. Finding such a job may not be easy, but the rewards of doing so are immeasurable. In fact, you should focus laser-like on finding a good job. Like many other job seekers, you'll experience many rejections. But if you persist with a positive attitude, supportive relationships, and a resume and/or application that commands attention, you should be able to land job interviews that lead to a decent job you both do well and enjoy doing. But without the proper job search skills and information for navigating today's job market, you may become too disheartened and disillusioned with your failure to find a good job as you encounter many rejections.

That's our mission throughout this book – to help you land a decent job that can well change your life for the better. Without such a job, you may quickly become another "recidivism statistic" – 70 percent of ex-offenders return to jails and prisons within three years of release. Failing to find rewarding employment, they tend to revert to old relationships and predictable patterns of behavior that lead them back to the same controlling institutions. That's not a life – that's a sentence. You should be free to succeed in an increasingly forgiving, accepting, and entrepreneurial world that rewards individuals who demonstrate talent, hard work, and perseverance.

10 Steps to a New Life in the Work World

This is not a book about the whole re-entry process. Rather, the following pages focus on proven strategies for finding a job. But not for just finding any job. Our goal is to help you connect with the **right job** – one that you do well and enjoy doing. Such a job should relate to your unique talents, values, and goals.

While your first job out may not pay well, it should give you an opportunity to prove yourself and thus establish a good employment record of performance. It should lead to other jobs that pay better and have a brighter future. The important thing is to land that first job out from which you can launch a satisfying career. If you closely follow our 10 steps to job search success, you should be successful in finding a good job and starting a new and productive worklife. Since this book includes strategies that you can use over and over again as you change jobs and careers, you'll want to keep it for future reference after you land your first job.

The figure on page 5 illustrates our 10 steps to job search success. The first step, **Examine and Change Your Attitudes**, is found in Chapter 3. The final step, **Negotiate Salary and Benefits Like a Pro**, is detailed in Chapter 12. Chapter 2 sets the stage for the 10 steps by examining 20 key myths and realities as well as 22 key principles for success. The final chapter, "Starting Right, Surviving, and Advancing Your Career," puts the whole job search within the context of the actual job – what you need to do to be successful on the job as well as to advance your career.

We wish you well as your embark on this next phase in your life. Like many other people in transition, you face a new world with dreams and a renewed sense of purpose. If you follow our advice, we're confident you'll eventually achieve your dreams as well as avoid many disappointments along the way. As we note throughout this book, **you have within you the power to change your life**. With the help of this book and your network of supporters, you can unleash that power in today's job market. Just be sure you take the necessary **actions** to make your dreams come true!

10 Steps to Job Search Success

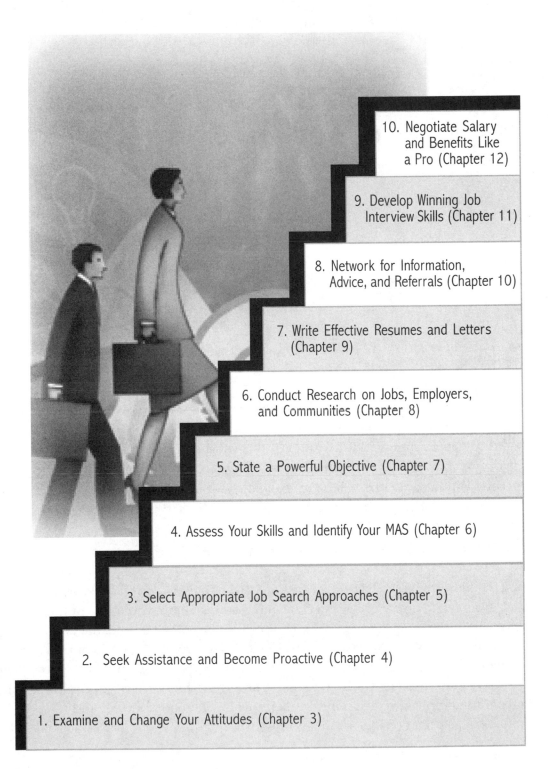

10. Negotiate Salary and Benefits Like a Pro (Chapter 12)

9. Develop Winning Job Interview Skills (Chapter 11)

8. Network for Information, Advice, and Referrals (Chapter 10)

7. Write Effective Resumes and Letters (Chapter 9)

6. Conduct Research on Jobs, Employers, and Communities (Chapter 8)

5. State a Powerful Objective (Chapter 7)

4. Assess Your Skills and Identify Your MAS (Chapter 6)

3. Select Appropriate Job Search Approaches (Chapter 5)

2. Seek Assistance and Become Proactive (Chapter 4)

1. Examine and Change Your Attitudes (Chapter 3)

2

Be Truthful, Realistic, and Focused on Shaping Your Future

BEFORE YOU TAKE YOUR FIRST STEP on the road to re-entry, you must be truthful, realistic, and focused on shaping your future. The road is all about taking **responsibility** for your past, present, and future. The **truth** is that you have a record. The **reality** is that your record will most likely affect your employability to some degree. If you are a convicted felon, it will literally follow you throughout your worklife. However, this truth and reality should not become a major impediment to your future if you follow our 10-step approach to job search success. While employers will be concerned about your past record, they are more concerned about your **future** truthfulness, character, and value in their workplace!

Employers Want to Hire Your Future

Ex-offenders are often their own worst enemies. Many live in the past by replaying their troubled lives, harboring anger, blaming others, finding excuses, conning themselves and others, lacking goals, being unwilling to follow a schedule, and fearing employers won't hire an ex-con. Other ex-offenders are psychologically troubled by the whole incarceration experience and thus may require some form of therapy; they may have low self-esteem, exhibit signs of learning disabilities, lack good information, have difficulty making decisions on their own, make poor choices, and often have unrealistic expectations about themselves, others, and the job market.

Forget about your criminal record for a moment and think of yourself as being like any other job seeker. In many respects, you are similar to other candidates employers encounter – someone with the potential to do the job. Employers want to hire your future rather than your past. Focusing on your attitudes and behavior, they look at your past as an indication of your future potential to be productive in their company. They look for **patterns of behavior**, especially your strengths or achievements – those things that are right rather than wrong about you – that will transfer to their workplace. While they look for weaknesses, possible red flag behaviors (see our extensive discussion of red flags in *Job Interview Tips for People With Not-So-Hot Backgrounds*, Impact Publications, 2004), and evidence that you have changed your attitudes and behaviors, they primarily want to know what you do well and enjoy doing. Above all, they are looking for competent individuals who are enthusiastic and energetic. How you present your past in relation to your future with the employer will largely determine how successful you will be in landing a job.

Take Responsibility and Make Changes

Let's examine several myths and realities as well as numerous success principles for better understanding how this first step affects the remaining nine steps of a successful job search for ex-offenders. As we do this, we place the whole job search within the larger context of special re-entry and transition issues affecting ex-offenders. Taking responsibility for yourself and making the necessary changes that will create new outcomes for you and those around you is essential. If you do nothing differently than you have done in the past, don't expect things will change for you. You'll merely repeat the same patterns that will produce

> *Nothing positive is going to happen unless you make it happen by changing your attitudes and behaviors. You have within you the power to shape your future.*

similar results. The truth is that nothing positive is going to happen unless you **make** it happen by **changing** your attitudes and patterns of behaviors. You have within you the **power** to shape your future. But first you need to learn how to harness that power by following several proven principles of success.

20 Myths and Realities to Build Effectiveness

You should be able to relate to most of the following myths and realities. The myths can stall your effective re-entry into the workplace as well as prevent you from making smart decisions and taking effective action. The realities clarify what you should and can do to become more effective in today's job market.

Your Background and Employers

MYTH #1:   **Employers don't want to hire people with a criminal background.**

REALITY: It depends on the particular employer, the ex-offender, and position. Let's deal with some hard facts. While employers ostensibly cannot discriminate against individuals solely on the basis of their criminal record (implicit in Title VII of the Civil Rights Act and protected by the Equal Employment Opportunity Commission, www.eeoc.gov), they can refuse to hire if they can show that your background will negatively affect their workplace and business. Also, several federal laws specify certain occupations that are off limits or restricted for individuals with various types of criminal convictions, and certain jobs require mandatory criminal background checks for public safety purposes:

- Financial institutions insured by the Federal Deposit Insurance Corporation (if your conviction involved dishonesty, breach of trust, or money laundering).

- Insurance industry (for certain classes of felons).

- High-level positions in unions and companies managing employee benefit plans (barred for 13 years).

- Health care services that receive Medicare and Medicaid payments and the pharmaceutical industry (for certain types of crimes).

- Child care services (requires criminal history background checks for positions involving child care).

- Prisoner transportation services (requires criminal history background checks)

- Aviation (since 2001 many positions with airlines and airports require background checks to further ensure public safety)

- Law enforcement and other criminal justice positions (prohibited from entering most such jobs).

State and local governments may include additional restrictions on certain occupations, especially any positions that deal with public safety and welfare, such as driving a bus or taxi. Most states also prohibit ex-offenders from acquiring certain professional licenses and vocational certifications. You need to inquire about these restrictions before looking for a job or acquiring training and certification. Many government agencies have unwritten rules not to hire ex-offenders, even though they are not supposed to discriminate.

If you challenge an employer for discriminating against you because of your criminal record, they can successfully argue that your background will have an adverse effect on their workplace and business – you are untrustworthy and a potential risk to other employees and the public. Surveys show that many employers simply don't want to take the risk of hiring ex-offenders, especially those convicted of sex or violent crimes. The reluctance to hire ex-offenders in part may be due to the fear of legal

> *You are well advised to seek out jobs, employers, and temporary employment agencies that are receptive to ex-offenders.*

liabilities if such a hire posed a danger to co-workers or the public. Indeed, studies show that employers have lost 72 percent of negligent hiring cases involving ex-offenders, which on average cost them $1.6 million to settle per case (Mary Connerly, Richard Arvey, and Charles Bernardy, "Criminal Background Checks for Prospective and Current Employees, *Public Personnel Management*, 2001, page 20). Also, over 95 percent of employers conduct background checks as part of their routine screening process. Understandably, given the potential for expensive lawsuits and judgments against employers, ex-offenders are viewed by many employers as more trouble than they are worth, rather than more worth than they are trouble.

On the other hand, many employers who hire individuals for unskilled, low-wage, entry-level, temporary, and high-turnover positions ask few background questions. Many are dead-end jobs with no future. These are the types of positions ex-offenders quickly find and involve minimal disclosure of their backgrounds. Finding a job becomes more problematic as ex-offenders move toward more skilled and higher-wage positions and those involving greater responsibilities. Such positions usually require background checks and disclosure of a criminal record.

Employers differ in how they view and hire ex-offenders. Many employers are open to hiring low-level drug offenders who seem to pose few workplace problems. Other employers have no problem hiring ex-offenders who appear to have changed their lives as well as demonstrate the right attitudes and skills for doing the job. In fact, many employers in the construction, manufacturing, and hospitality trades regularly hire ex-offenders for low-wage and blue-collar jobs. Other employers attend job fairs organized for hiring ex-offenders. Several temporary employment agencies, such as Labor Finders, regularly work with ex-offenders in placing them in similar types of temporary and permanent jobs. Employers in the retail and service sectors, especially with jobs that require a great deal of customer contact, are least likely to hire ex-offenders.

Not surprisingly, you are well advised to seek out jobs, employers, and temporary employment agencies that are especially receptive to individuals with criminal backgrounds. While they may not offer the best jobs, at least they give you an opportunity to acquire **experience** and thus start building a new employment record. This is especially important for young ex-offenders who never established a stable and coherent work history prior to their incarceration. In the long run, experience does count in the job market. It will help you move to other jobs that pay more and involve greater responsibilities.

At the same time, you need to change certain aspects of your background that are within your power to change. Hopefully, you are among the 50 percent who took part in educational and vocational training programs while you were incarcerated. If, for example, you lack a high school diploma or equivalent (GED), don't expect to attract many employers regardless of your criminal history. In fact, 95 percent of all low-skilled jobs today require a high school diploma or some work experience. Unfortunately, nearly 40 percent of ex-offenders lack a high school diploma and relevant work experience. If you fall into this disadvantaged group, it's time you did something about it. Get smart by seeing your probation or parole officer (P.O.) as well as various community groups that can assist ex-offenders with education, training, apprenticeships, and job placement. Low-skilled jobs that pay well, which in the past were primarily found in manufacturing and through unions, are quickly disappearing and moving overseas where they become low-paying jobs.

It's safe to assume that most employers want to hire individuals who can best do the job regardless of their backgrounds. Be concerned about your past, but focus on your future by being prepared to communicate the things you have changed in your life and what it is you can do for the employer. You can do this most effectively by following our advice in Chapters 6 and 7 on assessing skills and setting goals.

MYTH #2:   **I'll have to lie about my background in order to get a good job.**

REALITY: The **truth** will set you free and help you shape a positive and productive future. When you feel down, remember this important principle of life: **This, too, will pass**. Give yourself time and your best effort. Your past will quickly pass if you are truthful. Commit yourself to the truth – no more lies, cover-ups, or excuses to yourself or to others. If you can't tell the truth, then don't expect to get a job or keep a job for very long. This is especially true for jobs, employers, and companies with a future – those offering higher wages and greater responsibilities that lead to a long-term career. Keep in mind this fact of employment life: More and more employers are suspicious of job seekers who **lie** about their backgrounds. As a result, they increasingly conduct background and reference checks, administer a variety of revealing tests (drug, aptitude, psychological, polygraph), and subject candidates to multiple interviews to determine the truthfulness and appropriate fit of candidates.

> _This, too, will pass. The truth will set you free and help you shape a positive and productive future._

If you think you can hide your record from employers, think again. You're a person with both a paper and electronic trail. Once you get your documents – birth certificate, driver's license, Social Security number, or state ID – you're real easy to find in systems employers regularly access when doing background checks. In today's increasingly high-tech, database-driven, and security-conscious society, there's no place to hide (see _No Place to Hide_, Robert O'Harrow, Jr., Free Press, 2005). Employers can easily and inexpensively access your employment, criminal, and credit records through a variety of electronic databases they routinely consult when doing background checks. And if by chance you fool an employer about your background, chances are your criminal record will eventually catch up with you on the job. Your P.O. may check on you by calling your employer, an old prison buddy may unexpectedly show up, or someone you secretly told about your record may talk too much. Word gets around. When you come up for a promotion or make a job change involving a background check, your criminal record will probably surface. When it does, your lie will be exposed and you'll be fired or passed over. Everything you worked for now changes for the worse because of your **failure to disclose**.

Rather than try to live a lie, **tell the truth in a positive way** – that you were incarcerated but changed your life by participating in educational, vocational, substance abuse, or anger control programs. Much of our society forgives those who make sincere efforts to change their lives and tell the truth. When you tell the truth, you're not expected to go into all the details, but at least tell the truth that matters most to employers – that you're not a risky hire.

We all at times stumble and fall. It's how we pick ourselves up and move on with our lives that really counts. Americans especially admire people who overcome adversity. We strongly believe in come-backs, fresh starts, and second acts – that you can be anything you want to be if only you will work hard at being the person you want to be.

MYTH #3: I'll be able to quickly find a job and start a new life.

REALITY: Chances are your transition to the free world will not be quick and easy or trouble-free. Expect to encounter many land mines along the way that may discourage you as well as tempt you to make some bad choices.

In today's job market, the average job seeker takes from three to six months to find a job and experiences many psychological ups and downs as he or she encounters numerous **rejections** on the road to finding a job. You, too, will experience many rejections, which may or may not have anything to do with your criminal record.

In fact, studies consistently show that ex-offenders have great difficulty in finding employment. Those who quickly (within 30 days of release) find a job are usually hired by former employers or received help from family and friends with their job search. Few ex-offenders find full-time employment on their own. As a result, many remain unemployed or move into "casual" jobs or illegal activities. These studies also confirm what we know about job-finding approaches of the general population – the most effective approach involves networking with family, friends, and former employers. Without a **support network**, finding a job may take a long time. We'll address this critical issue in Chapter 4 on support groups and in Chapter 10 on networking.

Whatever you do, don't confuse your experiences with those of people without your background. Indeed, **rejections** are part of the job hunting process for people with or without a criminal record. How you handle those rejections may determine how long you continue job hunting. If you are like many other job seekers who take rejections personally, your enthusiasm and motivation to continue looking for a job will be negatively affected. As a result, you may prematurely stop looking for a job because of your fear of getting more rejections.

At the same time, the job hunting situation of many ex-offenders is very different from that of the average job seeker:

- Ex-offenders may re-enter communities with limited resources for becoming successful – little money, few possessions, no housing or transportation, and often heavily indebted because of child support, victim restitution, and court claims.

- Ex-offenders face several decisions, challenges, and psychological adjustments relating to community, family, friends, housing, transportation, clothing, health, and finances that affect their attitude toward conducting an effective job search.

- Ex-offenders usually return to the same dysfunctional communities and circles of associates that were in part responsible for their incarceration. These communities often have high rates of unemployment and crime. Unsuccessful in finding meaningful employment in these communities, many ex-offenders soon repeat their same patterns of behavior and become another crime statistic, joining 70 percent of ex-offenders who re-enter the criminal justice system within three years.

One of the major reasons most ex-offenders have difficulty finding employment is because they are in the wrong place at the wrong time. Since most ex-offenders relocate into communities with limited employment opportunities, high crime rates, and poverty – places with lots of illegal temptations for the unemployed – they often feel they have nowhere to go but back into the criminal life.

> *Change your life by first changing your community. Find individuals who will lift you up rather than drag you down.*

Here's one of the best tips for re-entry: Change your life by first changing your community; relocate to a place of hope rather than to one of despair; and associate with winners rather than losers. Find individuals in your community who will **lift you up** rather than drag you down. If you do this, you'll be well on your way to winning the re-entry game. Chapter 8 includes tips on choosing communities of hope.

The irony is that you need to find a job faster than the average job seeker, but your background will make it more difficult for you to find a job quickly. Accordingly, this whole process may be challenging and it will take time. The good news, as we outline in Chapter 4, is that several government programs, churches, unions, and community-based nonprofit organizations provide much needed assistance to ex-offenders in dealing with the important re-entry issues, such as housing, health, education, and employment. Your P.O. also can provide assistance. These **support groups** and individuals offer many helping hands to those who are serious about changing their lives for the better. Reach out to them for help as early as possible in your transition. Above all, heed the wise words of ex-offender and author/trainer Ned Rollo in *Man, I Need a Job* (Open Inc., 2004, page 10):

> No matter how crazy things may get, don't do anything stupid that would place you in danger of losing your freedom or chances for a rewarding future. And above all, don't give up!

With some help from well-meaning groups and a positive attitude and a great deal of persistence on your part, you should be able to make a successful transition. You **will** find a job that will help you rebuild your life.

Attitude and Responsibility

MYTH #4: **It's not my fault that I'm in this situation – I've had lots of bad luck and lousy relationships.**

REALITY: The first step to changing your life is to admit responsibility for your own situation. Life doesn't just happen or fall out of the sky. You make **choices** that have consequences. Some people make lots of bad choices that result in difficult situations. Let's look at some of your choices and their consequences. What five bad and five good choices have you made during the past 10 years?

Bad Choices	Consequences
_____	_____
_____	_____
_____	_____
_____	_____
_____	_____

Good Choices	**Consequences**
_____	_____
_____	_____
_____	_____
_____	_____
_____	_____

Who was responsible for each of the bad and good choices?

Once you take responsibility for your choices, you can begin discarding the baggage that continues to weigh you down. Since you have the power within you to change your life, you need to become better acquainted with your ability to create your future. It won't be easy, but nothing worthwhile is ever easy. You have to work at it day after day until your new attitudes and actions become positive and productive behaviors.

Maybe you've had bad luck, but so have many other successful people, and you're not dead yet. Start by asking yourself these questions:

- Do you have dreams that motivate you to do your very best?

- Do you run with winners or hang around losers?

- What have you done to change your luck?

- Do you have goals and a detailed plan of action for taking charge of your life?

- How many people have you truthfully told your story to and asked for their advice on how you can change your life?

- When tomorrow comes, what five things do you have on a "To Do" list that will help you get ahead?

- Will you develop a new relationship with a person who can assist you?

- Will you take advantage of education and training opportunities?

- Will you visit your local library or One-Stop Career Center to learn something new about jobs and employers?

- Will you call two or three employers to see if they have any job opportunities?

- Have you used to your best ability both pre- and post-release re-entry resources, from educational programs to your P.O.?

The point here is very simple: If you do nothing to get ahead, you'll get nothing in return. Indeed, people who don't take responsibility for themselves most likely become a victim of circumstances. You need to develop a positive and proactive attitude that constantly puts you in new places and with new people who can assist you with your re-entry.

In real estate, the three most important words are location, location, location. For ex-offenders, the three

The three most important words for ex-offenders are relationships, relationships, relationships. Your most important resource will be the new relationships you develop with successful people.

most important words are **relationships, relationships, relationships**. Your most **important resource** will be the new relationships you develop with successful people in the days, weeks, and months ahead. As we will later see in our discussion of networking in Chapter 10, one of the keys to your future success will be your ability to build, maintain, and expand your network of personal and professional relationships. As ex-offenders eventually admit, many of their past problems directly relate to the many dysfunctional relationships they developed with family members, friends, and acquaintances. It's time to take responsibility for your fate by being **proactive**. Abandon those negative relationships as you move into the next phase of your life.

MYTH #5: **Since I don't have money, a car, a job, or permanent housing, I can't do much to get ahead.**

REALITY: You'll never get ahead with such a self-defeating attitude and by making excuses. In fact, you may be the source of your problems. It's time you had a major attitude adjustment. Yes, life is unfair, but you also live in a land of seemingly unlimited opportunities for those who take initiative to succeed. Start thinking like the **immigrant** who arrives in America with nothing but the shirt on his back, a few dollars, but dreams of a better future. They pick themselves up and run.

Indeed, many immigrants come here with horrendous stories of bad luck, war, and family deaths. Many have questionable backgrounds, and most go through very difficult times. Many don't speak English the day they arrive, but they learn quickly. Our typical immigrant has nothing to lose and everything to gain through a positive attitude, hard work, drive, and persistence. *"No"* and *"can't do"* are not in his vocabulary. His attitude and approach to life is one of *"Yes," "I'll try,"* or *"I can do this."* He takes jobs no one wants but eventually ends up in a job he loves. Against what initially appears to be all odds, he succeeds beyond most people's dreams. Within a few years he has a great job or owns a thriving business, lives in a wonderful community, has a large and supportive network of relationships, and has a wonderful family with well-educated children who excel in many ways. He becomes the model of the American dream. And guess what? He did it on his own and through the many relationships he built and nurtured.

In fact, there are thousands of such success stories in America today among both old and new immigrants – Vietnamese, Korean, Chinese, Indian, Mexican, Cuban, Russian, Ghanian, Ethiopian, Nigerian, Jamaican, Italian, Irish, Japanese, and German immigrants. Many had nothing but became something. The most successful immigrant groups have networks of their own countrymen who provide support and strong family relationships. Ex-offenders in America actually have an advantage over most of those immigrants – a network of groups and numerous free resources aimed at helping ex-offenders make a positive transition. Ex-offenders' major disadvantage is **dysfunctional attitudes** that center around negative thinking, anger, and excuses.

The next time you make excuses for not being successful, think of the thousands of new immigrants today who will soon become extremely successful. If you think and behave like an immigrant – positive and proactive – you may succeed beyond your wildest dreams!

Jobs and Employers

MYTH #6:   No one will hire me!

REALITY: The truth is that lots of people may hire you. But you have to do things differently in order to connect with the right people who will hire you. You first need to understand the job market, employers, and the most effective methods for landing a job. Unfortunately, many job seekers quit looking for a job after a few frustrating weeks of receiving no responses or encountering several rejections. Making numerous mistakes in their job search, they conclude that the job market is bad and thus employers aren't hiring people with their experience and skills. This is really an excuse for not taking the necessary action to land a job. The mistakes most job seekers make relate to knowledge as well as a variety of attitudes and skills:

- Abandon dreams and lack goals
- Harbor self-defeating and bad attitudes
- Fail to do first things first
- Hang around the wrong crowds and networks
- Disregard or overlook skills and accomplishments
- Write and distribute awful resumes and letters
- Mess up the critical job interview
- Fail to develop an attractive pattern of work behavior
- Appear honest but stupid, or dishonest but smart
- Project an image of need or greed
- Conduct an outdated job search or over-rely on technology
- Be unwilling to take risks and handle rejections
- Fail to implement and follow through
- Avoid professional advice and seeking help
- Resist changing behavior and acquiring new habits of success

We examine each of these 15 mistakes most job seekers make – regardless of their backgrounds – and show how they can go on to win the job in *No One Will Hire Me! Avoid 15 Mistakes and Win the Job* (Impact Publications, 2004).

MYTH #7:   **There are no jobs in my community.**

REALITY: That may be true, but you also have the power to change your community or neighborhood and thus your environment for employability. Many ex-offenders return to the same dysfunctional neighborhoods they came from. Indeed, a recent study by the Urban Institute *(From Prison to Work*, Washington, DC, October 2004) confirms what many correctional personnel already suspect:

> Communities that receive large concentrations of released prisoners are already struggling with high rates of unemployment and poverty and a dearth of available jobs.

Other studies have found that ex-offenders disproportionately relocate to the worst neighborhoods within metropolitan areas – those that are extremely poor and have the highest unemployment and crime rates. For example, each year over 9,000 ex-offenders relocate to the city of Baltimore. Within the city, nearly 80 percent of these ex-offenders move to the very worst neighborhoods in terms of unemployment, poverty, and high crime rates. Many of these places might be best called "neighborhoods of despair" rather than neighborhoods or communities of hope. Understandably, when ex-offenders have no place to go upon release, they tend to return to their old communities where they have family, friends, and acquaintances who may be able to assist them with their initial needs – food and housing. While these individuals may become an important support network, they may not be very helpful for finding a job if they are located in communities with few if any job opportunities.

The simple fact of employment life is this: You have to go where the jobs are – in another neighborhood, suburb, city, or town. Finding a job outside your community involves conducting a long-distance job search as well as dealing with important issues, such as transportation, housing, family, terms of your release, and your P.O. If your re-entry thrusts you into a community with high unemployment and limited job opportunities, you need to seriously consider relocating to a community that has more opportunities for someone with your interests, skills, and abilities. This may initially appear difficult to do, but each week thousands of people successfully make such employment relocation decisions. Using a network of community-based organizations that provide assistance to ex-offenders (see Chapter 4), you eventually should be able to make such a move. Consider breaking out of this vicious circle by moving to a community of hope – growing communities with low unemployment and crime rates. These communities are often found outside major cities. For a list of the best places to live and work in America, visit these websites:

- **Sperling**   www.bestplaces.net
- **Fortune Magazine**   www.fortune.com
- **City Rating**   www.cityrating.com
- **Money/CNN**   http://money.cnn.com/bestplaces

MYTH #8:   **I don't have skills employers want in today's job market.**

REALITY: You may have more skills than you think you possess. Indeed, as we'll see in Chapter 6 on self-assessment, most people have over 300 skills, but they may not be aware of these skills, nor are they prepared to talk about three or four skills they regularly use. You first need to take an **inventory of your skills** in order to best present yourself to employers. The most sought-after skills in today's workplace include:

- Communication
- Analytical
- Research
- Technical competence

- Organization
- Interpersonal
- Problem-solving

Employers want more than just technical skills related to preforming a job. Most employers want to recruit individuals who are intelligent, communicate well, take initiative, and are trainable and honest. They especially look for candidates who have **strong communication skills**, which include written, oral, interpersonal, and nonverbal communication. At the same time, many employers provide on-the-job training. Depending on the position, especially in the case of entry-level jobs, employers often look for individuals who are enthusiastic, energetic, and trainable. **Your ability and willingness to learn new skills** may be more important to an employer than your current stock of ready-to-work skills. If you took advantage of educational and vocational programs while you were incarcerated, you can provide evidence of your learning skills.

The Job Search

MYTH #9: **The best way to find a job is to respond to classified ads, use employment agencies, and submit applications to personnel offices.**

REALITY: Except for certain types of organizations, such as government, these formal application procedures are not the most effective ways of finding jobs. Such approaches assume the presence of an organized, coherent, and centralized job market – but no such thing exists. The job market is highly decentralized, fragmented, and chaotic. Classified ads, employment agencies, and personnel offices tend to list low-paying yet highly competitive jobs or high-paying, highly skilled positions that are hard to fill. Most jobs are neither listed nor advertised; they are most likely discovered through word-of-mouth contacts. Your most fruitful strategy will be to conduct research and informational interviews on what career counselors call the "hidden job market." At the same time, many ex-offenders who attend job fairs find this method to be especially effective in landing a job. We address these and other effective methods in Chapter 5.

MYTH #10:   **I can't use the Internet in my job search because I don't have a computer and can't afford a monthly Internet connection fee.**

REALITY: This is another excuse that indicates a potential attitude or knowledge problem. If you don't know how to use a computer or the Internet, you can easily learn the basics within an hour or two. You also don't need to own a computer nor pay for Internet access to use the Internet. Your local public library most likely has computers with Internet connections that are free of charge to use. Library personnel may even give you some basic instruction on how to use the Internet. Your local One-Stop Career Center, which is operated by the government, also may have computers and Internet connections you can use free of charge. Be sure to contact the One-Stop Career Center nearest you, which can be found through your municipal or county government office or through this website:

www.careeronestop.org

Many nonprofit and church groups that work with ex-offenders also may permit you to use their computers. In only a few minutes you can learn how to use the Internet and e-mail. You also can set up free e-mail accounts through Hotmail, Yahoo, Google, and other websites. Many employment websites also offer free e-mail accounts for managing your online job search.

MYTH 11:   **Employers are in the driver's seat; they have the upper hand with applicants.**

REALITY: Most often no one is in the driver's seat since both the employer and the job seeker have a problem to solve. Not knowing what they want, many employers make poor hiring decisions. They frequently let applicants define their hiring needs. If you can define employers' needs as your skills, you might end up in the driver's seat!

MYTH 12:   **Employers hire the best qualified candidates. Without a great deal of experience and qualifications, I don't have a chance.**

REALITY: Employers hire people for all kinds of reasons. Most rank experience and qualifications third or fourth in their pecking order of hiring criteria. Employers seldom hire the best qualified candidate, because "qualifications" are difficult to define and measure. Employers normally seek people with the following characteristics: competent, intelligent, honest, enthusiastic, and likable. "Likability" tends to be an overall concern of employers – will you "fit in" and get along well with your superiors, co-workers, customers, or clients? Employers want **value** for their money. Therefore, you must communicate to employers that you are such a person. You must overcome employers' objections to any lack of experience or qualifications. But **never** volunteer your weaknesses. The best qualified person is the one who knows how to get the job – convinces employers that he is the **most** desirable for the job.

MYTH 13:   **It's best to use an employment firm to find a job.**

REALITY: It depends on the firm and the nature of employment you are seeking. Employment firms that specialize in your skill area may be well worth contacting. For example, many law firms use employment firms to hire paralegals rather than directly recruit such personnel themselves. Many employers now use temporary employment firms to recruit both temporary and full-time employees at several different levels, from labor and clerical to professional. Indeed, many temporary employment firms have temp-to-perm programs that link qualified candidates to employers who are looking for full-time employees. But make sure you are working with a legitimate employment firm. Such firms get paid by employers or they collect placement fees from applicants only **after** the applicant has accepted a position. Beware of firms that want up-front fees for promised job placement assistance.

MYTH 14:   **I must be aggressive in order to find a job.**

REALITY: Aggressive people tend to be offensive and obnoxious people. They also make pests of themselves. Try being purposeful, persistent, and pleasant in all job search activities. Such behavior is well received by potential employers!

MYTH 15:   **Once I apply for a job, it's best to wait to hear from an employer.**

REALITY: Waiting is not a good job search strategy. If you want action from employers, you must first take action. The key to getting a job interview and offer is follow up, follow up, follow up. You do this by making follow-up telephone calls as well as writing follow-up and thank-you letters to employers.

MYTH 16:   **I don't need a resume. I can get a job based on completing applications, using contacts, and interviewing for jobs.**

REALITY: While you may complete several applications during your job search, more and more employers for both blue- and white-collar positions want to see a resume. If you attend a job fair, you'll need to take several copies of a resume with you. While networking is one of the most effective methods for finding employment, it does not erase the need for a resume. The resume is your calling card; it provides a prospective employer with a snapshot of your background and skills. Employers often want to first see you on paper (resume) **before** meeting you in person (interview). Whether you like it or not, chances are you'll need a resume very early in your job search, especially when a contact asks you to "Send me your resume."

MYTH 17:   **A good resume is the key to getting a job.**

REALITY: While resumes play an important role in the job search process, they are often overrated. The purpose of a resume is to communicate your qualifications to employers who, in turn, invite you to job interviews. The key to getting a job is the job interview. No job interview, no job offer.

MYTH 18:   **I should include my salary expectations on my resume or in my cover letter.**

REALITY: You should **never** include your salary expectations on your resume or in a cover letter, unless specifically requested to do so. Salary should be the very **last** thing you discuss with a prospective employer. You do so only after you have had a chance to **assess the worth of the position** and **communicate your value** to the employer. This usually occurs at the end of your final job interview, just before or after being offered the job. If you prematurely raise the salary issue, you may devalue your worth.

MYTH 19:   **My resume should emphasize my work history.**

REALITY: Employers are interested in hiring your **future** rather than your past. Therefore, your resume should emphasize the skills and abilities you will bring to the job as well as your interests and goals. Let prospective employers know what you are likely to do for them **in the future**. When you present your work history, do so in terms of your major skills and accomplishments.

MYTH 20: **It's not necessary to write letters to employers – just send them a resume or complete an application.**

REALITY: You should be prepared to write several types of job search letters – cover, approach, resume, thank-you, follow-up, and acceptance. In addition to communicating your level of literacy, these job search letters enable you to express important values sought after by employers – your tactfulness, thoughtfulness, enthusiasm, likability, and follow-up ability. Sending a resume without a cover letter devalues your resume and application.

22 Key Principles for Success

Why are some people more successful than others? Many people frequently ask and answer this question. Indeed, many motivational speakers, success seminar gurus, and authors have made a career of preaching positive thinking and principles of success. Some take a religious- or faith-based perspective on this question:

The Purpose-Driven Life (Rick Warren)
How to Find Your Mission in Life (Richard Nelson Bolles)
The Path (Laurie Beth Jones)
Don't Throw Away Tomorrow (Dr. Robert H. Schuller)
The Power of Positive Thinking (Dr. Norman Vincent Peale)
Your Best Life Now (Joel Osteen)

Others use a non-religious approach that primarily emphasizes the power of positive thinking and incorporates many sales-related analogies:

The Success Principles (Jack Canfield)
How to Get What You Really, Really, Really, Really Want (Wayne Dyer)
Success Through a Positive Mental Attitude (Napoleon Hill and
     W. Clement Stone)
Think and Grow Rich (Napoleon Hill)
Unlimited Power (Anthony Robbins)
Create Your Own Future (Brian Tracy)
Maximum Achievement (Brian Tracy)
The Magic of Thinking Big (David Schwartz)
The 7 Habits of Highly Effective People (Stephen R. Covey)
The 8th Habit (Stephen R. Covey)
How to Win Friends and Influence People (Dale Carnegie)
How to Get What You Want (Zig Ziglar)
Secrets of Success (Og Mandino)

If you need to re-examine your attitudes and motivations, we strongly recommend reading a few of these books, which are available in many libraries or through Impact Publications (www.impacpublications.com). Focusing on faith, attitudes, motivations, and behaviors, they may well change your life or at least have a significant impact on the way you approach each day of your life.

Some of the general success principles apply to people engaged in finding employment and to ex-offenders in transition. Indeed, over the years we have worked with thousands of individuals in conducting a job search as they transition from one stage of life to another. We've learned that job search success is determined by more than just carrying out a good plan. We know success is not determined primarily by intelligence, time management, positive thinking, or luck. Based upon experience, theory, research, and common sense, we believe you will achieve job search success by following most of these 22 principles:

1. **You should work hard at finding a job:** Make this a daily endeavor, challenge yourself, and involve your family. Focus on specifics such as how many phone calls you will make each day to uncover job leads and schedule interviews.

2. **You should not be discouraged by setbacks:** You are playing the odds, so expect disappointments along the way and handle them in stride. You will get many "no's" before finding the one "yes" which is right for you.

3. **You should be patient and persevere:** Expect several weeks or even months of hard work before you connect with the job that's right for you. While you may need to take a temporary job to make ends meet, don't abandon your goal to find a job you do well and enjoy doing.

4. **You should be honest with yourself and others:** Honesty is always the best policy. But don't be naive and stupid by confessing your negatives and shortcomings to others.

5. **You should develop a positive attitude toward yourself:** Nobody wants to employ guilt-ridden people with inferiority complexes and low self-esteem. Focus on your positive characteristics.

6. **You should associate with positive and successful people:** Finding a job largely depends on how well you relate to others. Avoid associating with negative and depressing people who complain and have a "you-can't-do-it" attitude. Run with winners who have a positive "can-do" outlook on life.

7. **You should set goals:** You should have a clear idea of what you want and where you are going. Without these, you will present a confusing and indecisive image to others. Clear goals direct your job search into productive channels. Setting high goals will help make you work hard in getting what you want. Challenge yourself to be your very best.

8. **You should plan:** Convert your goals into action steps that are organized as short, intermediate, and long-range plans. Then make sure you **implement** those plans on a daily basis. Planning without implementation is a waste of time and indicates a serious lack of motivation.

9. **You should get organized:** Translate your plans into activities, targets, names, addresses, telephone numbers, and materials. Develop an efficient and effective filing system and use a large calendar to set time targets, record appointments, and compile useful information.

10. **You should be a good communicator:** Take stock of your oral, written, and nonverbal communication skills. How well do you communicate? Since most aspects of your job search involve communicating with others, and communication skills are one of the most sought-after skills, always present yourself well both verbally and nonverbally. If you have bad grammar, pronunciation, and spelling, by all means get professional help to improve your communication skills **before** you make a bad impression on employers.

11. **You should be energetic and enthusiastic:** Employers are attracted to positive people. They don't like negative and depressing people who toil at their work. Generate enthusiasm both verbally and nonverbally. Check on your telephone voice with a friend or relative – it may be more unenthusiastic than your face-to-face voice.

12. **You should be prepared to answer questions:** You should be able to anticipate at least 80 percent of all questions an employer will ask during a job interview. Prepare positive answers that express your attitude, skills, and abilities. However difficulty, be prepared to disclose your record when asked about any convictions.

13. **You should address possible red flag questions:** While employers want to know about your strengths, they also probe for weaknesses. Be sure to prepare answers to any red flag questions that could knock you out of the competition, especially those relating to your criminal background, work habits, education, and training.

14. **You should ask questions:** Your best information comes from asking questions. Learn to develop intelligent questions that are non-aggressive, polite, and interesting to others. But don't ask too many questions and thereby become a bore.

15. **You should be a good listener:** Being a good listener is often more important than being a good questioner, talker, or motormouth. Learn to improve your face-to-face listening behavior (nonverbal cues) as well as remember and use information gained from others. Make others feel they enjoyed talking with you, i.e., you are one of the few people who actually **listens** to what they say.

16. **You should be civil, which means being polite, courteous, and thoughtful:** Treat gatekeepers, especially receptionists, like human beings. Avoid being aggressive. Try to be polite, courteous, and gracious. Your social graces are being observed. Remember to send thank-you letters – a very thoughtful thing to do in a job search. Even if rejected, thank employers for the "opportunity." They may later have additional opportunities, and they will **remember** you.

17. **You should be tactful:** Watch what you say to others about people. Don't be a gossip, back-stabber, or confessor. Word does get around about your behavior, which could be negative.

18. **You should maintain a professional stance:** Be neat in what you do and wear, and speak with the confidence, authority, and maturity of a professional.

19. **You should demonstrate your intelligence and competence:** Present yourself as someone who gets things done and achieves results – a **producer**. Employers generally seek people who are bright, hard working, responsible, communicate well, have positive personalities, maintain good interpersonal relations, are likable, observe dress and social codes, take initiative, are talented, possess expertise in particular areas, use good judgment, are cooperative, trustworthy, and loyal, generate confidence and credibility, and are conventional. In other words, they like people who score in the "excellent" to "outstanding" categories of a performance evaluation.

20. **You should be open-minded and keep an eye open for "luck":** Too much planning can blind you to unexpected and fruitful opportunities. You should welcome the unexpected. Learn to re-evaluate your goals and strategies. Seize new opportunities if appropriate.

21. You should evaluate your progress and adjust: Take two hours once every two weeks and evaluate your accomplishments. If necessary, tinker with your plans and reorganize your activities and priorities. Don't get too set in a routine and thereby kill creativity and innovation.

22. You should believe in yourself and seize your Second Act. You've stumbled and fallen, but you also can pick yourself up and become the Comeback Kid. Life comes in seasons and passes quickly. Past failures should not become impediments to future successes. While there is a season for everything, this is **your season** to start fresh as you move into the next stage of your life.

These principles should provide you with an initial orientation for starting your job search. As you become more experienced, you will develop your own set of operating principles that should work for you.

3

Examine and Change Your Attitudes

T HE OLD CAUTIONARY SAYING that "your attitude is showing" and the old sports and sales adage that "attitude is everything" are especially appropriate for ex-offenders in transition. After all, finding a job involves presentation, competition, and selling yourself. Employers look for **truthfulness, character, and value** in candidates by examining their attitudes during a job interview. Certain attitudes raise red flags and thus quickly knock candidates out of consideration. Whether or not you are aware of it, your attitude may show more than the clothes you wear to the job interview!

Ex-Offender Attitudes and Motivation

After months and possibly years of incarceration, few ex-offenders re-enter society with a positive, can-do attitude. Many feel worthless, hopeless, and unwanted. Their negative attitudes are often obvious to family members, friends, and employers. Not surprisingly, those attitudes affect their motivation to take actions that lead to success in finding a job.

More often than not, ex-offenders' re-entry is filled with anxiety and uncertainty – uncertain how people will receive them, uncertain about their families, uncertain about their housing and financial situations, and uncertain whether or not they will find a job, succeed on the outside, or become another recidivism statistic. If they harbor anger and negative attitudes, chances are they also lack the necessary motivation to become successful. Older ex-offenders, who may have been incarcerated for several years, especially fear re-entering the job market. Unlike many young offenders, older ex-offenders often lack self-motivation skills that are essential for making a successful transition.

What's Your Attitude?

If you have nothing to start with, at least you have an attitude that will potentially motivate you and thus propel you to success. On the other hand, your attitude might drag you down a road to failure. Take a moment to examine your attitude. Is it negative much of the time? Do you often make excuses? Does your attitude often show in what you say and do? Are others attracted to you in a positive manner? What exactly motivates you to succeed?

One of the first things you need to do is check the state of your attitude. You can do this by completing the following exercise. Check whether or not you primarily agree ("Yes") or disagree ("No") with each of these statements:

		Yes	No
1.	Other people often make my work and life difficult.	❑	❑
2.	When I get into trouble, it's often because of what someone else did rather than my fault.	❑	❑
3.	People often take advantage of me.	❑	❑
4.	When I worked, people less qualified than me often got promoted.	❑	❑
5.	I avoid taking risks because I'm afraid of failing.	❑	❑
6.	I don't trust many people.	❑	❑
7.	Not many people trust me.	❑	❑
8.	Not many people I know take responsibility.	❑	❑
9.	Most people get ahead because of connections, schmoozing, and politics.	❑	❑
10.	When I worked, I was assigned more duties than other people in similar positions.	❑	❑
11.	I expect to be discriminated against in the job search and on the job.	❑	❑

12. I don't feel like I can change many things; I've been dealt this hand, so I'll have to live with it.   ❑   ❑

13. I've had my share of bad luck.   ❑   ❑

14. I usually have to do things myself rather than rely on others to get things done.   ❑   ❑

15. People often pick on me.   ❑   ❑

16. Employers try to take advantage of job seekers by offering them low salaries.   ❑   ❑

17. I didn't like many of the people I worked with.   ❑   ❑

18. There's not much I can do to get ahead.   ❑   ❑

19. My ideas are not really taken seriously.   ❑   ❑

20. I often think of reasons why other people's ideas won't work.   ❑   ❑

21. I sometimes respond to suggestions by saying _"Yes, but . . . ,"_ _"I'm not sure . . . ,"_ _"I don't think it will work . . . ,"_ _"Let's not do that . . ."_   ❑   ❑

22. Other people are often wrong but I have to put up with them nonetheless.   ❑   ❑

23. I don't see why I need to get more education and training.   ❑   ❑

24. I often wish other people would just disappear.   ❑   ❑

25. I sometimes feel depressed.   ❑   ❑

26. I have a hard time getting and staying motivated.   ❑   ❑

27. I don't look forward to going to work.   ❑   ❑

28. Friday is my favorite workday.   ❑   ❑

29. When I worked, I sometimes came to work late or left early.   ❑   ❑

30. The jobs I've had didn't reflect my true talents.   ❑   ❑

31. I should have advanced a lot further than where I am today.   ❑   ❑

32. I'm worth a lot more than most employers are willing to pay.   ❑   ❑

33. I sometimes do things behind my boss's back that could get me into trouble.   ❑   ❑

                                                    TOTALS   ___   ___

Not all of these statements necessarily reflect bad attitudes or negative behaviors. Some may be honest assessments of realities ex-offenders frequently encounter. In fact, some organizations are dysfunctional and thus they breed negative attitudes and behaviors among their employees. However, if you checked "Yes" to more than six of these statements, you may be harboring some bad attitudes that affect both your job search and your on-the-job performance. You may want to examine these attitudes as possible barriers to getting ahead in your job search as well as on the job. Indeed, you may want to change those attitudes that may be preventing you from making good choices and getting ahead. We'll examine how to make such changes later in this chapter (pages 35-39).

What Excuses Do You Make?

Many negative and dysfunctional attitudes are related to excuses we make for our behavior. Take, for example, the following list of "100 Excuses for Choosing Poor Behavior" compiled by Rory Donaldson on www.brainsarefun.com. While many of these excuses apply to school children, many also relate to everyone else, including the elderly. He prefaces this list with Rudyard Kipling's observation that *"We have forty million reasons for failure, but not a single excuse"*:

1. It's your fault.	29. I hurt my finger.
2. I'm not happy.	30. I don't feel well.
3. It's too hot.	31. You didn't tell me.
4. I'm too busy.	32. It was cold.
5. I'm sad.	33. I'm not good at that.
6. I didn't sleep well.	34. I left it in my pocket.
7. It's not fair.	35. He made a face at me.
8. I wanted to watch TV.	36. I wasn't.
9. I didn't write it down.	37. I was rushed.
10. It's too hard.	38. You didn't give it to me.
11. It's too far away.	39. We did that last year.
12. The teacher didn't explain it.	40. That's not the way we learned at school.
13. I forgot.	41. His mother said it was O.K.
14. The dog was sick.	42. I already did it.
15. There was too much traffic.	43. It was right here.
16. I tried.	44. It's too much work.
17. My pencil broke.	45. It stinks.
18. My grandmother wouldn't let me.	46. I didn't know it was sharp.
19. You're mean.	47. I was scared.
20. I didn't know it was today.	48. I was frustrated.
21. I'm too tired.	49. I did already.
22. My brother was sick.	50. It wasn't in the dictionary.
23. The car broke down.	51. I lost it.
24. It was snowing.	52. Nobody likes me.
25. I hurt my foot.	53. I have poor self esteem.
26. I thought it was due tomorrow.	54. I'm too happy.
27. The ice was too thin.	55. I'm sleepy.
28. I ran out of time.	

56. He hit me.
57. I already know that.
58. I left it at school.
59. It's too easy.
60. It's not important.
61. I couldn't get into my locker.
62. I dropped it.
63. I have a learning disorder.
64. I lost my pencil.
65. My pen leaked.
66. I have an excuse.
67. It got wet.
68. It got dirty.
69. My dog threw up.
70. I missed the bus.
71. I have a different learning style.
72. It was raining.
73. My grandfather was visiting.
74. I didn't know.
75. No one told me.
76. I don't have to.
77. My neck hurts.
78. I ran out of paper.
79. The electricity went out.
80. I don't know how.
81. I can't.
82. I don't know where it is.
83. He hit me first.
84. It's the weekend.
85. I ran out of money.
86. I'm too stupid.
87. My teacher said to do it this way.
88. I watched it at my friend's house.
89. I just cleaned it.
90. My friend got one.
91. You lost it.
92. It takes too much time.
93. He told me I didn't have to.
94. I'm hungry.
95. I couldn't open the door.
96. I'm too important.
97. It spilled.
98. I ran out of batteries.
99. I'm doing something else.
100. I didn't know it was hot.

We and other employers have often encountered 20 additional excuses related to the workplace. Some are even used by candidates during a job interview to explain their on-the-job behavior! Most of these excuses reflect an attitude lacking in truthfulness, responsibility, and initiative:

1. No one told me.
2. I did what you said.
3. Your directions were bad.
4. It's not my fault.
5. She did it.
6. It just seemed to happen.
7. It happens a lot.
8. What did he say?
9. I had a headache.
10. I don't understand why.
11. I don't know how to do it.
12. That's your problem.
13. It wasn't very good.
14. Maybe you did it.
15. I thought I wrote it down.
16. That's not my style.
17. He told me to do it that way.
18. I've got to go now.
19. Where do you think it went?
20. We can talk about it later.

We all make excuses. Many are harmless excuses that help us get through the day. Identify a few excuses you frequently make:

1. _____
2. _____
3. _____
4. _____
5. _____

On the other hand, certain excuses may prevent you from getting and keeping a job. Identify any excuses that may work against your employability:

1. _____

2. _____

3. _____

4. _____

5. _____

When you express such excuses, you literally **show an attitude** that is not appreciated by employers. People with positive attitudes and proactive behavior do not engage in behaviors that reflect such excuses. They have a "can do" attitude that helps focus their goals on doing those things that are most important to achieving their goals. For example, rather than show up 10 minutes late for a job interview and say they got lost or had bad directions, people with positive attitudes and proactive behavior scope out the interview location the day before in anticipation of arriving 10 minutes early. They make no excuses because they plan ahead and engage in no-excuses behavior!

Does Your Attitude Show?

The job search is all about making good first impressions on strangers who know little or nothing about your background and capabilities but who have the power to hire. Whether completing an application, writing a resume, or interviewing for a job, your attitude will show in many different ways, both verbally and nonverbally.

Many job seekers show attitudes of disrespect, deceit, laziness, irresponsibility, and carelessness – all red flags that will quickly knock you out of the competition. Most of these attitudes are communicated during the critical job interview when employers have a chance to read both verbal and nonverbal behavioral cues. Here are some common mistakes job seekers make that show off some killer attitudes that also reflect on their character:

Mistake	Attitude/Character
▪ Lacks a job objective	Confused and unfocused
▪ Misspells words on application, resume, and letters	Careless and inconsiderate
▪ Uses poor grammar	Uneducated and illiterate
▪ Sends resume to the wrong person	Careless and error-prone
▪ Arrives late for the job interview	Unreliable and lacks punctuality
▪ Dresses inappropriately	Unperceptive and insensitive
▪ Doesn't know about the company	Lazy and thoughtless

- Talks about salary and benefits   Greedy and self-centered
- Bad-mouths previous employer   Disrespectful and angry
- Doesn't admit to any weaknesses   Disingenuous and calculating
- Boasts about himself   Obnoxious and self-centered
- Lies about background   Deceitful and untrustworthy
- Lacks eye contact   Shifty and dishonest
- Blames others for problems   Irresponsible and immature
- Interrupts and argues   Inconsiderate and impatient
- Has trouble answering questions   Unprepared and nervous
- Fails to ask any questions   Disinterested in job and employer
- Jumps from one extreme to another   Manic and disorganized
- Fails to close and follow up interview   Doesn't care about the job

On the other hand, employers look for attitudes that indicate a candidate has some of the following positive characteristics:

- Accurate
- Adaptable
- Careful
- Competent
- Considerate
- Cooperative
- Dependable
- Determined
- Diligent
- Discreet
- Educated
- Efficient
- Empathic
- Energetic
- Enthusiastic
- Fair
- Focused
- Good-natured
- Happy
- Helpful
- Honest
- Intelligent
- Loyal
- Nice
- Open-minded
- Patient
- Perceptive
- Precise
- Predictable
- Prompt
- Purposeful
- Reliable
- Resourceful
- Respectful
- Responsible
- Self-motivated
- Sensitive
- Sincere
- Skilled
- Tactful
- Team player
- Tenacious
- Tolerant
- Trustworthy
- Warm

Change Your Attitudes

If you have negative attitudes and often need to make excuses for your behavior, you are probably an immature and unhappy person. It's time you took control of both your attitudes and behaviors. Start by identifying several of your negative attitudes and try to transform them into positive attitudes. As you do this, you will begin to identify the positive attitude (person) you want to be. For starters, examine these sets of negative and positive attitudes that can arise at various stages of the job search, especially during the critical job interview:

Negative Attitude	Positive Attitude
I've just got out of prison and need a job.	While incarcerated, I turned my life around by getting my GED, learning new skills, and controlling my anger and addictions. I'm really excited about becoming a landscape architect and working with your company.
I didn't like my last employer.	It was time for me to move on to a more progressive company.
I haven't been able to find a job in over three months. I really want this one.	I've been learning a great deal during the past several weeks of my job search.
My last two jobs were problems.	I learned a great deal about what I really love to do from those last two jobs.
Do you have a job?	I'm in the process of conducting a job search. Do you know anyone who might have an interest in someone with my qualifications?
I can't come in for an interview tomorrow since I'm interviewing for another job. What about Wednesday? That looks good.	I have a conflict tomorrow. Wednesday would be good. Could we do something in the morning?
Yes, I flunked out of college in my sophomore year.	After two years in college I decided to pursue a career in computer sales.
I really hated studying math.	Does this job require math?
Sorry about that spelling error on my resume. I was never good at spelling.	(Doesn't point it out; if asked, say *"It's one that got away."*)
I don't enjoy working in teams.	I work best when given an assignment that allows me to work on my own.
What does this job pay?	How does the pay scale here compare with other firms in the area?

Will I have to work weekends?

What are the normal hours for someone in this position?

I have to see my parole officer once a month. Can I have that day off?

I need to keep an appointment the first Friday of each month. Would it be okay if I took off three hours that day?

I'm three months pregnant. Will your health care program cover my delivery?

Could you tell me more about your benefits, such as health and dental care?

Can you think of any particular negative attitudes you might have that you can restate in positive language? Identify five that relate to your job search and work. State them in both the negative and positive:

Negative Attitude	**Positive Attitude**
1. _____	_____
_____	_____
_____	_____
2. _____	_____
_____	_____
_____	_____
3. _____	_____
_____	_____
_____	_____
4. _____	_____
_____	_____
_____	_____
5. _____	_____
_____	_____
_____	_____

Resources for Changing Attitudes

You'll find numerous books, audiotapes, videos, and software specializing in developing positive thinking and productive attitudes. Most are designed to transform the thinking and perceptions of individuals by changing negative attitudes. One of the major themes underlying these products is that you can change your life through positive thinking and new attitudes. Individuals whose lives are troubled, for example, can literally transform themselves by changing their thinking in new and positive directions. These products are especially popular with people in sales careers, such as real estate and insurance, who must constantly stay motivated and positive in the face of making cold calls that result in numerous rejections. Positive thinking helps them get through the day, the week, and the month despite numerous rejections that would normally dissuade most people from continuing to pursue more sales calls that result in even more rejections.

One of the most influential books on self-transformation through positive thinking is Napoleon Hill's *Think and Grow Rich*. This single book has had a tremendous impact on the development of the positive thinking industry, which now includes hundreds of motivational speakers and gurus who produce numerous seminars, books, and audio programs for the true believers. Other popular books and authors include:

Keith Harrell	■ *Attitude Is Everything*
Napoleon Hill and W. Clement Stone	■ *Success Through a Positive Mental Attitude*
Dr. Norman Vincent Peale	■ *The Power of Positive Thinking* ■ *Six Attitudes for Winners*
Anthony Robbins	■ *Personal Power* ■ *Unlimited Power* ■ *Awaken the Giant Within* ■ *Live With Passion!*
Dr. Robert H. Schuller	■ *You Can Become the Person You Want to Be* ■ *Be Happy Attitudes*
Dale Carnegie	■ *How to Win Friends and Influence People*
Les Brown	■ *Live Your Dream*
David Schwartz	■ *The Magic of Thinking Big*
Zig Ziglar	■ *How to Get What You Want*

Og Mandino   ■ *Secrets of Success*

Brian Tracy   ■ *Change Your Thinking, Change Your Life*
                              ■ *Create Your Own Future*
                              ■ *Eat That Frog!*
                              ■ *Focal Point*
                              ■ *Maximum Achievement*

Steve Chandler   ■ *100 Ways to Motivate Yourself*
                              ■ *Reinventing Yourself*

Bay and Macpherson   ■ *Change Your Attitude*

As you will quickly discover, a positive attitude that focuses on the future is one of the most powerful motivators for achieving success. Any of these recommended books will get you started on the road to changing your attitudes as well as your life. They are filled with fascinating stories of self-transformation, motivational language, and exercises for developing positive attitudes for success.

Here's an important life-changing tip: Get serious about shaping your future by committing yourself to reading at least one of these books over the next two weeks. If reading is a problem for you, try to find audio tapes that include similar material. You can find the books and audio tapes in many libraries. Set aside at least one hour each day to read a book or listen to a tape that can literally change your life. Such books and tapes will both exercise your mind and inspire you to be your best.

4

Seek Assistance and Become Proactive

WHILE YOU MAY AT TIMES feel lonely, frustrated, and angry, always remember you are not alone unless you choose to be alone. Many helping hands are available to assist ex-offenders in transition. Experienced in working with ex-offenders and other disadvantaged groups, these individuals and groups have lots of street smarts that can be of great benefit to you in finding a job and dealing with other important re-entry issues. If you are under supervision, for example, your P.O. will be one of your most important helping hands. Despite a sometimes overwhelming case load, your P.O. can put you in touch with community organizations that assist ex-offenders. Numerous government agencies, nonprofit organizations, and faith-based groups provide all types of assistance, from housing, health care, and counseling to training and employment. Become familiar with various community organizations and programs so you can literally hit the ground running when you re-enter **your** community.

Community-Based Programs and Services

Not all communities are alike when it comes to assisting ex-offenders in transition. Some communities are well organized to assist ex-offenders while others are not focused on re-entry issues, or they absorb ex-offenders into existing services designed to assist disadvantaged groups. Ex-offenders living in Chicago and the Quad Cities area of Illinois and Iowa (Safer Foundation), New York City (Center for Employment Opportunity), Baltimore (Mayor's Office of Employment Development), and Texas

(Project RIO), for example, can benefit greatly from local efforts to provide employ-ment programs and services for ex-offenders. Some of the programs, such as the Safer Foundation in Chicago and Project RIO in Texas, actually start in detention centers, jails, and prisons and involve both pre- and post-release services. Other communities have employment placement and training programs, such as One-Stop Career Centers, and nonprofit organizations, such as Goodwill Industries, which increasingly service ex-offenders along with other hard-to-employ populations, including welfare recipients and people with disabilities. Many of these programs offer housing, health care, job training, transportation, and child care services to individuals as well as financial incentives, such as bonding and tax credits, to employers who hire hard-to-employ populations.

The following discussion is designed to help you to both understand and navigate communities that may or may not have programs and services designed for ex-offenders. If you relocate to Chicago, New York City, or Texas, you will find programs and services that deal with the immediate and long-term needs of ex-offend-ers – short-term jobs, skills training, job placement, and job retention. Other communities, such as Balti-more, may have a loose coalition of government agencies, nonprofit organizations, and churches and experimental programs focused on ex-offender re-entry and employability issues. In many other com-munities, you may be on your own in a sea of hope and fear; these may be the toughest communities for ex-offenders who need a support system beyond just family and friends to help them make a successful transition.

> *With 660,000 ex-offenders released each year, all communities and the many organizations that deal with disadvantaged groups more or less work with ex-offenders.*

However, many communities offer hope if you know how to **navigate them properly**. Indeed, you should be aware of alternative programs and services available in many communities, such as One-Stop Career Centers, nonprofit organizations, and churches that assist disadvantaged groups, including ex-offenders in transition. In the end, with a flood of 660,000 ex-offenders re-entering communities each year, all communities and the many organizations that deal with disadvantaged groups more or less work with ex-offenders. So let's focus on getting some new street smarts by identifying services, where to go, and whom to contact for re-entry assistance.

Safety Nets and Opportunity Networks

Once you've been released, you will most likely return to your former community of family and friends. The terms of your release may require that you become docu-mented, reside in a specific community, report any movement, regularly see your

P.O., disclose your criminal history to employers, and avoid certain jobs because of your background. You face certain legal restrictions you need to acknowledge and work with. If you don't, you may be in violation of your terms of release.

If you're lucky, you may be quickly hired by a former employer or land a job through a family connection or referral from a friend. In fact, these are the best sources for finding a job, regardless of your background – informal, word-of-mouth contacts that also screen you for employment and thus help you deal with the troubling issue of disclosure.

However, not everyone is fortunate to have great personal connections to assist them in finding a job. And you don't have the luxury to spend three to six months looking for a job. Many ex-offenders, who quickly exhaust their meager gate money, are in a scary survival mode – they need to get a job **now** just to pay for basic food, housing, and transportation. Contrast their situation with individuals who lose their jobs: they often have savings and family to fall back on, or they qualify for unemployment compensation and public welfare – services beyond the reach of many ex-offenders who may only qualify for Food Stamps. Except for family, you don't have many standard safety net options in today's job market. You need a job, and the sooner, the better.

> *If you're lucky, you may be quickly hired by a former employer or land a job through a family connection or referral from a friend – the best sources for finding a job.*

The first thing you need to do is to develop some **community smarts** by rethinking how you fit into a community and how it relates to you. We don't mean acquiring traditional street smarts, since such smarts may have gotten you into trouble in the first place. We're talking about how you approach a community as part of your lifeline and support system. Your community has various safety nets to assist ex-offenders in transition, which you need to know about and at times use to jump-start your new life in the free world.

A community is more than just a place in which you live, work, and raise a family. A community also is a place of opportunities to fulfill your dreams. It's made up of many individuals, groups, organizations, institutions, and neighborhoods that come together for achieving different goals. Perhaps it's best to view them as playing different competitive and cooperative games. As they compete, cooperate, come into conflict, and co-op one another, they provide **opportunity structures** for finding jobs through informal, word-of-mouth channels. They become important **networks** for locating job opportunities. Some of these networks serve as safety networks, but most should be viewed as **networks of opportunity**. It's where many good jobs can be found for those who know how to network their way to a new job and life. (See Chapter 10 for details on how to make networking literally work for you!)

The Yellow Pages of any telephone book will give you a good overview of the major organizational players in a community that define both safety nets and opportunity networks. Banks, mortgage companies, advertising firms, car dealers, schools, churches, small businesses, industries, hospitals, law firms, government agencies, and civic and volunteer organizations all coexist as well as periodically cooperate and compete with one another. Banks, for example, need to loan money to the businesses, churches, and individuals. The businesses, in turn, need the educational institutions to purchase their goods and services as well as provide an educated and skilled workforce. And the educational institutions need the businesses to absorb their graduates. Churches need members and money. Therefore, individuals tend to cooperate in seeing that people playing the other games also succeed.

> *You should view communities as made up of both **safety nets** and **opportunity networks** – groups and organizations that can help you quickly get back on your feet and find employment.*

The larger the community, the more safety nets and opportunity networks will be available to you. For example, the safety nets for ex-offenders in Chicago, Houston, New York City, Baltimore, and Washington, DC are much greater than in Sioux Falls, South Dakota or Grand Prairie, Texas. However, the opportunity networks may be fewer in large poor cities that have high unemployment rates than in smaller cities and suburbs that have booming economies with very low unemployment.

Key Community Players for Ex-Offenders

Let's outline the key community players who can provide both a safety net and job opportunities for ex-offenders. They generally fall into these categories:

- **Government agencies and programs:** Social services, public health, courts, P.O.s, halfway houses, homeless shelters, and One-Stop Career Centers.

- **Nonprofit and volunteer organizations:** Substance abuse centers, housing groups, public health groups, mental health organizations, legal services, and education and training organizations. Some of the most prominent such organizations that regularly work with ex-offenders include Goodwill Industries and the Salvation Army.

- **Churches and other faith-based organizations:** Includes a wide range of denominations that offer everything from evangelical to social services as well as faith-based organizations involved in the federal government's new

Ready4Work Prisoner Reentry Initiative jointly funded by the U.S. Department of Labor (Center for Faith-Based and Community Initiatives), the U.S. Department of Justice, and a consortium of private foundations.

A good way to look at communities is to visualize the safety nets and opportunity networks relating to you as found in the diagram on page 45.

Model Job Placement and Retention Programs

To illustrate our community approach, let's look at a few communities with programs and services available for ex-offenders.

Chicago and the Quad Cities Area
(Safer Foundation)

For more than 30 years, the Chicago-based Safer Foundation (www.saferfoundation. org) has focused on assisting ex-offenders with finding and keeping jobs in the Chicago and Quad Cities areas of Illinois and Iowa. Working with over 4,000 clients each year, the Safer Foundation has developed a model program for dealing with a hard-to-employ population that has similar characteristics in many other communities across the country:

- Young and poor
- Little or no work history
- Less than a 10th grade education
- Unrealistic expectations
- Substance abuse and mental health issues

The Safer Foundation offers both prison- and community-based services to ex-offenders. Working with the Illinois Department of Correction in two adult transition centers and the Sheridan Correctional Facility, their programs provide basic education and life skills training. Once released, ex-offenders are encouraged to attend vocational classes as well as receive job placement assistance from employment specialists. Once placed in a job, the employment specialist follows up with the ex-offender and employer during the first 30 days. Program participants also are assigned case managers who offer assistance during the first 12 months of employment. Over 40 percent of program participants remain employed after six months, which is a significantly higher job retention rate than for ex-offenders outside this program.

Community Safety Nets and Opportunity Networks

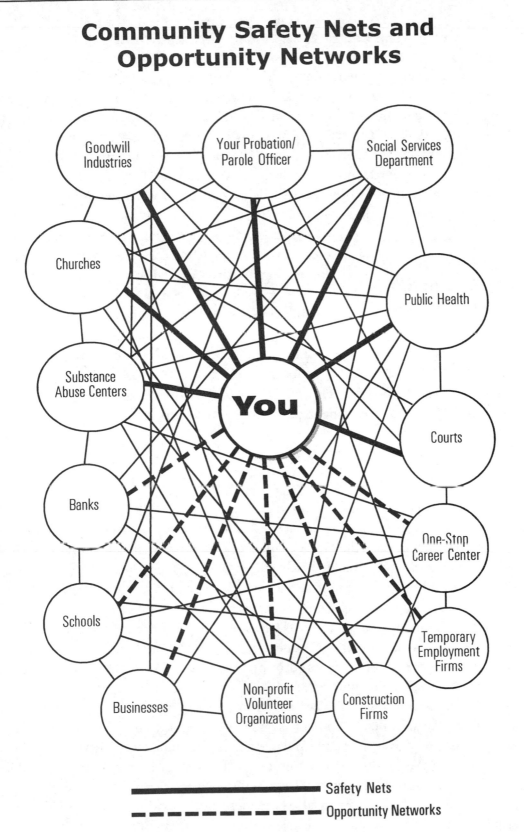

Goodwill Industries

Your Probation/ Parole Officer

Social Services Department

Churches

Public Health

Substance Abuse Centers

You

Courts

Banks

One-Stop Career Center

Schools

Temporary Employment Firms

Businesses

Non-profit Volunteer Organizations

Construction Firms

————————— Safety Nets

– – – – – – – Opportunity Networks

New York City
(The Center for Employment Opportunities)

The Center for Employment Opportunities (www.ceoworks.org) offers job readiness and placement services to ex-offenders returning to New York City as well as to others under community supervision. Its model work experience program – the Neighborhood Work Project (NWP) – provides participants with immediate, paid, and short-term employment while they take part in a program to develop skills for rejoining the workforce and restarting their lives. The program provides an intensive four-day job readiness workshop that deals with resume writing, job search skills, interview preparation, dress, and discussing one's conviction and incarceration. It also assesses individual needs for support services, such as housing, clothing, child care, transportation, and documentation. Participants undergo vocational assessment (reading, math, job-related skills), develop an employment plan, regularly meet with a job coach, and receive paid transitional employment (NWP) four days a week. Sixty percent of program participants are placed in permanent jobs within two to three months. The program closely supervises those placed as well as continues to offer participants post-placement, job coaching, and support services for an additional 12 months.

> *The CEO program (www.ceoworks.org) includes useful online job search advice.*

State of Texas
(Project RIO)

Project Reintegration of Offenders (RIO) is a state-wide program operated by the state employment office, the Texas Workforce Commission, in collaboration with the Texas Department of Criminal Justice (www.workforcelink.com/html/rio/default_rio.html). Offering both pre- and post-release services to participants, Project RIO links education, training, and employment during incarceration with employment, training, and education after release. Prior to release, Project RIO staff members encourage participants to take advantage of educational and vocational services; assist them in getting the necessary documents (driver's license, birth certificate, Social Security card, etc.) for employment; and provide placement services to gain practical work experience. After release, Project RIO provides job preparation and job search assistance. Participants attend job search workshops that focus on completing applications, preparing a resume, and participating in mock interviews. The primary focus is on quickly landing a job. Project RIO also works with employers in certifying them for the Work Opportunity Tax Credit program (provides tax incentives for hiring economically disadvantaged ex-offenders) and providing bonding services upon request (issue fidelity bonds at no cost for up to six months).

Baltimore
(Mayor's Office of Employment Development)

The city of Baltimore, Maryland represents both a private/public coalition approach and an experimental program approach to assisting ex-offenders in transition. Each year nearly 9,000 ex-offenders are released into this city, which is anything but a hotbed of economic development and employment. This is a hopeful but troubled city with one of the highest homicide rates in the nation. Like ex-offenders in many other large cities, nearly 80 percent in Baltimore move into the worst neighborhoods. Recognizing that both the city and ex-offenders face a major challenge, Baltimore has been very aggressive in dealing with the recidivism problem and pulling together major community resources for dealing with the re-entry issue. The Mayor's Office of Employment Development facilitated the creation of the Baltimore Citywide Ex-offender Task Force in October 2002 to focus on ex-offender re-entry issues (www. oedworks.com/exoffender.htm). The Task Force included more than 100 government agencies and community partners. In March 2004, the Task Force was succeeded by a mayoral-appointed Ex-Offender Employment Steering Committee. The Committee recently published a resource directory for ex-offenders, which outlines the major government and community-based organizations providing services to ex-offenders:

Ex-offender Resource Guide: Baltimore Community Services for Individuals With Criminal Backgrounds (December 2004)

Many of these agencies and organizations function as safety nets and opportunity networks for individuals who are unemployed, homeless, hungry, sick, victims of domestic violence, mentally ill, HIV-positive, or drug and alcohol abusers. Examples of such service providers include:

Employment

- Baltimore Works One-Stop Career Center
- Career Development and Cooperative Education Center
- Caroline Center
- Damascus Career Center
- Goodwill Industries of the Chesapeake
- Maryland New Directions
- Prisoners Aid Association of Maryland, Inc.
- Southwest One-Stop Career Center
- The GATE

Health

- First Call for Help
- Health Care for the Homeless
- Jai Medical Center
- Maryland Youth Crisis Hotline
- Rape Crisis Center
- Sisters Together and Reaching, Inc.
- The Men's Health Center
- Black Educational AIDS Project

Housing

- 20th Street Hope House
- AIDS Interfaith Residential Services
- At Jacob's Well

- Baltimore Rescue Mission
- Helping Up Mission
- Light Street Housing
- Maryland Re-Entry Program
- Safe Haven
- Salvation Army
- SSI Outreach Project

Legal

- Homeless Persons Representation Project
- House of Ruth, Domestic Violence Legal Clinic
- Lawyer Referral & Information Service
- Legal Aid Bureau
- Office of the Public Defender
- University of Baltimore School of Law

Mental Health

- Baltimore Crisis Response Center
- Department of Social Services

- Family Help Line
- Gamblers Anonymous
- North Baltimore Center
- People Encouraging People
- Suicide Prevention Hotline
- You Are Never Alone

Substance Abuse

- Bright Hope House
- I Can't, We Can, Inc.
- Addict Referral and Counseling Center
- Crossroads Center
- Day Break Rehabilitation Program
- Friendship House
- Quarterway Outpatient Clinic
- SAFE House

Food and Clothing

- Salvation Army
- Bethel Outreach Center, Inc.
- Our Daily Bread
- Paul's Place

Baltimore has also initiated a transitional jobs project, Project Bridge, for ex-offenders. It's a collaborative effort involving Goodwill Industries of the Chesapeake; Associated Catholic Charities; the Center for Fathers, Families, and Workforce Development; and the Second Chance Project. Targeted toward ex-offenders who are unlikely to find employment on their own, the project provides eligible ex-offenders returning to Baltimore with transitional employment, support services, and job placement, followed by 12 months of post-placement retention services.

Many communities offer ex-offender assistance programs similar to those found in Baltimore.

For street-smart ex-offenders who understand the many service providers focused on their re-entry challenges, the City of Baltimore looks like a loosely structured set of safety nets and opportunity networks. Ex-offenders entering Baltimore are well advised to learn how they can best use these organizations to quickly find employment as well as deal with other pressing re-entry issues.

Many communities offer assistance programs for ex-offenders similar to those cited above. Start with several of the organizations listed on the next page to uncover programs in your area.

Useful Re-Entry Resources

For an excellent summary of governmental agencies and community-based organizations assisting ex-offenders with employment, legal, and other re-entry issues, including referrals to other relevant organizations, be sure to visit the **National H.I.R.E. Network** website, which identifies key re-entry resources in all 50 states:

www.hirenetwork.org/resource.html

Other useful websites include:

Government

- Center for Employment Opportunities (New York City)   www.CEOworks.org
- Federal Bureau of Prisons   www.bop.gov
- U.S. Parole Commission   www.usdoj.gov/uspc/parole.htm
- U.S. Office of Justice Programs   www.ojp.usdoj.gov/reentry
- U.S. Department of Labor, Center for Faith-Based and Community Initiatives   www.dol-tlc.org
- Volunteers of America   www.voa.org

Associations

- American Correctional Association   www.aca.org
- American Jail Association   www.corrections.com/aja.indcx.shtml
- Corrections Connection   www.corrections.com

Nonprofit/Volunteer

- The Safer Foundation   www.saferfoundation.org
- OPEN, INC.   www.openinc.org
- Just the Necessities   www.justthenecessities.org
- The Sentencing Project   www.sentencingproject.org
- Family and Corrections Network   www.fcnetwork.com
- Legal Action Center   www.lac.org
- Criminal Justice Policy Foundation   www.cjpf.org/clemency/clemency.html
- Annie E. Casey Foundation   www.aecf.org
- The Fortune Society   www.fortunesociety.org
- Second Chance/STRIVE (San Diego)   www.secondchanceprogram.org

Faith-Based

- Prison Fellowship Ministries   www.pfm.org
- Re-entry Prison and Jail Ministry   www.reentry.org/cgi-bin/resource.cfm#resources

- **Conquest Offender Reintegration
  Ministries** (Washington, DC)   www.conquesthouse.org/links.html
- **Breakthrough Urban Ministries**   www.breakthroughministries.com
  (Chicago)
- **Exodus Transitional Community,
  Inc.** (New York)   www.etcny.org

Using Your Community Resources

A similar pattern of networks and relationships will be found in other large communities across the country. The city of Washington, DC, for example, operates a faith-based mentoring program for ex-offenders through its Faith Community Partnership, which is made up of a network of over 40 congregations. The sponsoring agency, the Court Services and Offender Supervision Agency (www.csosa.com), provides supervisory and treatment services to over 26,000 individuals in pretrial release and on probation and parole. Pinellas County in Florida operates a re-entry program sponsored by the Pinellas County Ex-Offender Re-Entry Coalition (www. exoffender.org). In 2004 the U.S. Department of Justice Office of Community Oriented Policing Services (COPS) provided $1.2 million in grants under the Justice Department's Value-Based Reentry Initiative (VBRI) grant program to organizations in five cities (Boston, Detroit, Kansas City, Oakland, and Washington, DC) to continue programs for successfully re-integrating ex-offenders into their communities. The U.S. Department of Labor's Center for Faith-Based and Community Initiatives (www.dol-tlc.gov), in collaboration with the U.S. Department of Justice and a consortium of private foundations, recently sponsored a three-year, $22.5 million program – the Ready4Work Prisoner Reentry Initiative – to assist faith-based and community programs in providing mentoring and other transition services.

What is different among communities is the degree to which a community actually recognizes – as in the cases of Chicago, New York City, Baltimore, Boston, Detroit, Kansas City, Oakland, and the state of Texas – the need to focus on issues surrounding the re-entry of ex-offenders into their communities. If you enter a community that does not provide specific assistance and services to ex-offenders, you'll be on your own in a sea of government agencies and community-based organizations that primarily provide employment and safety net services for disadvantaged groups, similar to the ones we identified for Baltimore. Therefore, one of your most important initial jobs will be to **understand how your particular community is structured in terms of such networks and relationships**. Once you understand your community, you should be prepared to take advantage of the many services and opportunities available to someone in your situation.

You can start identifying your community networks by completing the following exercise. Specify the actual names of at least three different government agencies and community-based organizations for each category that you need to know about and possibly use in the coming weeks and months. If you don't have this information, ask your P.O. for assistance, visit your local library and ask personnel at the information desk for assistance, do an Internet search, or contact your local government social services department.

Employment

1. _____

2. _____

3. _____

Housing

1. _____

2. _____

3. _____

Health

1. _____

2. _____

3. _____

Other (legal, mental health, substance abuse, food, etc.)

1. _____

2. _____

3. _____

One-Stop Career Centers

One community group you should become familiar with is your local One-Stop Career Center. Indeed, make sure you visit a One-Stop Career Center soon after release. It may well become one of your most important lifelines for landing your first job out.

Usually operated by the state employment office, One-Stop Career Centers provide numerous resources for assisting individuals in finding employment, such as computerized job banks, job listings, counseling and assessment services, job search assistance, and training programs. Since career professionals staffing these centers increasingly work with ex-offenders, you'll be no stranger to their offices. Be sure to disclose your criminal background to their personnel, since knowing about your record may result in their providing you with special contacts and services. You can easily find the center nearest you by visiting this website:

- **One-Stop Career Centers**   www.careeronestop.org

If you're using the Internet, you'll also want to visit these two related websites operated by the U.S. Department of Labor:

- **America's CareerInfoNet**   www.acinet.org
- **America's Service Locator**   www.servicelocator.org

Temporary Employment Agencies

You also may want to contact various temporary employment agencies or staffing firms. This is good way to quickly get employed and acquire work experience. With temporary employment agencies, you work for the agency which, in turn, places you on temporary assignments with their clients. While these companies primarily recruit individuals for temporary or part-time positions, many of these firms also have temp-to-perm programs. With these programs, you may work two to three months with one employer who hopes to hire you full-time once your contract expires with the temporary employment agency and you have met their performance expectations. Many large cities have over 200 such firms operating. Many of these agencies specialize in particular occupations, such as construction, accounting, information technology, law, and health services. Other agencies may recruit for all types of positions, including many low-skill, low-wage labor positions. Some of the most popular temporary employment agencies with a nationwide presence include Labor Finders (www.laborfinders.com), Manpower (www.manpower.com), Olsten (www.olsten.com), and Kelly Services (www.kellyservices.com).

Become More Proactive

Many ex-offenders have limited knowledge about the job market, unrealistic expectations about employers and how quickly they will find a full-time job, and a history of limited work experience. If you approach your re-entry with a positive attitude and realistic expectations – this transition will be difficult but not impossible – and take sensible actions, you should be successful. You must hit the ground running by taking actions that make a difference in your future. If you were used to spending lots of time sleeping, watching television, and exercising your body while incarcerated, it's time to spend more of your waking hours exercising your mind (read and do research) and becoming involved in activities that will advance your job search. As we noted throughout this chapter, you can make things happen if you will:

- Work with your P.O.
- Acquaint yourself with groups and organizations that assist ex-offenders.
- Approach your community as a network of opportunity structures.
- Use resources that can quickly lead to job search success and a new record of work experience.
- Avoid individuals, groups, and organizations that may waste your time by taking you down the wrong road.

When you get up in the morning, follow the advice of Brian Tracy in *Eat That Frog* – first do those things you hate to do (eat the frog first) so that the rest of your day will be devoted to more enjoyable activities! Don't procrastinate by avoiding those things you hate to do. Clear the least enjoyable activities in the day by getting them over with immediately. There is much to be done in finding a job. Let's now turn to developing some realistic expectations as to how best to find a job.

5

Select Appropriate Job Search Approaches

HOW WILL YOU GO ABOUT finding a job? Are you going to do this on your own or rely on others to find you a job? Will you primarily respond to classified ads in the newspaper with a letter and resume or visit companies to fill out applications? Do you plan to knock on doors to introduce yourself to employers or hang around a busy corner for someone to hire you for the day? What about using the telephone to call employers, or searching for job vacancies on bulletin boards or on the Internet? Will you look for jobs through a One-Stop Career Center, employment agencies, placement services, or friends and family? Do you plan to attend a job fair or some other type of career or job event?

Most anyone can find a job, especially in an economy where demand for workers outstrips available supply. You can always rake leaves, trim lawns, clean buildings, paint, lift boxes, drive a vehicle, pick up trash, or use a shovel. The real questions are (1) what type of work will you find? and (2) how rewarding will the job be in terms of salary, benefits, and job satisfaction? How you approach your job search will make a big difference in what type of work you will do as well as the next job you may move to in your worklife. If you choose an appropriate job search approach, you should be able to find a job that's right for you.

Become a Self-Reliant Job Seeker

Most ex-offenders have difficulty finding a job on their own. Many lack basic education and work skills, few have ever held a full-time job, and many have never conducted a well organized job search on their own. Few know where to start, what they want to do, whom to contact, how to dress, how to answer and ask questions, or how to ask for the job. As a result, many rely on job placement services designed to assist ex-offenders or other hard-to-employ people, or they join the underground economy of day laborers and illegal activities. In other words, they rely on others to find or give them a job rather than try to find a job on their own. While a job seeker may learn how to best complete an application, write a resume, or interview for the job, a placement specialist initially locates employers who might be interested in screening such candidates.

While it's nice to have other people do this critical job search work for you, this is not the best approach for finding a job. Instead, you should be developing the knowledge and skills to find a job through your own efforts.

There are many ways to find a job that don't rely on job placement services. The most effective job search methods require you to take responsibility for your employment and your future career. While you will conduct a job search within your support system, you start by acquiring important job search skills for contacting employers. These are important **self-management skills** that you will most likely use throughout your life as you go through several job changes. In fact, individuals first entering the job market today will go through 15 job changes and three to five career changes. The more self-reliant you become in finding a job, the easier it should be for you to change jobs and careers in the years ahead. One of your major goals should be to acquire the necessary job search skills to land a job on your own. You can acquire many of these skills by completing the remaining chapters of this book.

> *You need to take responsibility and acquire important self-management skills. The more self-reliant you become in finding a job, the easier it should be for you to change jobs and careers in the years ahead.*

The Best Job Search Methods

As indicated in the questions at beginning of this chapter, there are many ways to find a job. In fact, every day hundreds of people find jobs using a variety of methods. However, some of these methods are more effective in finding a job than others.

The best methods are ones that lead to good paying jobs with a future – not just any job. Studies consistently show that the most effective job search method (used by 50 to 80 percent of successful candidates) is **networking** – finding job leads through family members, friends, and acquaintances. The job search experiences of ex-offenders also confirm this finding – those who quickly enter the job market do so through the assistance of family and friends. The least effective job search method, which ironically is the most widely used method, is responding to classified ads and job postings. If you want to use your time wisely, focus the largest amount of your time on those methods that appear to have the greatest payoff in terms of job leads and interviews.

Let's examine the most widely used job search methods. Our advice: Don't rely on any one method; use several of these methods throughout your job search.

Respond to Classified Ads

Pick up any newspaper and thumb through the classified ad section in search of a job related to your interests, skills, and experience. Chances are you will identify several interesting jobs, but few of them will relate to your skills and experience. Believing that most job vacancies are found in the newspapers, thousands of job seekers explore the classified ads each day. Engaging in wishful thinking, they often respond to ads with a resume, letter, or phone call. Unfortunately, two things happen at this stage:

1. Many other people also respond to the same ad and thus they face a great deal of competition for a single position.

2. Lacking the required skills and experience, they stretch their qualifications in the hopes that the employer might hire them anyway.

Not surprisingly, employers often receive numerous responses to their ads. They can immediately disregard 80 percent of the responses, because the candidates do not appear qualified for the position. Indeed, many candidates seem to waste their time applying for a position that does not relate to their skills and experience.

In some cases, an ad may not be for an actual job. Some employers place ads in order to collect resumes or sell candidates on self-employment schemes. Don't assume just because an ad appears in the newspaper that it represents a legitimate job vacancy.

Your chances of getting a job by responding to classified ads are not very good – at best a five percent chance of getting a positive or negative response from an employer! However, many job seekers spend most of their job search time on this single, ineffective job search method. They read the newspaper, respond to a few job listings, and then sit and wait for employers to call them for an interview. When they don't get a response, they conclude there are no jobs available for them at present.

Here's the truth about classified job ads:

1. **They represent no more than 15 percent of available job vacancies.** Some of the remaining 85 percent of job vacancies may be advertised elsewhere (on the Internet, in employment offices, on bulletin boards, with unions), but most of the jobs (50 to 75 percent) are found on the "hidden job market," which primarily operates by word-of-mouth, and are found through networking.

2. **They tend to represent jobs at the two extreme ends of the job market** – low-wage, high-turnover positions and high-wage, highly skilled positions. In other words, they represent difficult-to-fill positions. Most jobs, which fall between these two extremes, are not well represented in the classifieds.

3. **They create unrealistic expectations – false hopes** that you will actually get the job or that you are basically unqualified for most jobs.

Our point here is that you should not waste a great deal of time focused on classified ads. It's an ego-bruising experience to get rejected by many employers. Explore classified ads for a few minutes each day, but move on to more productive job search methods.

If you see a job that seems to be a perfect fit, you can increase your odds of getting a job interview by doing the following:

1. **Respond immediately** with a phone call and ask for an interview.

2. **Follow the application instructions.** How does the employer want you to contact him – by e-mail, fax, or mail your resume or call for a telephone screening interview? What does he want you to send him – resume, letter, references, examples of work?

3. **Dissect the ad carefully and then write a cover letter** in which you respond to each requirement with corresponding examples of your qualifications. If you applying for a position as an electrician, your letter might include the following statements:

Your Requirements	My Qualifications
■ One year experience	Completed one-year apprenticeship and served two years as an electrician's helper on complex commercial projects
■ Responsible	Praised by previous employer and co-workers as being a quick starter who takes initiative, is responsible, and gets the job done well and on time.

4. **Follow up your application within five days** with a phone call, fax, or e-mail. We prefer a phone call. This will be the single most important action you can take to move your application to the top of the pile and get it read and remembered. Ask if the employer has any questions about

your application, restate your qualifications and interest in the position, and ask for a job interview. If you don't ask for the job interview, chances are the employer won't contact you for an interview! Your phone call also gives you a chance to be interviewed over the telephone by the employer – the first screening step in the job interview process.

A good resource for handling classified job ads in your job search is Kenton W. Elderkin's classic *How to Get Interviews From Classified Job Ads*. It's now only available through the publisher, Impact Publications (www.impactpublications.com).

Use the Internet

During the past 10 years the Internet has become a very popular resource for both employers and job seekers. In fact, much of today's job market and recruitment/job search activities have moved to the Internet. If you are not using the Internet in your job search, you are not up-to-date in your job search, and you will be missing out on important segments of the job market. In addition, employers may view you as unprepared for today's workplace, which increasingly values technical skills.

> *The largest and most popular employment websites provide a wealth of information about jobs, employers, and the job search in general.*

Many employers use the Internet to recruit candidates through employment websites, such as Monster.com and Careerbuilder.com, as well as through their own company websites. Job seekers use the Internet to find job vacancies, post their resumes to online resume databases, and research jobs, companies, and employers. Approximately 15 percent of job seekers actually find jobs based upon using the Internet. This percentage has steadily increased – from just five percent five years ago.

In many respects, using the Internet is similar to finding a job through classified ads. Indeed, many classified ads appear on employment websites and are called "job postings." Employers who might normally place classified ads for positions in newspapers find it's cheaper and more effective to post their jobs on websites. They also find resume databases useful for identifying candidates who best meet their hiring requirements.

The largest and most popular employment websites provide a wealth of information for job seekers about jobs, employers, and the job search in general: job search tips, featured articles, career experts, career assessment tests, community forums, chat groups, salary calculators, resume and interview advice, relocation information, success stories, newsletters, career events, online job fairs, polls and surveys, contests, online education and training, company ads, and special channels for students, freelancers, military, and other groups. The 10 most popular employment websites are:

- www.ajb.org
- www.monster.com
- www.careerbuilder.com
- www.careerjournal.com
- www.directemployers.com

- http://hotjobs.yahoo.com
- www.nationjob.com
- www.flipdog.com
- www.careerflex.com
- www.employment911.com

As you explore the Internet, you should at least visit these large employment websites. Altogether, over 25,000 websites focus on employment. Hundreds of thousands of additional employer websites include information on employment with specific companies and organizations.

However, you should be aware that jobs found on the Internet tend to be for individuals with at least a high school education and some college, and most jobs pay $25,000 or more a year; many lower-level jobs tend to be entry-level sales positions. A large percentage of jobs require a college education, technical skills, and work experience. Many employers use the Internet to find hard-to-recruit individuals, especially professionals, who have a great deal of work experience or some combination of exotic skills.

Individuals lacking a high school education, work experience, and marketable skills are unlikely to find employers on the Internet interested in their backgrounds for two reasons: (1) they don't have such jobs, and (2) it's cheaper to recruit low-wage earners by putting a sign on a busy street corner, in a window, or at a work site; visiting day-laborer centers; or listing the job free of charge with a public employment office or through a job developer working with hard-to-place individuals. If you lack basic education, work experience, and skills, you should use the Internet to primarily educate yourself about alternative jobs and careers, assess your skills, and learn how to acquire more education and training.

As you will quickly discover, the Internet is a wonderful information and communication tool if used properly. It's an especially frustrating medium for individuals who spend most of their job search time trying to find a job online by responding to job postings and entering their resume into online resume databases.

As we noted in Chapter 3 (Myth #10), if you don't have a computer or an Internet connection, contact your local library or One-Stop Career Center for assistance. Most of these places offer free public access to the Internet and some minimal help to get you up and running on the Internet.

Even though you may not qualify for jobs found on the Internet, learn how to use the Internet early in your job search. It will open a whole new world of employment to you as well as give you many great ideas for thinking about and planning your future.

While the Internet can be extremely useful for job seekers, few of them know how to use this tool properly. Many mistakenly believe that employers actually hire over the Internet! When you are looking for a job, the Internet is best used for:

1.   Conducting research on jobs, employers, companies, and communities.

2.   Acquiring useful advice and referrals.

3.   Communicating with individuals via e-mail.

Your most productive online activities will relate to **research** and **communication**. While you may, depending on your qualifications, want to post your resume on various employment websites and periodically review online job listings, don't spend a great deal of time doing so and then waiting to hear from employers based on such activities. This whole process is similar to working classified employment ads in newspapers – a low probability of getting a response from employers. Move on to other more productive activities, especially visiting **employer websites**, which are more likely to yield useful information, job listings, and applications than the more general and popular employment websites.

In fact, since more and more employers recruit directly from their own websites, rather than use general employment websites, you are well advised to explore employer websites for employment information. If, for example, you have a college education, a strong technical background, and are exceptionally talented, companies such as Microsoft (www.microsoft.com/careers) and Boston Consulting Group (www.bcg.com) provide a wealth of information for such job seekers interested in their companies. Even if you don't qualify for employment with these companies, you can learn a great deal about job hunting by visiting those two websites alone.

But your most useful online job search activity relates to **research**. Thousands of websites can yield useful information for enhancing your job search. For example, use the Internet to explore different jobs (www.bls.gov/oco) and employers (www.hoovers.com), community-based employment assistance (www.careeronestop.org), career counselors (www.nbcc.org), networking groups (www.linkedin.com), salary ranges (www.salary.com), best communities (www.findyourspot.com), relocation (www.monstermoving.com), job search tips (www.winningthejob.com), and career advice (www.wetfeet.com). You can even use the Internet to conduct an online assessment (www.careerlab.com), blast your resume to thousands of employers (www.resumeblaster.com), contact recruiters (www.recruitersonline.com), and explore hundreds of professional associations (www.ipl.org/div/aon) and nonprofit organizations (www.guidestar.org) that are linked to thousands of employers.

The Internet also is a terrific way to **communicate** with people, especially with employers. If you don't have an e-mail address, you can always set up a free e-mail account through one of the major search engines, such as MSN (www.hotmail.com) or Yahoo (www.yahoo.com), or create a dedicated job search e-mail through one of the major employment websites, such as Monster.com or CareerBuilder.com.

For more information on how to wisely use the Internet in your job search, see Ron and Caryl Krannich's *America's Top Internet Job Sites* (Impact Publications), Margaret Dikel's *Job Searching on the Internet* (McGraw-Hill), and Richard Nelson Bolles's *Job Hunting on the Internet* (Ten Speed Press), which are available through www.impactpublications.com or see the order form at end of this book.

Contact Employers Directly

One of the most effective methods for finding a job is making direct contact with employers. You can do this many different ways:

1. **Use the telephone:** Few people enjoy making cold calls to strangers, especially since doing so results in many rejections. However, job seekers who contact numerous employers by phone do generate job interviews. In fact, this is the fastest way to get job interviews. Make 100 phone calls to inquire about job vacancies and you may be able to generate one or two job interviews. Since this is largely a numbers game, and you are playing the odds, you must be willing to make many phone calls and endure numerous rejections. Most people you call will politely tell you they have no jobs available at present. But persistence will pay off. You will eventually uncover job vacancies for which you qualify. Use the Yellow Pages as your directory for identifying potential employers. When making such calls, have a prepared outline of points to cover in front of you from which you (1) quickly introduce yourself, (2) ask about job vacancies, (3) request a job interview, and (4) thank the person for his or her time and consideration. Don't write it out word for word and read it. If you do this, you will sound as if you are reading it. You want to sound spontaneous. If you receive a rejection, that's okay. In the process, you may acquire some useful information about jobs elsewhere. And you can now move on to call the next potential employer!

2. **Send e-mail:** If you use the Internet, you should explore the websites of employers. While many of these websites will post employment opportunities, others may not. If they don't, send an e-mail inquiring about such opportunities. However, if you can find a phone number, it's best to make a telephone call rather than wait for an e-mail reply. Many companies automatically delete unsolicited e-mail inquiries. E-mail is no substitute for using the telephone, which is more efficient and effective than e-mail.

3. **Go door to door:** Many job seekers are successful in finding jobs by literally showing up at the doors or work sites of employers and asking about job opportunities. This approach requires a great deal of initiative, entrepreneurship, and a willingness to accept rejections as part of the game. This is the in-your-face version of the cold telephone call. Many businesses, such as large retail stores (Wal-Mart, K-Mart, Target, Home Depot), grocery stores, restaurants, and banks, are well organized to handle walk-in job seekers. You may be asked to sit at a computer terminal or "job kiosk" to complete an electronic application, or you will be given a paper application to complete (see Chapter 9). Others, such as construction firms, often welcome individuals to show up at their job sites for work. If you walk into a small business, such as a warehouse, auto repair shop, or construction company, you may be able to meet directly with the owner and ask about job opportunities. Timing is the key to such walk-in approaches – if you happen to arrive at the right time, when a job needs to be filled immediately, you may get lucky and be offered the job. If that happens, be prepared to interview (see Chapter 11) for a job while inquiring about opportunities. If you use this approach, be prepared for many rejections. However, if you persist and visit 100 employers, chances are you will uncover one or two job opportunities for which you qualify. If you visit 500 employers, you may uncover five job opportunities. But you will probably experience a few hundred rejections in the process of uncovering the right job for you.

4. **Hang around busy corners:** Day-laborer sites, both formal and informal, are used a great deal by illegal immigrants and individuals with limited skills and education. Day-laborer sites may be found on a busy street corner or adjacent to a convenience store or vacant lot. Large day-laborer markets of Hispanics (*jornaleros*) are especially prevalent in Southern California, Arizona, Texas, and Florida where they have recently become very controversial political issues.

   Employers – usually home owners or subcontractors who need cheap day laborers – may stop to check who is available for a few hours or a day or two of temporary work. Most work is physical labor – landscaping, roofing, gardening, construction – and wages are usually negotiated on an hourly, daily, or per job basis. In many communities, informal day-laborer sites represent a gray market of undocumented workers (illegal immigrants) and cash wages (no tax or Social Security deductions). Cities in some states, such as California, Washington, Arizona, Illinois, New York, Connecticut, Maryland, Georgia, Florida, and Washington, DC, actually sponsor formal day-laborer sites where employers can come to hire laborers. In California and Arizona, these markets are 95 percent His-panic. In Chicago, many homeless African Americans participate in these markets. In New York City a large number of Polish and Indian (Sikh) immigrants also participate.

Despite controversies concerning the illegal immigrant and taxation questions, day-laborer centers offer employment options for poor people who lack sufficient education and skills, and who are willing to tolerate unstable and often exploitative work (many are cheated by unscrupulous employers) situations. In fact, some studies show that nearly 25 percent of day laborers prefer such unstable work situations to other types of employment. Many can make $80 to $100 or more a day by just showing up when they want to work. In some cases day laborer experiences turn into full-time jobs, especially with subcontractors who decide to hire the best of the many day laborers they have worked with and thus have a chance to screen their on-the-job behavior.

Register With Employment Agencies and Placement Services

Public employment services operate One-Stop Career Centers (www.careeronestop.org), which post many vacancies listed by employers in their communities. These centers also are linked to America's Job Bank (www.ajb.dni.us), an electronic job bank which includes over 1 million job listings. Be sure to visit your local center and acquaint yourself with the many useful free services available to the public. Many employment agencies and placement services look for candidates they can place with their clients. Register-ing with these agencies and services can result in temporary or permanent jobs. However, beware of any

Beware of any agency or service that wants you to pay them for employment services. The legitimate firms are paid by employers.

agency or service that wants you to pay them for employment services. The legitimate firms are paid by employers – not by job seekers. Anyone who asks you to pay them money to find you a job should be avoided. You can find legitimate agencies through a One-Stop Career Center (ask their personnel for recommended agencies and services). Two of the best known temporary labor and staffing firms found in hundreds of communities across the country are LaborFinders (www.laborfinders.com) and Manpower (www.manpower.com). You may want to visit these firms early in your job search since they may be able to help you quickly find employment with their many clients. Also, check on dozens of other temporary employment firms that may operate in your community. If your community has a specialized program to assist ex-offenders, chances are they also have a placement program designed to quickly place ex-offenders in jobs with employers who are interested in hiring ex-offenders. If you are a college graduate, you can use the placement services of the career center or alumni office. For recent college graduates this means signing up for on-campus job interviews through the career services center.

Attend Job Fairs

Job fairs are great ways to survey job opportunities, meet employers, network, practice resume and interview skills, learn about salaries and benefits, and possibly get hired on the spot. While you will find many job fairs operating in large cities (check the classified section of your Sunday newspaper for large ads announcing such events), many correctional institutions also sponsor job fairs for ex-offenders.

The typical job fair is held in a large conference room of a hotel or a public building and takes place over one day – often from 9am to 4pm. Many employers have representatives at tables or booths who advertise their company or organization and are looking for candidates who meet their hiring requirements. Job seekers circulate among the various displays (booths and tables) as they try to learn more about the organizations, pick up literature, talk with a representative, and leave a resume. Job fairs can be very enlightening experiences for job seekers, especially if they find a good selection of employers and if the job fair also includes special job search workshops, such as writing resumes, interviewing for jobs, or using a job fair in your job search. Job fairs for ex-offenders are great places to find employment since employers already indicate, by their participation, that they are willing to hire ex-offenders. However, employers attending such job fairs are not looking for just any ex-offenders – they want to hire the best of the best who have basic education and workplace skills.

You should keep the following eight tips in mind when planning to attend a job fair:

1. **Check to see if you qualify for the job fair.** Some job fairs are open to the general public and involve many different types of employers. These general job fairs are sometimes sponsored by a single company that is opening a new business and needs to recruit hundreds of people, such as a large hotel and conference center, sports arena, or an amusement park, Many job fairs specialize in a particular skill or occupational area. For example, some job fairs only focus on high-tech and computer skills. Others may specialize in clerical skills or the construction trades. And still others may be organized for government-related jobs, including specialized job fairs of government contractors looking for individuals with military backgrounds as well as those with security clearances.

Special career events, such as career conferences sponsored by a single company, may be by invitation only.

2. **Be sure to pre-register for the job fair.** Many job fairs require you to register before the event – not just show up at the door. One of the registration requirements is to submit a resume which, in turn, is entered into a resume database. This database enables employers attending the job fair to review the resumes online both before and after the job fair.

3. **Plan ahead.** Prior to attending the event, try to get a list of companies that will be attending. Research several of the companies on the Internet. Discover what they do, who they employ, and what is particularly unique or different about them. When you go the job fair, you will have some knowledge of those employers you want to meet. Better still, you'll impress the representatives when you indicate you know something about what they do. You'll avoid asking that killer question – _"What do you do?"_ Being prepared in this manner also means you will be more at ease in talking with employers, because you have some common ground knowledge for engaging in an intelligent job-oriented conversation.

4. **Bring copies of your resume to the job fair.** Since you will be meeting many employers at the job fair as you circulate from one table or booth to another, your calling card is your resume. A good rule of thumb is to bring 25 to 50 copies of your resume to the job fair. If the employer is interested in you, they will want to see your resume. Best of all, they will give you instant feedback on your qualifications. In many cases, they will interview you on the spot and may even hire you that day! So make sure you write a terrific resume as well as bring enough copies for every employer you are interesting in meeting.

5. **Dress appropriately.** Job fairs are places where first impressions are very important. Be sure to dress as if you were going to a formal job interview – conservative, neat, and clean. If, for example, you have tattoos on your arm, wear a long-sleeve shirt. While your tattoos may be an interesting conversation piece with some friends and strangers, they are negative distractions for many employers, who may question your choices.

6. **Prepare a 30-second pitch.** Your 30-second pitch should tell an employer who you are and what skills and experience you have that should be of interest to the employer. Tell them why they should consider interviewing and hiring you.

7. **Be prepared to interview for the job.** Since some employers will actually interview candidates and hire them at the job fair, don't assume a job fair is merely a casual "get together" to just meet employers. Prepare for a job fair in the same way you would prepare for a job interview – bring a positive attitude, be enthusiastic and energetic, anticipate questions, prepare your own questions, and observe all the verbal and nonverbal rules for interview success (see Chapter 11).

8. **Follow up your contacts within five days.** Job fairs are all about networking with employers. If you're interested in an employer and you've had a chance to meet a representative and get his or her name and business card, be sure to follow up with a phone call and/or e-mail within five days of your meeting. This communication will remind the individual of your continuing interest and may result in a formal job interview with other company representatives.

If you are currently incarcerated, check with your library or education department to see if they have a copy of this excellent video: *An Ex-Offender's Guide to Job Fair Success*.

Network With Family, Friends, and Others

The single most effective way of getting a job is through networking. Your network consists of family, friends, your P.O., former supervisor, acquaintances, minister, people you do business with, and even strangers whom you meet and with whom you develop a relationship. These people can be of assistance in finding a job, because many have useful information, advice, and referrals to others who know about jobs appropriate for you. You want to plug into these informal yet rich channels of job information and communications.

*Through networking, you tap into the **hidden job market** where many of the best jobs can be found.*

As we noted earlier, most jobs are not advertised. Through networking, you tap into the **hidden job market** where many of the best jobs can be found. These jobs are located through word-of-mouth. People in your network – family members, friends, P.O., and others – know about such jobs, or they may know people who may know, and thus they refer you to others in the know. The more networking you do, the more likely you will find a job on the hidden job market.

However, many people are reluctant to network because it involves initiating conversations and meetings with others. The twin fears of embarrassment (I'm unemployed and an ex-offender) and rejection (they may say *"No, I can't help you"*) work against many job seekers. But these are false fears that seldom materialize. Instead, people who learn to network well are surprised how supportive others are in giving them useful information, advice, and referrals. Many of these people have been in similar situations and others helped them with their job search. Most people enjoy helping others, as long as they are not put on the spot and asked to take responsibility for your employment fate! Networkers are not beggars – they are nice people who are in search of information and advice, and hopefully useful referrals to people who have the power to hire.

We devote Chapter 10 to the whole process of networking in the job search. We show you how to launch an effective networking campaign. Read it carefully and put it into practice immediately. It may well become your most important approach to landing a job that's right for you!

6

Assess Your Skills and Identify Your MAS

S ELF-ASSESSMENT IS THE BASIS for conducting a successful job search. You first need to know who you are in terms of your interests, skills, and abilities **before** you can state a clear objective and communicate your strengths to employers. Without this self knowledge and lacking a clear sense of purpose, you are likely to be confused as you wonder where to search for a job that will best fit your interests, skills, abilities, and values.

Discover the Truth About You

Discovering who you are and what you really want to do is by no means easy. It requires conducting a long and honest conversation with your best friend – yourself – in which you get to meet and know yourself in greater depth.

You probably talk to yourself a lot – that little inner voice that goes from fear, worry, and anger to optimism, joy, and happiness. If you are a con artist, scammer, or sociopath, your conversation may be directed toward manipulating and taking advantage of others. If you have low self-esteem, your inner voice may focus, like a broken record, on what's wrong with you and avoid taking positive steps.

More often than not, our conversation with ourselves is negative, confusing, and disorganized – jumping from one subject to another, but never really focused on taking actions that produce positive outcomes. That's about to change, at least we hope it will within a few hours of reading this chapter and relating it to Chapter 7.

We need to get your inner voice focused on what's **positive** about you and your future. You must be brutally **honest** with yourself. No games, no tricks, no lies, no manipulation, no scamming – just the truth about you. This truth may initially hurt, but it, too, will set you free as you go on to landing a good job and leading a productive life based on an understanding of your unique talents. It will have a surprising effect on your self-esteem – you will actually meet a new you who has lots of good things to say about you. Best of all, your self-assessment may transform you from the person you thought you were to the person you want to be.

Bear with us. This and Chapter 7 are long and tedious chapters on two of the most important subjects you will ever deal with – discovering the **real you** and changing the **direction of your life**. Since these closely related chapters are the most important chapters of this book, spend some serious time completing the exercises. You will be well rewarded!

Ask yourself:

- *What do I do well?*
- *What do I do poorly?*
- *What do I enjoy doing?*
- *What do I dislike doing?*
- *What do I want to do during the next 12 months? Five years?*
- *What do I want to do with the rest of my life?*
- *What kind of person do I want to become?*

Ask Powerful Questions About Yourself

Through a series of probing questions and exercises, your self-assessment activities enable you to answer this two-part question:

*What do I **do well** and **enjoy doing**?*

This question focuses on **specifying your interests, skills, and abilities** and prepares you for answering the next critical question:

*What do I **really** want to do?*

When you answer this question, you are prepared to **state your job or career objective**. Taken together, these two questions will help you organize a powerful job search that clearly focuses on your major strengths and goals. These two questions also will help improve the quality of your conversation with both yourself and others!

What Employers Want From You

It's not surprising what employers want from their employees – truthfulness, character, and value. They want to better **predict your future behavior** based upon a clear understanding of your past patterns of behavior. You can help them achieve this understanding by organizing this step in your job search around the qualities of truthfulness, character, and value.

As we noted earlier (Chapter 2) in our discussion of myths and realities centered around "qualifications," employers attempt to hire individuals who are competent, intelligent, honest, enthusiastic, and likable. At the same time, many employers are suspicious of candidates, because they have encountered manipulators, scammers, and deceivers among job applicants. They actually hired some people who turned out to be the wrong choice for the job, costing the company money, embarrassing the hiring manager, and even endangering other employees in the workplace.

In fact, recent surveys indicate that nearly two-thirds of job seekers include inaccurate information on applications and resumes, from fictitious degrees, schools, and accomplishments to nonexisting employers, employment dates, positions, responsibilities, and awards. Some of these inaccuracies are unintentional, but others are deliberate lies in order to cover up not-so-hot backgrounds and to get the job. Many of these inaccuracies surface during job interviews as candidates give deceptive answers to questions, or during the first 90 days on the job when an employer has the chance to observe actual on-the-job behavior.

> *Employers want* **truthfulness**, **character**, *and* **value** – *no lies, no scamming, no cheating about you and your work.*

Employers aren't stupid. Dealing with people they really don't know well – basically strangers – they are suspicious about putting such people on the company payroll. If you assume you can manipulate employers, think again. Get over your misplaced sense of power, which indicates you may be headed for trouble in both the job market and the workplace.

Employers anticipate all types of personalities, motivations, and behaviors – positive, negative, and manipulative – from strangers who want a job. Books such as *Don't Hire a Crook*, *101 Mistakes Employers Make and How to Avoid Them*, *Hiring the Best*, *Hiring Smart*, and *The Safe Hiring Manual: The Complete Guide to Keeping Criminals, Imposters, and Terrorists Out of Your Workplace* are on the reading lists of many employers. In fact, employers can tell you lots of stories about the characters they have met, hired, and fired!

While employers may appear to trust what you say, they also want to verify your credentials and observe what you actually do. This means conducting background checks (over 95 percent of employers do this), asking probing behavior-based questions, subjecting candidates to multiple job interviews, and administering a variety of revealing tests (aptitude, drug, personality, psychological, and polygraph) to discover the truth about you. **Verification and observation** are the real basis for trust – not questionable resumes and clever conversations with strangers.

Above all, employers want **value** for their money – people who can do the job well. Take, for example, a recent survey by the National Association of Colleges and

Employers (www.naceweb.org/press). It found that college graduates with strong communication skills and integrity have a distinct advantage in the job market. The most highly valued candidates were ones who demonstrated strong communication skills, honesty/integrity, interpersonal/teamwork skills, and a strong work ethic. These skills were more highly valued than computer, leadership, and organizational skills. These tend to be the same skills employers look for in candidates who do not have a college degree. As an ex-offender, you need to make sure these highly desired skills are part of your skill set and clearly communicate them to employers.

At this stage in your job search, it's extremely important that you take a complete inventory of your skills so you can better communicate with employers what it is you do well and enjoy doing. Once you do this and formulate a clear objective, you will be on the road to finding the right job for you. Your self-assessment will end much of your confusion as you begin charting an exciting path to renewed job and life success.

Your Skills and Abilities

Most people possess two types of skills that define their strengths as well as enable them to move within the job market: work-content skills and functional skills. These skills become the key **language** – both verbs and nouns – for communicating your qualifications to employers through your resumes and letters as well as in interviews.

Functional skills can be transferred from one job or career to another.

We assume you have already acquired certain **work-content skills**. These "hard skills" are easy to recognize since they are often identified as "qualifications" for specific jobs, they are the subject of most education and training programs and often relate to a specialized skill language that non-specialists may consider to be jargon. Work-content skills tend to be technical and job-specific in nature. Examples of such skills include welding, painting, cooking, cleaning, landscaping, repairing air conditioners, programming computers, selling real estate, wiring a room, or operating a complicated piece of machinery. They may require formal training, are associated with specific trades or professions, and are used only in certain job settings. While these skills do not transfer well from one occupation to another, they are critical for entering and advancing within specific occupations.

At the same time, you possess many **functional/transferable skills** employers readily seek along with work-content skills. These are "soft skills" associated with **numerous** job settings. They are mainly acquired through experience rather than formal training, and can be communicated through a general vocabulary. Functional/transferable skills are less easy to recognize since they tend to be linked to certain **personal characteristics** (energetic, intelligent, likable) and the ability to **deal with**

processes (communicating, problem-solving, motivating) rather than **doing things** (programming a computer, building a house, repairing air conditioners).

Most people view the world of work in traditional occupational job skill terms. This is a **structural view** of occupational realities. Occupational fields are seen as consisting of separate and distinct jobs which, in turn, require specific work-content skills. From this perspective, occupations and jobs are relatively self-contained entities. Social work, for example, is seen as being different from paralegal work; social workers, therefore, are not "qualified" to seek paralegal work.

Ex-offenders as a group possess few marketable occupational skills, because of their youth, limited education, and spotty work experience. If, on the other hand, you have participated in pre-release education and vocational programs, you will have some work-content skills to include on your applications, in your resume, and during job interviews.

On the other hand, a **functional view** of occupations and jobs emphasizes the similarity of job characteristics as well as common links among different occupations. For example, if you work with people, data, processes, and objects in one occupation, you can transfer that experience to other occupations which have similar functions. Ex-offenders who have been involved in illegal activities have many transferable skills – from planning, organization, and communication to persistence, leadership, and problem-solving – that can be applied to legitimate work activities.

The skills we identify and help you organize in this chapter are the functional skills that define your **strengths**. While most people have only a few work-content skills, they may have numerous – as many as 300 – functional/transferable skills. These skills enable job seekers to more easily change jobs and careers without acquiring additional education and training. They constitute an important bridge for moving from one occupation to another. But you must first be aware of your functional skills before you can relate them to the job market.

Before you decide if you need more education or training, you should first assess both your functional and work-content skills to see how they best fit into different jobs and occupations. Once you do this, you should be better prepared to communicate your qualifications to employers with a rich skills-based vocabulary.

Focus on Key Strengths and Questions

If you begin your job search by focusing on your **strengths**, you'll be able to quickly identify your work-content and functional skills. While you should be aware of your weaknesses, your strengths give you needed direction and keep you focused on what's really important to employers.

Without knowing your strengths, you will lack focus and your motivation may suffer accordingly. After all, your goal should be to find a job that is fit for you rather than one you think you might be able to fit into. You can best do this by asking the right questions about your strengths and then assessing what you do best – your skills and abilities.

Knowing the right questions to ask will save you time and steer you into productive job search channels from the very beginning. Asking the wrong questions can leave you confused and frustrated. The questions must be understood from the perspectives of both employers and applicants.

Two of the most humbling questions you will encounter in your job search are *"Why should I hire you?"* and *"What are your weaknesses?"* While employers may not directly ask these questions, they ask them nonetheless. If you can't answer these questions in a positive manner – directly, indirectly, verbally, or nonverbally – your job search will be in trouble, and you will join the ranks of the unsuccessful and disillusioned job searchers who feel something is wrong with them. Ex-offenders and individuals who have lost their jobs are especially vulnerable to these questions, since many already have low self-esteem and a negative self-image. Many such people focus on what is wrong rather than what is right about themselves, which tends to be self-destructive. By all means avoid such negative thinking!

> *Employers want to hire your **value or strengths** – not your weaknesses.*

Employers want to hire your **value or strengths** – not your weaknesses. Since it is easier to identify and interpret weaknesses, employers look for indicators of your strengths by trying to identify your weaknesses. The more successful you are in communicating your strengths, the better off you will be in relation to both employers and fellow applicants.

Your Strengths and Weaknesses

Unfortunately, many people work against their own best interests. Not knowing their strengths, they market their weaknesses by first identifying job vacancies and then trying to fit their "qualifications" into job descriptions. This approach often frustrates applicants; it presents a picture of a job market which is not interested in the applicant's strengths and it leads to the often-heard complaint of frustrated job seekers – *"No one will hire me!"* This leads some people toward acquiring new skills which they hope will be marketable, even though they do not enjoy using them. Millions of individuals find themselves in such misplaced situations: the divorce lawyer who would rather be teaching in a university; the computer programmer who enjoys cooking and would love to be a top chef; the surgeon who is an accomplished pianist; or the salesman who is good at managing a community fund-raising drive. Your task is to avoid joining the ranks of the misplaced and unhappy workforce by first understanding your skills and then relating them to your values, interests, and goals. In so doing, you will be in a better position to target your job search toward jobs that should become especially rewarding and fulfilling.

Your Functional/Transferable Skills

We know most people stumble into jobs by accident. Some are in the right place at the right time to take advantage of opportunities. Others work hard at trying to fit into jobs posted on the Internet; listed in classified ads, employment agencies, and personnel offices; identified through friends and acquaintances; or found by knocking on doors or just showing up. After several years in the work world, many people wish they had better planned their careers from the very start. All of a sudden they are unhappily locked into jobs because of retirement benefits and family responsibilities of raising children and meeting monthly mortgage payments.

If you are an ex-offender with limited work experience and few strengths, you especially need to understand and identify your transferable or functional skills. Once you have done this, you will be better prepared to identify what it is you want to do. Moreover, your self-image and self-esteem will improve. Better still, you will be prepared to communicate your strengths to others through a rich skills-based vocabulary. These outcomes are critically important for completing applications and writing your resume and letters (Chapter 9) as well as for networking and interviewing (Chapters 10 and 11).

Your goal should be to find a job that is fit for you rather than one you think you might be able to fit into.

Let's illustrate the concept of functional/transferable skills for ex-offenders who are currently incarcerated. Many of them view their skills in strict work-content terms – knowledge of a particular job or a specific education and training experience, such as cleaning buildings, dishwashing, cooking, repairing radios, working in the laundry, grounds keeping, landscaping, repairing machinery, welding, fixing air conditioners, plumbing, using computers, or making furniture. While there are many general labor and trade jobs on the outside directly related to these prison experiences (carpentry, construction, janitorial work, kitchen jobs, culinary work, electrical work, automotive repair, office work, pipefitting, welding, and electronic), many other jobs may relate to your transferable skills which may be your major strengths.

Ex-offenders possess several skills that are directly transferable to a variety of jobs. Unaware of these skills, they may fail to communicate their strengths to others. For example, if you have participated in educational and vocational programs, you may have demonstrated several of the following **transferable organizational and interpersonal skills**:

1. Communication
2. Decision-making
3. Following orders/instructions
4. Selling/persuading
5. Logical thinking
6. Team building/playing
7. Organizing/prioritizing
8. Reviewing/evaluating
9. Trouble-shooting
10. Problem solving

In addition, you may have demonstrated some of these **transferable personality and work-style traits** sought by employers in many occupational fields:

1. Quick learner/astute
2. Diligent/patient
3. Honest/trustworthy
4. Loyal/motivated
5. Patient/calm
6. Punctual/reliable
7. Assertive/initiative
8. Responsible/cooperative
9. Intelligent/sensitive
10. Accurate/talented

If you have done a good job, your supervisor will likely focus on complimenting you about these skills and traits, which also gives your P.O. some idea of your major strengths. Both individuals may be important to your job search, especially when it comes time to provide references.

As just noted, most functional/transferable skills can be classified into these two general skills and trait categories – organizational/interpersonal skills and personality/work-style traits:

Organizational and Interpersonal Skills

___ communicating
___ trouble-shooting
___ problem solving
___ implementing
___ analyzing/assessing
___ self-understanding
___ planning
___ understanding
___ decision-making
___ setting goals
___ innovating
___ conceptualizing
___ thinking logically
___ generalizing
___ evaluating
___ managing time
___ identifying
    problems

___ creating
___ synthesizing
___ judging
___ forecasting
___ controlling
___ tolerating
    ambiguity
___ organizing
___ motivating
___ persuading
___ leading
___ encouraging
___ selling
___ improving
___ performing
___ designing
___ reviewing
___ consulting

___ attaining
___ teaching
___ team building
___ cultivating
___ updating
___ advising
___ coaching
___ training
___ supervising
___ interpreting
___ estimating
___ achieving
___ negotiating
___ reporting
___ administering
___ managing
___ multi-tasking
___ defending

Personality and Work-Style Traits

___ diligent
___ honest
___ patient

___ reliable
___ innovative
___ perceptive

___ persistent
___ assertive
___ tactful

___ sensitive	___ receptive	___ candid
___ loyal	___ resourceful	___ frank
___ astute	___ diplomatic	___ adventuresome
___ successful	___ determining	___ cooperative
___ risk taker	___ self-confident	___ firm
___ versatile	___ creative	___ dynamic
___ easygoing	___ tenacious	___ sincere
___ enthusiastic	___ open	___ self-starter
___ calm	___ discreet	___ initiator
___ outgoing	___ objective	___ precise
___ flexible	___ talented	___ competent
___ expressive	___ warm	___ sophisticated
___ competent	___ empathic	___ diplomatic
___ adaptable	___ orderly	___ effective
___ punctual	___ tidy	___ efficient
___ democratic	___ tolerant	___ cool and collected

These are the types of skills you need to identify and then communicate to employers in your resumes and letters as well as during interviews.

Identify Your Skills

You should take some vocational tests and psychological inventories to identify your values, interests, skills, aptitudes, and temperament. Most are pencil-and-paper or computerized tests which are administered and interpreted by a career professional. Several prisons, jails, and detention centers administer assessment devices as part of their pre-release programs. Once you enter your community, several of these inventories are available at low cost ($20) through the career services centers of local community colleges. Also, check with your local One-Stop Career Center for information on such inventories and tests.

The most widely used assessment devices are the *Myers-Briggs Type Indicator*®, *Strong Interest Inventory*®, *Self-Directed Search*®, and *Campbell*™ *Interest and Skill Survey*:

- **Myers-Briggs Type Indicator® (MBTI®):** This is the most popular personality inventory in the world used by psychologists and career counselors. It has multiple applications for everything from marital counseling to executive development programs. It attempts to measure personality dispositions and interests – the way people absorb information, decide, and communicate. It analyzes preferences to four dichotomies (extroversion/introversion, sensing/intuiting, thinking/feeling, judging/perceiving) which result in 16 personality types. The MBTI® comes in a variety of forms. Available through CPP, Inc. (www.cpp.com and www.skillsone.com) and most colleges, universities, and testing centers.

- **Strong Interest Inventory®:** Next to the *Myers-Briggs Type Indicator®* and the *Self-Directed Search®* , this remains one of the most popular assessment devices used by career counselors. Individuals respond to 317 multiple-choice items to determine their occupational interests according to six occupational themes, 25 interest scales, occupational scales, and personal style scales. Used extensively for career guidance, occupational decisions, employment placement, educational choices, and vocational rehabilitation programs. Available through CPP, Inc. (www.cpp.com) and most schools, colleges, universities, and testing centers.

- **Self-Directed Search® (SDS):** One of the most widely used and adapted interest inventories in career counseling. Designed to assist individuals in making career choices based on an analysis of different orientations toward people, data, and things. It matches interests with six types (realistic, investigative, artistic, social, enterprising, and conventional) that are, in turn, related to different types of occupations that match these types. Used in helping determine how one's interests fit with various occupations. Available through Psychological Assessment Resources (www.parinc.com).

- **Campbell™ Interest and Skill Survey (CISS®):** One of the most popular assessments devised for measuring interests and skills. Includes 320 items divided into 200 interest and 120 skill categories. Available through NCS Pearson (www.pearsonassessments.com).

Other popular assessment devices, which measure different aspects of personality and behavior, include:

Personality and Motivation

- *California Psychological Inventory Form 434 (CPI™ 434)* (www.cpp.com)
- *Edwards Personal Preference Schedule* (www.harcourtassessment.com)
- *Enneagram* (www.enneagraminstitute.com)
- *Keirsey Character Sorter* (http:// kcirsey.com)
- *16-Personality Factor Questionnaire* (16PF) (www.pearsonassessments.com)

Values

- *Career Beliefs Inventory (CBI)* (www.cpp.com)
- *Minnesota Importance Questionnaire (MIQ)* (www.psych.umn.edu)
- *Survey of Interpersonal Values (SIV)* (www.pearsonreidlondonhouse.com)
- *Temperament and Values Inventory*
- *O*NET Career Values Inventory* (http://jist.com)

Interests and Attitudes

- *Career Assessment Inventory™ – Enhanced Version (CAI-E)* (www.pearsonassessments.com)
- *Career Exploration Inventory* (http://jist.com)
- *Career IQ and Interest Test (CIQIT)* (www.proedinc.com)
- *Guide to Occupational Exploration Interest Inventory* (http://jist.com)
- *Harrington-O'Shea Career Decision-Making System* (www.agsnet.com)
- *Jackson Vocational Interest Survey (JVIS)* (http://jvis.com)
- *Job Search Attitude Inventory (JSAI)* (http://jist.com)
- *Kuder Occupational Interest Survey* (www.kuder.com)
- *Leisure to Occupational Connection Search (LOCS)* (http://jist.com)
- *Leisure/Work Search Inventory* (http://jist.com)
- *Ohio Vocational Interest Survey* (www.harcourtassesment.com)
- *Vocational Interest Inventory* (http://jist.com)

Skills, Behaviors, Aptitudes

- *Barriers to Employment Success Inventory* (http://jist.com)
- *BRIGANCE® Diagnostic Employability Skills Inventory* (www.curriculumassociates.com)
- *Career Decision Scale* (www.parinc.com)
- *FIRO-B®* (www.cpp.com)

Multiple Indicators

- *APTICOM* (www.vri.org)
- *Armed Services Vocational Battery (ASVAB)*
- *Assessment of Career Decision Making (ACDM)* (www.wpspublish.com)
- *The Birkman Method* (www.birkman.com)
- *CAM Computerized Computerized One-Stop* (www.pesco.org)
- *Career Scope* (www.vri.org)
- *Key Educational Vocational Assessment System (KEVAS)*
- *Vocational Interest, Temperament, & Aptitude System (VITAS)* (www.vri.org)

At the same time, you'll find several assessment devices available online. The following seven websites are well worth exploring for both free and fee-based online assessments tools:

- **SkillsOne**   www.skillsone.com
  (CPP's online assessment system)   www.cpp-db.com
- **CareerLab.com**   www.careerlab.com
- **Self-Directed Search®**   www.self-directed-search.com
- **Personality Online**   www.personalityonline.com
- **Keirsey Character Sorter**   www.keirsey.com
- **MAPP™**   www.assessment.com
- **PersonalityType**   www.personalitytype.com

These 16 additional sites also include a wealth of related assessment devices that you can access online:

- **Analyze My Career**   www.analyzemycareer.com
- **Birkman Method**   www.birkman.com
- **Career Key**   www.careerkey.org/english
- **CareerLeader™**   www.careerleader.com
- **CareerPlanner.com**   www.careerplanner.com
- **CareerPerfect.com**   www.careerperfect.com
- **Careers By Design®**   www.careers-by-design.com
- **CollegeBoard.com**   www.myroad.com
- **Enneagram**   www.ennea.com
- **Humanmetrics**   www.humanmetrics.com
- **Jackson Vocational Interest Inventory**   www.jvis.com
- **My Future**   www.myfuture.com
- **People Management International**   www.sima-pmi.com
- **Profiler**   www.profiler.com
- **QueenDom.com**   www.queendom.com
- **Tests on the Web**   www.2h.com

We present several good alternatives to the above assessment devices in the remainder of this chapter that are designed to identify both your work-content and transferable skills and then relate them to your interests, values, and motivations. These self-assessment techniques stress your positives or strengths rather than identify your negatives or weaknesses. Each exercise requires a different investment of your time and effort as well as varying degrees of assistance from other people.

These exercises, however, should be used with caution. They provide you with a clear picture of your **past**, which may or may not be particularly useful for charting your future. Nonetheless, these exercises do help individuals:

1. Organize data on themselves.
2. Target their job search around clear objectives and skills.
3. Generate a rich vocabulary of skills and accomplishments for communicating their strengths to potential employers.

If you feel these exercises are inadequate for your needs, by all means seek professional assistance from a testing or assessment center staffed by a licensed psychologist or certified career counselor. Many such centers can do in-depth testing which goes further than these self-directed skill exercises.

Checklist Method

This is the simplest method for identifying your strengths. Review the different types of transferable skills outlined on pages 75-76. Place a "1" in front of the skills that **strongly** characterize you; assign a "2" to those skills that describe you to a **large extent**; put a "3" before those that may or may not describe you to **some extent**. When finished, review the lists and identify, in order of importance, the top 10 characteristics that best describe you on each list.

Autobiography of Accomplishments

Write a lengthy essay about your **life accomplishments**. This could range from 10 to 25 pages. After completing the essay, go through it page by page to identify what you most enjoyed doing (working with different kinds of information, people, and things) and what skills you used most frequently as well as enjoyed using. Finally, identify those skills you wish to continue using. After analyzing and synthesizing this data, you should have a relatively clear picture of your strongest skills.

Computerized Assessment Programs

While the previous self-directed exercises required you to either respond to checklists of skills or reconstruct and analyze your past job experiences, several computerized self-assessment programs are designed to help individuals identify their skills. Many of the programs are available in career centers, and some can be accessed online. Some of the most widely used programs include:

- *Career Navigator*
- *Choices*
- *Discover*
- *Guidance Information System* (GIS)
- *Self-Directed Search* (SDS) Form R
- *SIGI-Plus*

Most of these programs do much more than just assess skills. They also integrate other key components in the career planning process – values, interests, goals, related jobs, college majors, education and training programs, and job search plans. These programs are widely available in schools, colleges, One-Stop Career Centers, and libraries across the country and many are free of charge in your community. You might check with the career or counseling center at your local community college or your local One-Stop Career Center (visit www.servicelocator.org and www.careerone-stop.org for various locations) to see what computerized career assessment programs are available for your use.

Relatively easy to use and taking one to two hours to complete, these programs generate a great deal of valuable career planning and job search information. Many will print out a useful analysis of how your interests and skills are related to specific jobs and careers. Such programs come closest to our notion of a magic bullet – they generate a great deal of personal and professional data for such a small investment of time, effort, and money.

Your Interests and Values

Just knowing your abilities and skills will not give your job search the direction it needs for finding a job that's right for you – one you both do well and enjoy doing. You also need to know your **work values and interests**. These are the basic building blocks for setting goals and targeting your abilities toward certain jobs and careers.

Take, for example, the ex-offender who does a superb job cleaning floors, hauling trash, or typing. While he possesses marketable skills (janitors, trash haulers, computer operators are in demand), if he doesn't regularly use these job-related skills and is more interested in working outdoors or with people, his abilities will not become **motivated skills**. In the end, your interests and values will determine which skills should play a central role in your job search.

Work, Leisure, and Home-Based Interests

We all have interests. Most change over time. Many of your interests may center on your past jobs, whereas others relate to activities that define your hobbies and leisure activities. Still other interests may relate to your dreams.

While many of the tests we previously identified focus on identifying and analyzing interests, the following exercises are more open-ended and require self analysis rather than assistance from a professional. Two good places to start identifying your interests are *The Guide to Occupational Exploration* and *The Enhanced Guide to Occupational Exploration*, which classify all jobs into 12 interest areas.

Examine the following list of interest areas. In the first column check those work areas that appeal to you. In the second column rank order those areas you checked in the first column. Start with "1" to indicate the most interesting:

Your Work Interests

Yes/No (x)	Ranking (1-12)	Interest Area
___	___	**Artistic:** An interest in creative expression of feelings or ideas.
___	___	**Scientific:** An interest in discovering, collecting, and analyzing information about the natural world, and in applying scientific research findings to problems in medicine, the life sciences, and the nature sciences.

___ ___ **Plants and animals:** An interest in working with plants and animals, usually outdoors.

___ ___ **Protective:** An interest in using authority to protect people and property.

___ ___ **Mechanical:** An interest in applying mechanical principles to practical situations by using machines or hand tools.

___ ___ **Industrial:** An interest in repetitive, concrete, organized activities done in a factory setting.

___ ___ **Business detail:** An interest in organized, clearly defined activities requiring accuracy and attention to details (office settings).

___ ___ **Selling:** An interest in bringing others to a particular point of view by personal persuasion, using sales and promotion techniques.

___ ___ **Accommodating:** An interest in catering to the wishes and needs of others, usually on a one-to-one basis.

___ ___ **Humanitarian:** An interest in helping others with their mental, spiritual, social, physical, or vocational needs.

___ ___ **Leading and influencing:** An interest in leading and influencing others by using high-level verbal or numerical abilities.

___ ___ **Physical performing:** An interest in physical activities performed before an audience.

The Guide to Occupational Exploration also includes other checklists relating to home-based and leisure activities. You may discover that some of your home-based and leisure activity interests should become your work interests. Examples of such interests include:

Leisure and Home-Based Interests

___ Acting in a play or amateur variety show.

___ Advising family members on their personal problems.

___ Announcing or emceeing a program.

___ Applying first aid in emergencies as a volunteer.

___ Building model airplanes, automobiles, or boats.

___ Building or repairing radios, televisions, or other electronic equipment.

___ Buying large quantities of food or other products for an organization.

___ Campaigning for political candidates or issues.

___ Canning and preserving food.

___ Carving small wooden objects.

___ Coaching children or youth in sports activities.

___ Collecting experiments involving plants.

___ Conducting house-to-house or telephone surveys for a PTA or other organization.

___ Creating or styling hairdos for friends.

___ Designing your own greeting cards and writing original verses.

___ Developing film/printing pictures.
___ Doing impersonations.
___ Doing public speaking or debating.
___ Entertaining at parties or other events.
___ Helping conduct physical exercises for disabled people.
___ Making ceramic objects.
___ Modeling clothes for a fashion show.
___ Mounting and framing pictures.
___ Nursing sick pets.
___ Painting the interior or exterior of a home.
___ Playing a musical instrument.
___ Refinishing or re-upholstering furniture.
___ Repairing electrical household appliances.
___ Repairing the family car.
___ Repairing or assembling bicycles.
___ Repairing indoor plumbing.
___ Speaking on radio or television.
___ Taking photographs.
___ Teaching in Sunday School.
___ Tutoring pupils in school subjects.
___ Weaving rugs or making quilts.
___ Writing articles, stories, or plays.
___ Writing songs for club socials or amateur plays.

Indeed, many people turn hobbies or home activities into full-time jobs after deciding that such "work" is what they really enjoy doing.

For more sophisticated treatments of work interests, which are also validated through testing procedures, contact career counselors, women's centers, testing and assessment centers, or the appropriate publishers for information on these tests:

- *Career Assessment Inventory*
- *Career Exploration Inventory*
- *Jackson Vocational Interest Survey*
- *Kuder Occupational Interest Survey*
- *Leisure/Work Search Inventory*
- *Ohio Vocational Interest Survey*
- *Strong Interest Inventory*®
- *Vocational Interest Inventory*

Your Key Work Values

Work values are those things you like to do. They give you pleasure and enjoyment. Most jobs involve a combination of likes and dislikes. By identifying what you both like and dislike about jobs, you should be able to better identify jobs that involve tasks you most enjoy. Several exercises can help you identify your work values. First, identify what most satisfies you about work by completing this exercise:

My Work Values

I prefer employment which enables me to:

____ contribute to society	____ be creative
____ have contact with people	____ supervise others
____ work alone	____ work with details
____ work with a team	____ gain recognition
____ compete with others	____ acquire security
____ make decisions	____ make money
____ work under pressure	____ help others
____ use power and authority	____ solve problems
____ acquire new knowledge	____ take risks
____ be a recognized expert	____ work at own pace

Select four work values from the above list which are the most important to you and list them in the space below. List any other work values (desired satisfactions) which were not listed above but are nonetheless important to you:

1. _____

2. _____

3. _____

4. _____

Another approach to identifying work values is outlined in *The Guide to Occupational Exploration* below. If you feel you need to go beyond the above exercises, try this one. In the first column check those values that are most important to you. In the second column rank order the five most important values:

Ranking Work Values

Yes/No (x)	Ranking (1-5)	Work Values
____	____	**Adventure:** Working in a job that requires taking risks.
____	____	**Authority:** Working in a job in which you use your position to control others.
____	____	**Competition:** Working in a job in which you compete with others.
____	____	**Creativity and self-expression:** Working in a job in which you use your imagination to find new ways to do or say something.
____	____	**Flexible work schedule:** Working in a job in which you choose your hours to work.

____	____	**Helping others:** Working in a job in which you provide direct services to persons with problems.
____	____	**High salary:** Working in a job where many workers earn a large amount of money.
____	____	**Independence:** Working in a job in which you decide for yourself what work to do and how to do it.
____	____	**Influencing others:** Working in a job in which you influence the opinions of others or decisions of others.
____	____	**Intellectual stimulation:** Working in a job which requires a great amount of thought and reasoning.
____	____	**Leadership:** Working in a job in which you direct, manage, or supervise the activities of other people.
____	____	**Outside work:** Working out-of-doors.
____	____	**Persuading:** Working in a job in which you personally convince others to take certain actions.
____	____	**Physical work:** Working in a job which requires substantial physical activity.
____	____	**Prestige:** Working in a job which gives you status and respect in the community.
____	____	**Public attention:** Working in a job in which you attract immediate notice because of appearance or activity.
____	____	**Public contact:** Working in a job in which you daily deal with the public.
____	____	**Recognition:** Working in a job in which you gain public notice.
____	____	**Research work:** Working in a job in which you search for and discover new facts and develop ways to apply them.
____	____	**Routine work:** Working in a job in which you follow established procedures requiring little change.
____	____	**Seasonal work:** Working in a job in which you are employed only at certain times of the year.
		Travel: Working in a job in which you take frequent trips.
____	____	**Variety:** Working in a job in which your duties change frequently.
____	____	**Work with children:** Working in a job in which you teach or care for children.
____	____	**Work with hands:** Working in a job in which you use your hands or hand tools.
____	____	**Work with machines or equipment:** Working in a job in which you use machines or equipment.
____	____	**Work with numbers:** Working in a job in which you use mathematics or statistics.

Second, develop a comprehensive list of your past and present **job frustrations and dissatisfactions**. This should help you identify negative factors you should avoid in future jobs.

My Job Frustrations and Dissatisfactions

List as well as rank order as many past and present things that frustrate or make you dissatisfied and unhappy in job situations:

                                                                  Rank

1. _____ _____

2. _____ _____

3. _____ _____

4. _____ _____

5. _____ _____

6. _____ _____

7. _____ _____

8. _____ _____

9. _____ _____

10. _____ _____

Third, brainstorm a list of "Ten or More Things I Love to Do." Identify which ones could be incorporated into what kinds of work environments:

Ten or More Things I Love to Do

Item	Related Work Environment
1. _____	_____
2. _____	_____
3. _____	_____
4. _____	_____
5. _____	_____
6. _____	_____
7. _____	_____
8. _____	_____
9. _____	_____
10. _____	_____

Fourth, list at least 10 things you most enjoy about work and rank each item accordingly:

Ten Things I Enjoy the Most About Work

Rank

1. _____ _____

2. _____ _____

3. _____ _____

4. _____ _____

5. _____ _____

6. _____ _____

7. _____ _____

8. _____ _____

9. _____ _____

10. _____ _____

Fifth, you should also identify the types of interpersonal environments you prefer working in. Do this by specifying the types of people you like and dislike associating with:

Interpersonal Environments

Characteristics of people I like working with:	Characteristics of people I dislike working with:
_____	_____
_____	_____
_____	_____
_____	_____
_____	_____
_____	_____
_____	_____
_____	_____

No one test, instrument, or exercise will give you complete assessment information. You are well advised to use a variety of approaches to answer your self-assessment questions in the process of identifying what you really want to do.

Identify Your Motivated Abilities and Skills (MAS)

Once you know what you really do well and enjoy doing, your next task should be to analyze those interests, values, abilities, skills, and temperaments that form a **recurring motivated pattern**. This pattern is the single most important piece of information you need to know about yourself in the whole self-assessment process. Knowing your skills and abilities alone without understanding how they relate to your interests, values, and temperament will not give you the necessary direction for finding the job you want. You simply **must** know your pattern. Once you do, your job search activities may take on a whole new direction that will produce amazing results. You'll be able to state a clear objective (Chapter 7) that will guide you toward achieving your goals. So let's discover your pattern.

What's Your MAS?

Your pattern of motivated abilities and skills becomes evident once you analyze your **achievements or accomplishments**. For it is your achievements that tell us what you both do well and enjoy doing. If we analyze and synthesize many of your achievements, we are likely to identify a **recurring pattern** that probably goes back to your childhood and which will continue to characterize your achievements in the future.

> *Once you uncover your pattern, get prepared to acknowledge it and live with it in the future.*

An equally useful exercise is to identify your **weaknesses** by identifying your bad habits and analyzing your failures. These, too, would fall into recurring patterns. Understanding what your weaknesses are might help you avoid jobs and work situations that bring out the worst rather than the best in you. Indeed, you may learn more about yourself by analyzing your failures than by focusing solely on your accomplishments.

Another interesting approach is to examine how you have dealt with some of life's most **challenging situations**, such as your incarceration, an illness, accident, divorce, financial difficulties, starting a business, or a death in the family. Many of these difficult situations required character, drive, persistence, and problem-solving strategies beyond the ordinary. They may have drawn on inner strengths or a reservoir of skills you never knew you had but which occasionally came to the forefront when you were under extreme pressure. Moreover, your handling of these difficult situations might have led to life-altering consequences for you and those around you.

For now, let's focus on your positives rather than identify your negatives or how you coped with difficult situations. After you complete the strength exercises in this chapter, you may want to reverse the procedures to identify your weaknesses and challenges.

Numerous self-directed exercises can assist you in identifying your pattern of motivated abilities and skills. The basic requirements for making these exercises work for you are **time and analytical ability**. You must spend a great deal of time detailing your achievements by examining your history of accomplishments. Once you complete the historical reconstruction task, you must comb through your "stories" to identify **recurring** themes and patterns. This requires a high level of analytical ability which you may or may not possess. If analysis and synthesis are not two of your strong skills, you may want to seek assistance from someone who is good at analyzing and synthesizing information presented in narrative form.

Motivated Skills Exercise

One of the most useful exercises we and thousands of others use yields some of the best data on motivated abilities and skills. Initially developed by Dr. Bernard Haldane, the father of modern career counseling, this exercise is variously referred to as *"Success Factor Analysis," "System to Identify Motivated Skills,"* or *"Intensive Skills Identification."*

This exercise helps you identify which skills you **enjoy** using. While you can do it on your own, it is best to work with someone else. Since you will need six to eight hours to properly complete this exercise, divide your time into two or three work sessions.

The exercise consists of six steps. The steps follow the basic pattern of generating raw data, identifying patterns, analyzing the data through reduction techniques, and synthesizing the patterns into a transferable skills vocabulary. You need strong analytical skills to complete this exercise on your own. The six steps include:

1. **Identify 15-20 achievements:** While ideally you should inventory over 100-150 achievements, let's start by focusing on a minimum of 15-20 achievements. These consist of things you enjoyed doing, believe you did well, and felt a sense of satisfaction, pride, or accomplishment in doing. You can see yourself performing at your best and enjoying your experiences when you analyze your achievements. This information reveals your motivations since it deals entirely with your voluntary behavior. In addition, it identifies what is right with you by focusing on your positives and strengths. Identify achievements throughout your life, beginning with your childhood. Your achievements should relate to specific experiences – not general ones – and may be drawn from work, leisure, education, military, or home life. Put each achievement at the top of a separate sheet of paper

on which you will further elaborate. For example, your achievements might appear as follows:

Sample Achievement Statements

"When I was 10 years old, I started a small paper route and built it up to the largest in my district."

———————————

"I started playing basketball in ninth grade and became team captain in my junior year, the same year we had an undefeated season."

———————————

"When I was in junior high school, I sang tenor in the church choir and was asked to sing solos at several Sunday services."

———————————

"Designed, constructed, and displayed the Christmas nativity display at my church when I was 16 years old."

———————————

"Earned enough money as a cook at Jerry's Diner to help my grandmother buy a much-needed pair of eyeglasses."

———————————

"While I was small compared to other guys, I made the first string on my high school football team."

———————————

"Although incarcerated and struggling with reading, I was the first in my family to complete a GED and start working on a college degree."

———————————

"I helped a fellow inmate improve his reading and persuaded him to complete his GED and participate in the vocational program. I was so proud to learn he got a job three weeks after release and is now doing very well and has even enrolled in junior college."

———————————

"I proposed reorganizing the prison library and was put in charge of a team of four people who developed and implemented a plan that resulted in a 15-percent increase in the use of the library by fellow inmates. The warden complimented me on my excellent work."

———————————

2. Prioritize your seven most significant achievements.

    1. _____

    2. _____

3. _____

4. _____

5. _____

6. _____

7. _____

3. **Write a full page on each of your prioritized achievements.** You should describe:

    - How you initially became involved.
    - The details of **what you did** and **how you did it**.
    - What was especially enjoyable or satisfying to you.

    Use copies of the "Detailing Your Achievements" form on page 92 to outline your achievements.

4. **Elaborate on your achievements:** Have one or two other people interview you. For each achievement have them note on a separate sheet of paper any terms used to reveal your skills, abilities, and personal qualities. To elaborate details, the interviewer(s) may ask:

    - What was involved in the achievement?
    - What was your part?
    - What did you actually do?
    - How did you go about that?

    Clarify any vague areas by providing an example or illustration of what you actually did. Use these questions to get more details:

    - Would you describe in detail one example of what you mean?
    - Could you give me an illustration?
    - What were you good at doing?

    This interview should clarify the details of your activities by asking only "what" and "how" questions. It should take 45 to 90 minutes to complete. Make copies of the "Strength Identification Interview" form on page 93 to guide you through this interview.

5. **Identify patterns by examining the interviewer's notes:** Together, identify the recurring skills, abilities, and personal qualities **demonstrated** in your achievements. Search for patterns. Your skills pattern should be

Detailing Your Achievements

ACHIEVEMENT # ___: _____

_____

_____

1. How did I initially become involved? _____

_____

_____

_____

2. What did I do? _____

_____

_____

_____

_____

3. How did I do it? _____

_____

_____

_____

_____

4. What was especially enjoyable about doing it? _____

_____

_____

_____

_____

Strength Identification Interview

Interviewee _____   Interviewer _____

INSTRUCTIONS: For each achievement experience, identify the **skills** and **abilities** the achiever actually demonstrated. Obtain details of the experience by asking **what** was involved with the achievement and **how** the individual made the achievement happen. Avoid "why" questions which tend to mislead. Ask for examples or illustrations of **what** and **how**.

Achievement #1:

Achievement #2:

Achievement #3:

Recurring abilities and skills:

clear at this point; you should feel comfortable with it. If you have questions, review the data. If you disagree with a conclusion, disregard it. The results must accurately and honestly reflect how you operate.

6. **Synthesize the information by clustering similar skills into categories:** For example, your skills might be grouped in the following manner:

Synthesized Skill Clusters

Investigate/Survey/Read Inquire/Probe/Question	Teach/Train/Drill Perform/Show/Demonstrate
Learn/Memorize/Practice Evaluate/Appraise/Assess Compare	Construct/Assemble/Put together Organize/Structure/Provide definition/Plan/Chart course
Influence/Involve/Get participation/Publicize Promote	Strategize/Coordinate Create/Design/Adapt/Modify

This exercise yields a relatively comprehensive inventory of your skills. The information will better enable you to use a **skills vocabulary** when identifying your objective, writing your resume and letters, and interviewing. If you are like many others who have successfully completed this exercise, your self-confidence and self-esteem should increase accordingly.

Become a Purpose-Driven Ex-Offender

All of the exercises outlined in this chapter were designed to explore your **past** and **present**. At the same time, you need to project your skills and values into the **future**. What, for example, do you want to do over the next five, 10, or 20 years? We examine this question in the next chapter when we focus on developing a powerful objective for guiding your job search and perhaps your life.

Once you formulate your objective, you'll be prepared to take actions that should lead to a good job. Highly motivated and focused, you'll organize an effective job search that focuses laser-like on what you do well and enjoy doing. With an objective clearly reflecting your skills and values, a whole new world of work and satisfaction will open to you. You will become a purpose-driven ex-offender who knows exactly what he or she wants to do, and you'll become single-minded in achieving your goal.

As we noted earlier, you have the power within you to change your life. Unleashing that power requires relating all of the information you gathered on yourself in this chapter, especially your MAS, to the important work you will do in the next chapter to develop that all-important objective.

7

Develop a Powerful Objective

ONE YOU HAVE IDENTIFIED your motivated abilities and skills (MAS) in Chapter 6, you should be well prepared to develop a clear and purposeful objective for targeting your job search toward specific jobs, organizations, and employers. You should be able to clearly communicate to employers, with an appropriate set of examples and stories of success, that you are a talented and purposeful individual who **achieves results**.

Your objective must tell employers what you will **do for them** rather than what you want from them. It focuses your pattern of accomplishments on the needs of employers. As such, it should be employer-centered rather than self-centered.

Mission Statements, Goals, and Objectives

Your objective is not the same as a mission statement, which is usually associated with the kind of person you would like to become. A mission statement is more closely associated with your purpose or significance in life, and it might be identified through an obituary exercise – a statement of how you would like to be remembered after you die.

Goals and objectives are statements of what you want to do in the future. When combined with an assessment of your interests, values, abilities, and skills, and related to specific jobs, they give your job search needed direction and meaning for the purpose of targeting specific employers. Without them, your job search may become disorganized as you present an image of uncertainty and confusion to potential employers. Employers want to hire talented, enthusiastic, and purposeful individuals. Your goal should be to find a job or career that is compatible with your interests, motivations, skills, and talents as well as related to a vision of your future. In other words, try to find a job fit for you and your future rather than try to fit into a job that happens to be advertised and for which you think you can qualify. Your ultimate goal should be to find a job and career you really love.

Orient Yourself to Employers' Needs

Your objective should be a concise statement of what you want to do and what you have to offer to an employer. The position you seek is "what you want to do"; your qualifications are "what you have to offer."

Your objective should state your strongest qualifications for meeting employers' needs. It should communicate what you have to offer an employer without emphasizing what you expect the employer to do for you. In other words, your objective should be **work-centered**, not self-centered; it should not contain over-used terms that emphasize what **you** want, such as give me a(n) "opportunity for advancement," "position working with people," "progressive company," or "creative position." Such terms are viewed as "canned" job search language which say little of value about you, the candidate. Above all, your objective should reflect your honesty and integrity; it should not be "hyped."

Most job hunters lack clear objectives. Many engage in a random and somewhat mindless search for jobs by identifying available job opportunities and then adjusting their skills and objectives to fit specific job openings. While you can get a job using this approach, you may be misplaced and unhappy with what you find. You will fit into a job rather than find a job that is fit for you.

Be Purposeful and Realistic

Your objective should communicate that you are a **purposeful individual who achieves results**. It can be stated over different time periods as well as at various levels. You can identify short, intermediate, and long-range objectives and very general to very specific objectives. Whatever the case, it is best to know your prospective audience before deciding on the type of objective for your job search. Your objective should reflect **your career interests** as well as **employers' needs**.

Objectives also should be **realistic**. You may want to become president of the United States or solve all the world's problems. However, these objectives are unrealistic. While they may represent your ideals and fantasies, you need to be more realistic in terms of what you can personally accomplish in the immediate future given your particular skills, pattern of accomplishments, level of experience, and familiarity with the job market. What, for example, are you prepared to deliver to prospective employers over the next few months? While it is good to set challenging objectives, you can overdo it. Refine your objective by thinking about the next major step or two you would like to make in your career advancement. Develop a **realistic** action plan that focuses on the details of progressing your career one step at a time.

Project Yourself Into the Future

Even after identifying your abilities and skills, specifying an **objective** can be the most difficult and tedious step in the job search process; it can stall the resume writing process indefinitely. This simple one-sentence, 25-word statement can take days or weeks to formulate and clearly define. Yet, it must be specified prior to writing the resume and engaging in other job search steps. An objective gives meaning and direction to all other activities in your job search.

Your objective should be viewed as a function of several influences. Since you want to build upon your strengths and you want to be realistic, your abilities and skills will play a central role in formulating your work objective. At the same time, you do not want your objective to become a function solely of your past accomplishments and skills. You may be very skilled in certain areas, but you may not want to use these skills in the future. As a result, your values and interests will help determine which skills you will or will not incorporate into your work objective.

Overcoming the problem of historical determinism – your future merely reflecting your past – requires incorporating additional components into defining your objective. One of the most important is your ideals, fantasies, or dreams. Everyone engages in these, and sometimes they come true. Your ideals, fantasies, or dreams may include making $1,000,000 by age 40; owning a Mercedes-Benz and a Porsche; taking trips to Rio, Hong Kong, and Rome; owning your own business; developing financial independence; writing a best-selling novel; solving major social problems; or winning the Nobel Peace Prize. Since your fantasies require more money than you are now making, you will need to incorporate monetary considerations into your work objective.

Four major steps are involved in developing a realistic work objective. Each step can be implemented in a variety of ways:

STEP 1: Develop or obtain basic information on your functional/transferable skills, which we discussed in Chapter 6.

STEP 2: Acquire supportive information about yourself from others, tests, and yourself. Several resources are available for this purpose:

A. **From others:** Ask three to five individuals whom you know well to evaluate you according to the questions in the "Strength Evaluation" form on page 98. Explain to these people that you believe their candid opinion will help you better understand of your strengths and weaknesses from the

Strength Evaluation

TO: _____

FROM: _____

I am going through a career assessment process and thought you would be an appropriate person to ask for assistance. Would you please truthfully respond to the questions below? Your comments will be given to me by the individual named below; s/he will not reveal your name. Your comments will be used for advising purposes only. Thank you.

What are my strengths?

What weak areas might I need to improve?

In your opinion, what do I need in a job or career to make me satisfied?

Please return to: _____

perspectives of others. Make copies of this form and ask your evaluators to complete and return it to a designated third party who will share the information – but not the respondent's name – with you.

B. From vocational tests: Although we prefer self-generated data, vocationally oriented tests can help clarify, confirm, and translate your understanding of yourself into occupational directions. If you decide to use vocational tests, contact a professional career counselor who can administer and interpret the tests. Refer to our review of such tests in Chapter 6 (pages 76-78).

C. From yourself: Refer to the previous exercises in Chapter 6 that assist you in identifying your work values, job frustrations and dissatisfactions, things you love to do, things you enjoy most about work, and your preferred interpersonal environments.

STEP 3: Project your values and preferences into the future by completing simulation and creative thinking exercises:

A. Ten Million Dollar Exercise: First, assume that you unexpectedly received a $10,000,000 gift; now you don't have to work. Since the gift is restricted to your use only, you cannot give any part of it away. What will you do with your time? At first? Later on? Second, assume that you are given another $10,000,000, but this time you are required to give it all away. What kinds of causes, organizations, charities, etc. would you support? Complete the following form in which you answer these questions:

What Will I Do With Two $10,000,000 Gifts?

First gift is restricted to my use only:

_____

_____

_____

Second gift must be given away:

_____

_____

_____

B. Obituary Exercise: Make a list of the most important things you would like to do or accomplish before you die. Two alternatives are available for doing this. First, make a list in response to this lead-in statement: *"Before I die, I want to..."*

Before I Die, I Want to . . .

1. _____
    _____
2. _____
    _____
3. _____
    _____
4. _____
    _____
5. _____
    _____

Second, write a newspaper article which is actually your obituary for 10 years from now. Stress your accomplishments over the coming 10-year period.

C. My Ideal Work Week: Starting with Monday, place each day of the week as the headings of seven sheets of paper. Develop a daily calendar with 30-minute intervals, beginning at 7am and ending at midnight. Your calendar should consist of a 118-hour week. Next, beginning at 7am on Monday (sheet one), identify the **ideal activities** you would enjoy doing, or need to do, for each 30-minute segment during the day. Assume you are capable of doing anything; you have no requirements except those you impose on yourself. Furthermore, assume that your work schedule consists of 40 hours per week. How will you fill your time? Be specific.

D. My Ideal Job Description: Develop an ideal job. Be sure you include:

- Specific interests you want to build into your job
- Work responsibilities
- Working conditions
- Earnings and benefits
- Interpersonal environment
- Working circumstances, opportunities, and goals

STEP 4: Test your objective against reality. Evaluate and refine it by doing the following:

A. Market Research: Four steps are involved in conducting this research:

1. **Products or services:** Based upon all other assessment activities, make a list of what you **do** or **make**:

Products/Services I Do or Make

1. _____
2. _____
3. _____
4. _____
5. _____

2. **Market:** Identify who needs, wants, or buys what you do or make. Be very specific. Include individuals, groups, and organizations. Then, identify **what** specific **needs** your products or services fill. Next, assess the **results** you achieve with your products or services.

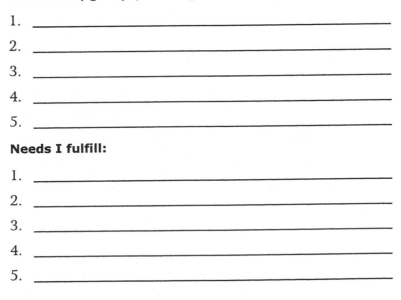

The Market for My Products/Services

Individuals, groups, and organizations needing me:

1. _____
2. _____
3. _____
4. _____
5. _____

Needs I fulfill:

1. _____
2. _____
3. _____
4. _____
5. _____

Results/outcomes/impacts of my products/services:

1. _____
2. _____
3. _____
4. _____
5. _____

3. **New Markets:** Brainstorm a list of **who else** needs your products or services. Think about ways of expanding your market. Next, list any new needs your current or new market has which you might be able to fill:

Developing New Needs

Who else needs my products/services?

1. _____
2. _____
3. _____
4. _____
5. _____

New ways to expand my market:

1. _____
2. _____
3. _____
4. _____
5. _____

New needs I should fulfill:

1. _____
2. _____
3. _____
4. _____
5. _____

4. **New products and/or services:** List any new products or services you can offer and any new needs you can satisfy:

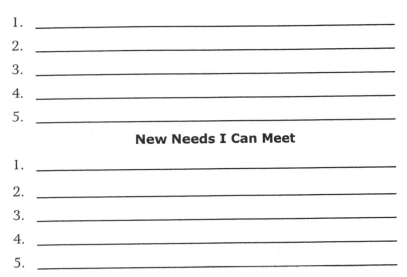

New Products/Services I Can Offer

1. _____
2. _____
3. _____
4. _____
5. _____

New Needs I Can Meet

1. _____
2. _____
3. _____
4. _____
5. _____

B. **Force Field Analysis:** Once you develop a tentative or firm objective, force field analysis can help you understand the various internal and external forces affecting the achievement of your objective. Follow this order of activities:

- **Clearly state your objective or course of action.** Make sure it's based upon your MAS from Chapter 6 and is employer-oriented rather than self-centered.

- **List the positive and negative forces affecting your objective.** Specify the internal and external forces working **for** and **against** you in terms of who, what, where, when, and how much. Estimate the impact of each on your objective.

- **Analyze the forces.** Assess the importance of each force upon your objective and its probable effect upon you. Some forces may be irrelevant to your goal. You may need additional information to make a thorough analysis.

- **Maximize positive forces and minimize negative ones.** Identify actions you can take to strengthen positive forces and to neutralize, overcome, or reverse negative forces. Focus on real, important, and probable key forces.

- **Assess the likelihood of attaining your objective** and, if necessary, modifying it in light of new information.

C. **Conduct Online and Library Research:** This research should strengthen and clarify your objective. Consult various reference materials on alternative jobs and careers. Many these resources are available in print form at your local library or bookstore. Some are available electronically and can be accessed through your local library. (Check to see if your library has online databases, such as Dun and Bradstreet's, which can be accessed from a home computer using your local library card.) If you explore the numerous company profiles and career sites available on the Internet, you should be able to tap into a wealth of information on alternative jobs and careers. Two good resources for beginning online research are Margaret Riley Dikel's *The Guide to Internet Job Search* (McGraw-Hill) and Ron and Caryl Krannich, *America's Top Internet Job Sites* (Impact Publications). See Chapter 8 for more information on conducting research.

D. **Conduct Informational Interviews:** This may be the most useful way to clarify and refine your objective. See Chapter 10 for details on networking and informational interviews.

After completing these steps, you will have identified what it is you **can** do (abilities and skills), enlarged your thinking to include what it is you would **like** to do (aspirations), and explored the realities of implementing your objective. Thus, setting a realistic work objective is a function of the many considerations outlined on page 105.

Your work objective is a function of both subjective and objective information as well as combines idealism with realism. We believe the strongest emphasis should be placed on your competencies and should include as much information on yourself as possible. Your work objective is realistic in that it is tempered by your past experiences, accomplishments, skills, and current research. An objective formulated in this manner permits you to think beyond your past experiences – a definite plus for ex-offenders who need to chart a new life after prison.

State a Functional Objective

Your job objective should be oriented toward skills and results or outcomes. You can begin by stating a functional job objective at two different levels: a general objective and a specific one for communicating your qualifications to employers both on resumes and in interviews. Thus, this objective-setting process sets the stage for other key job search activities. For the general objective, begin with the statement:

Objective Setting Process

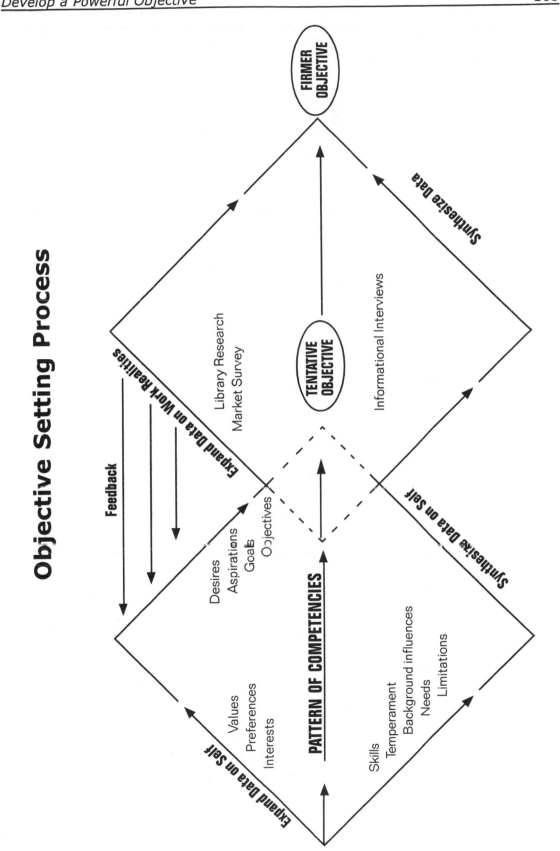

Stating Your General Objective

I would like a job where I can use my ability to _____*which will result in* _____.

The objective in this statement is both a **skill** and an **outcome**. For example, you might state:

Skills-Based and Results-Oriented Objective

I would like a job where my experience in landscaping, supported by strong design interests and maintenance abilities, will result in more customers and greater profits for the company.

At a second level you may wish to re-write this objective in order to target it at various landscaping companies. For example, on your resume it becomes:

Job-Targeted Objective

An increasingly responsible planning position in landscaping, where proven design and maintenance abilities will be used for expanding the company's clientele.

The following are examples of weak and strong objective statements. Various styles are also presented.

Weak Objectives

A challenging Landscaping position with a progressive company that leads to career advancement.

———————————

A position in Substance Abuse Counseling that will allow me to work with people in a helping capacity.

———————————

A position in Electronics with a progressive firm.

———————————

Sales Representative with opportunity for advancement.

———————————

Stronger Objectives

To use computer science training in **software development** *for designing and implementing operating systems.*

*To use innovative **landscape design** training for developing award-winning approaches to designing commercial properties.*

———————————

*A responsible **front desk position** with a major hotel that uses strong organization and communication skills for improving customer service.*

———————————

*A **masonry position** with a commercial construction firm that values creative stonework and rewards hard working, responsible, and loyal employees.*

———————————

*A challenging **sales position** in real estate where sales/customer service experience and strong communication and market skills will be used for expanding agency listings and commercial sales. Long term goal: top sales associate within five years and general manager of a branch real estate office within 10 years.*

———————————

Answer the Big Question

It is important to relate your objective to your audience. While you definitely want a good job that pays well, your audience wants to know what you can do for them in exchange for a good paying job. Remember, your objective should be work-centered, not self-centered.

We will return to this discussion when we examine how to develop the objective section on your resume. Your objective will become the key element for organizing all other elements on your resume. It

> *Your objective should be work-centered, not self-centered.*

gives meaning and direction to your job search. Your objective says something very important about how you want to conduct your life with the employer. It gives them an important indicator of the **value** you will bring to this job. Most important of all, it tells them who you really are in terms of your key values and accomplishments – a short answer to the big question of *"Why should I hire you?"*

8

Conduct Research on Jobs, Employers, and Communities

KNOWLEDGE IS POWER when conducting a job search. The more you know about yourself (Chapters 6 and 7), jobs, companies, and employers, the more effective you should be in making decisions that lead to landing the right job for you.

Life doesn't just happen. It involves making deliberate choices, which have both good and bad consequences. We believe you can make the best decisions based upon a good foundation of information rather than just doing things based upon emotions, guesses, or intuition. That's where research becomes important.

Research is the lifeblood of an effective job search. It is the process of acquiring information in order to make better choices. It involves reading, talking, listening, observing, analyzing, formulating conclusions, and selecting alternative courses of action.

Decisions, Decisions, Decisions

Once you are released, you have lots of important decisions to make – from housing to employment – that may have life-altering consequences. At times the pressure to make so many responsible decisions can be overwhelming, especially since most basic food, clothing, housing, work, and leisure decisions were made for you during your incarceration. Since you may be entering unfamiliar territory with new responsibilities, you want to gather as much information as possible before making important decisions. A simple decision, such as contacting a friend for information and advice or walking into a One-Stop Career Center to talk to a career counselor about job opportunities, can have important consequences if such contacts and resulting information lead to finding a job you can enjoy doing.

Let's look at how you can best conduct research for supporting a well organized and targeted job search. In so doing, you should be able to develop some useful research skills to better direct your job search.

Employment Decisions

Since you may know little about the job market, you need to acquire information in several important employment areas. These should become the central focus of your research activities:

1. **Job alternatives:** What jobs are available and which ones most interest you? What are the education and skill requirements, working conditions, and potential salary, benefits, and advancement opportunities?

2. **Employers and companies:** Who's hiring for what types of jobs? How do you reach the people who make the hiring decisions?

3. **Communities and neighborhoods:** Are you looking in the right places? Will you need to move or commute to your next job? Do you have probation or parole issues that may prevent you from relocating to another community?

Much research can be done during your pre-release. You can visit your prison library for resources, talk to correctional staff members, and write letters to family members, friends, and potential employers. If you do nothing else while incarcerated, read, read, read, and write, write, write about alternative jobs, employers, and communities. Talk to people in your institution about possible jobs and careers. Get focused on your future and develop new goals (Chapter 7). Learn to conduct informational interviews (see Chapter 10), which lead to acquiring information, advice, and referrals, by communicating with knowledgeable people.

Once you are released, your research options will increase dramatically. Now you can work with your P.O., who may have a list of local employers who regularly hire ex-offenders, and visit your local library, One-Stop Career Center, and several support groups that assist ex-offenders in transition. You can use the Internet and interview people by phone, e-mail, and in face-to-face meetings. Use these resources frequently. Start developing a plan of action for creating a new future centered around goals and employment.

Job Alternatives

A great deal of research can be done while you are incarcerated. Visit your library and look for any of these useful books and directories that examine alternative jobs and careers. Many are relevant to the interests, skills, and educational backgrounds of ex-offenders:

> *50 Best Jobs for Your Personality*
> *250 Best Jobs Through Apprenticeships*
> *300 Best Jobs Without a Four-Year Degree*
> *America's Top 100 Jobs for People Without a Four-Year Degree*
> *America's Top 101 Computer and Technical Jobs*
> *America's Top Jobs for People Re-Entering the Workforce*
> *Cool Careers for Dummies*
> *Enhanced Occupational Outlook Handbook*
> *Great Jobs in Two Years*
> *High-Tech Careers for Low-Tech People*
> *Occupational Outlook Handbook, 2004-2005*
> *The O*NET Dictionary of Occupational Titles*
> *Outdoor Careers*
> *Quick Prep Careers*
> *Top 100 Health Care Careers*

Most of these resources describe numerous jobs as well as include information on occupational outlook over the next 10 years, education and training requirements, working conditions, positions, salary ranges, and advancement opportunities.

We especially recommend reviewing the U.S. Department of Labor's *Occupational Outlook Handbook* and *The O*NET Dictionary of Occupational Titles*. Both books also can be viewed online by visiting these two websites:

- *Occupational Outlook Handbook*   www.bls.gov/oco
- *The O*NET Dictionary*   www.onetcenter.org

The *Occupational Outlook Handbook* reviews nearly 300 occupations covering over 85 percent of all jobs. *The O*NET Dictionary of Occupational Titles* provides details on nearly 1,110 jobs.

The U.S. Department of Labor gathers a great deal of information on growing and declining jobs. For example, their most recent surveys indicate the following jobs are the fastest growing jobs in the decade ahead. Each requires particular levels of education and training. As might be expected in today's high-tech and service economy, technical and service occupations will grow the fastest in the coming decade:

Fastest Growing Occupations, 2002-2012
(Numbers in thousands of jobs)

Occupational Title	Employment 2002	Employment 2012	Percent Change	Postsecondary Education or Training Needed
Medical assistants [3]	365	579	59	Moderate-term on-the-job training
Network systems and data communications analysts [1]	186	292	57	Bachelor's degree
Physician assistants [3]	63	94	49	Bachelor's degree
Social and human service assistants [3]	305	454	49	Moderate-term on-the-job training
Home health aides [4]	580	859	48	Short-term on-the-job training
Medical records and health information technicians [3]	147	216	47	Associate degree
Physical therapist aides [3]	37	54	46	Short-term on-the-job training
Computer software engineers, applications [1]	394	573	46	Bachelor's degree
Computer software engineers [1]	281	409	45	Bachelor's degree
Physical therapist assistants [2]	50	73	45	Associate degree
Fitness trainers and aerobics instructors [3]	183	264	44	Postsecondary vocational award
Database administrators [1]	110	159	44	Bachelor's degree
Veterinary technologists and technicians [3]	53	76	44	Associate degree
Hazardous materials removal workers [2]	38	54	43	Moderate-term on-the-job training
Dental hygienists [1]	148	212	43	Associate degree
Occupational therapist aides [3]	8	12	43	Short-term on-the-job training
Dental assistants [3]	266	379	42	Moderate-term on-the-job training
Personal and home care aides [4]	608	854	40	Short-term on-the-job training
Self-enrichment education teachers [2]	200	281	40	Work experience in a related occupation
Computer systems analysts [1]	468	653	39	Bachelor's degree
Occupational therapist assistants [2]	18	26	39	Associate degree
Environmental engineers [1]	47	65	38	Bachelor's degree
Postsecondary teachers [1]	1,581	1,284	38	Doctoral degree
Network and computer systems administrators [1]	251	345	37	Bachelor's degree
Environmental science and protection technicians, including health [2]	28	38	37	Associate degree
Preschool teachers, except special education [4]	424	577	36	Postsecondary vocational award
Computer and information systems managers [1]	284	387	36	Bachelor's or higher degree, plus Work experience
Physical therapists [1]	137	185	35	Master's degree
Occupational therapists [1]	82	110	35	Bachelor's degree
Respiratory therapists [2]	86	116	35	Associate degree

[1] Very high average annual earnings ($42,820 and over)
[2] High average annual earnings ($27,500 to $41,780)
[3] Low average annual earnings ($19,710 to $27,380)
[4] Very low average annual earnings (up to $19,600)

Employers and Companies

While it's important to know about alternative jobs and careers, including growing and declining occupations, in the end, you need specifics about who is actually hiring for what types of jobs in **your** community. After release, be sure to visit your local library and One-Stop Career Center, which will have a great deal of information on local businesses and employers. Ask for assistance in locating employers. The One-Stop Career Center may have a series of notebooks on local companies, including current job listings provided by various employers.

While many people primarily look to large companies for employment, don't forget to do research on small businesses and nonprofit organizations in your community which hire many more people than large companies. Indeed, small businesses account for nearly 85 percent of all employment in America. Many of these employers also are more willing to hire ex-offenders than large companies.

> *Don't forget to do research on small businesses and non-profit organizations. Many of these employers are more willing to hire ex-offenders than large companies.*

One of your best sources of information on employers and companies will be the Internet. Most businesses and organizations have their own websites, which include information about what they do and who and how they hire. Many also will have online application forms or information on submitting an electronic resume. You can easily find employers by using any major search engine, such as Google.com, Yahoo.com, MSN.com, or AskJeeves.com. Our favorite gateway websites or online directories to businesses and companies include:

- CEO Express   www.ceoexpress.com
- Hoover's Online   www.hoovers.com
- Dun and Bradstreet's Million
  Dollar Databases   www.dnbmdd.com/mddi
- Corporate Information   www.corporateinformation.com
- BizTech Network   www.brint.com

These are the top websites for conducting research on large companies and organizations. Small businesses can be accessed through some of these resources.

Websites that focus on **government jobs**, which you may or may not qualify for because of your background, include:

- FedWorld   www.fedworld.gov
- USA Jobs   www.usajobs.opm.gov
- FederalJobsCentral   www.fedjobs.com
- Federal Jobs Digest   www.jobsfed.com

Individuals interested in working in the **nonprofit sector** should visit these useful gateway websites:

- GuideStar   www.guidestar.org
- Action Without Borders   www.idealist.org
- Foundation Center   www.fdncenter.org
- Independent Sector   www.independentsector.org
- Internet Nonprofit Center   www.nonprofits.org

The following directories, which should be available through either your local library or One-Stop Career Center, are well worth reviewing:

- *Almanac of American Employers*
- *Almanac of American Employers: Mid-Size Firms*
- *The Directory of Corporate Affiliations: Who Owns Whom*
- *Dun & Bradstreet's Middle Market Directory*
- *Dun & Bradstreet's Million Dollar Directory*
- *Encyclopedia of Business Information Sources*
- *Standard & Poor's Industrial Index*
- *Standard Rate and Data Business Publications Directory*
- *Thomas' Register of American Manufacturers*

Communities

If the terms of your reentry include community restrictions because of probation, parole, or the nature of your crime, this section may be of limited usefulness in your job search. It also may be limited if you lack appropriate education and marketable skills for the job market. Nonetheless, it should become increasingly relevant in the years ahead after you have completed your post-release sentencing requirements.

Identifying the geographical area where you would like to work will be one of your most important decisions. Once you make this decision, other job search decisions and activities become easier. For example, if you live in a small town with limited job opportunities, you should consider moving to a city that has greater job opportunities or perhaps start your own business. If you decide to move, you will need to develop a long-distance job search campaign which would involve visiting community websites, writing letters, making long-distance phone calls, and visiting a community.

Deciding where you want to live involves researching various communities and comparing advantages and disadvantages of each. In addition to identifying specific job alternatives, organizations, and individuals in the community, you need to do research on other aspects of the community. After all, you will live in the community, buy or rent a residence, perhaps send children to school, and participate in community organizations and events. Often these environmental factors are just as important to your happiness and well-being as the particular job you accept. Renting an apartment in one community may run $300 a month whereas a similar apartment in another community may be over $1,000 a month. It would be foolish for you to take a new job without first researching several aspects of the community other than job opportunities.

Will you be living and looking for work in a community of hope or one of despair? Will you be relocating to one of the best or worst states for employment? Let's look at some revealing statistics on communities.

Unemployment By States (June 2004)

State	1,000's of Persons	Percentage
10 Lowest for Unemployment		
Vermont	11.3	3.2
South Dakota	14.4	3.3
North Dakota	12.3	3.4
Wyoming	9.6	3.4
Hawaii	21.5	3.5
Nebraska	36.9	3.7
Virginia	147.4	3.8
New Hampshire	28.8	3.9
Delaware	16.9	3.9
Maine	28.4	4.0
10 Highest for Unemployment		
District of Columbia	24.5	7.7
Alaska	24.8	7.0
Arizona	141.0	7.0
Louisiana	143.3	6.9
Michigan	348.1	6.8
Texas	719.8	6.5
New Mexico	59.2	6.5
California	1,110.4	6.3
Washington	196.6	6.1
Ohio	361.6	6.1

Employment and unemployment figures for states tell you nothing about the employment situation in particular cities and counties. For example, while Washington, DC has one of the highest unemployment rates in the country, three counties just 20 miles south and west of Washington, DC have the lowest unemployment rates in the country – Prince William, Fairfax, and Loudoun counties. Many of the best job opportunities will be found in thriving suburbs within 10 to 20 miles of large cities. Not surprisingly, many people move to these communities because of the abundance of good job opportunities.

You should consider moving to communities that are experiencing low unemployment coupled with steady job growth as well as offering attractive lifestyles. A *Fortune Magazine* survey in 2004 identified 25 cities as the best places for business and work. These cities are considered the top wealth creators which also offer attractive lifestyles and excellent quality of life. The first five cities are especially noted for their higher education institutions and high-tech orientation:

Fortune's Top 25 Metropolitan Area (2004)

Rank	Metro Area	Percent Job Growth (5 years)	Population
1	Madison, WI	32	443,000
2	Raleigh-Durham, NC	52	1,268,000
3	Austin, TX	30	1,349,000
4	Washington, DC	23	5,162,000
5	Atlanta, GA	50	4,386,000
6	Provo, UT	35	388,000
7	Boise, ID	12	465,000
8	Huntsville, AL	46	354,000
9	Lexington, KY	114	490,000
10	Richmond, VA	53	1,023,000
11	Omaha, NE	65	734,000
12	Albuquerque, NM	42	737,000
13	Knoxville, TN	29	704,000
14	Des Moines, IA	90	471,000
15	Houston, TX	55	4,420,000
16	Appleton, WI	78	367,000
17	San Diego, CA	15	2,907,000
18	Albany, NY	68	885,000
19	Minneapolis-St. Paul, MN	74	3,055,000
20	Ann Arbor, MI	54	603,000
21	Little Rock, AR	82	596,000
22	Charleston, SC	33	563,000
23	Fort Worth, TX	58	1,802,000
24	Colorado Springs, CO	47	544,000
25	Reno, NV	28	362,000

Communities in and around these metropolitan areas are likely to experience solid growth in the decade ahead. Many communities within the Washington (DC), Atlanta (GA), and Minneapolis/St. Paul (MN) metropolitan areas are already star performers, because of their extensive medical facilities and high-tech infrastructure as well as their attractive lifestyles. They will probably continue to be great growth communities. They will generate a disproportionate number of high paying jobs due to the high quality nature of their jobs and workforces.

Community growth and decline trends should be considered as part of your job and career options. If you live in a declining community with few opportunities for your skills and interests, seriously consider relocating to a growth community.

Depressed communities simply do not generate enough jobs for their populations, and the quality of jobs tends to be low. Many communities with populations of 100,000 to 500,000 offer a nice variety of job and lifestyle options.

Using several indicators of quality living, a 2004 study of the *American City Business Journals* identified the 20 best counties in the United States in terms of their incomes, education, housing, racial diversity, and short commuting times:

America's Top 20 Counties

Rank	Metro Area	Medium Income	Medium Home Value	Population
1	Los Alamos, NM	$78,993	$214,000	18,343
2	Olmsted, MN	$51,316	$114,700	124,277
3	Pitkin, CO	$59,375	$497,000	14,872
4	Douglas, CO	$82,929	$237,600	175,766
5	Loudoun, VA	$80,638	$202,300	169,599
6	Washington, MN	$66,305	$156,200	201,130
7	Johnson, KS	$61,455	$149,300	451,086
8	Hamilton, IN	$71,026	$163,600	182,740
9	Howard, MD	$74,167	$198,600	247,842
10	Fairfax, VA	$81,050	$222,400	969,749
11	Juneau, AK	$62,034	$179,200	30,711
12	Nantucket, MA	$55,522	$583,500	9,520
13	Wake, NC	$54,988	$156,200	627,846
14	Dakota, MN	$61,863	$148,500	355,904
15	Summit, UT	$64,962	$281,600	29,736
16	Dupage, IL	$67,687	$187,600	904,161
17	Chesterfield, VA	$58,537	$119,300	259,903
18	Fayette, GA	$71,227	$170,200	91,263
19	Hennepin, MN	$51,711	$141,100	1,116,200
20	Stafford, VA	$66,809	$155,100	92,446

For updated information, it's best to consult the latest surveys conducted by *Fortune Magazine* (www.fortune.com) and Sperling (www.bestplaces.net).

Research on different communities can be initiated from your local library or on a computer connected to the Internet. Several resources will provide you with a current profile of various communities. Statistical overviews and comparisons of states and cities, for example, are found in the **U.S. Census Data, The Book for the States,** and **The Municipal Yearbook.** Many libraries have a reference section of telephone books on various cities. If this section is weak or absent in your local library, check out several websites that function as **telephone directories**, such as:

- **Switchboard**   www.switchboard.com
- **SuperPages**   www.superpages.com
- **Yellow Pages**   www.yellow.com
- **Yahoo! Yellow Pages**   http://yp.yahoo.com

In addition to giving you names, addresses, and telephone numbers, the Yellow Pages are invaluable sources of information on local companies and organizations.

Many large libraries also have state and community directories as well as subscriptions to some state and community magazines and city newspapers. Using the Internet, you can explore hundreds of **newspapers and magazines** linked to these key websites:

- **Internet Public Library**   www.ipl.org/div/news
- **NewsDirectory.com**   http://newsdirectory.com
- **Newspapers.com**   www.newspapers.com

Research magazine, journal, and newspaper articles on different communities by consulting several print and online references available through your local library.

The Internet has a wealth of information on the best places to live and work. For information on the **best places to live**, visit these websites:

- **Find Your Spot**   www.findyourspot.com
- **Money Magazine**   www.money.cnn.com/real_estate/
                              index.html
- **Sperling's BestPlaces**   www.bestplaces.net

For information on the **best places to work**, check out these websites:

- **BestJobsUSA**   www.bestjobsusa.com/sections/
                              CAN-bestplaces2002/index.asp
- **Forbes Magazine**   www.forbes.com/lists
- **Fortune Magazine**   www.fortune.com (see "Rankings")
- **Great Place to Work**   http://greatplacetowork.com
- **Quintessential Careers**   www.quintcareers.com/best_
                              places_to_work.html
- **Working Mother**   www.workingmother.com
                              ("Working Mother Exclusives")

If you want to **explore various communities**, you should examine several of these gateway community sites:

- **Boulevards**   http://boulevards.com
- **Cities.com**   www.cities.com
- **CityGuides.Yahoo**   http://cityguides.local.yahoo.com
- **TOWD**   www.towd.com
- **Yahoo**   http://realestate.yahoo.com

Several relocation websites also provide a wealth of information on communities. Check these sites out for **linkages to major communities**:

- **Homestore.com**   http://homestore.com
- **Monstermoving.com**   www.monstermoving.monster.com
- **Relocation Central**   http://relocationcentral.com

Most major communities and newspapers have websites. You'll find a wealth of community-based information and linkages on such homepages, from newspapers and housing information to local employers, schools, recreation, and community services. Several employment sites include relocation information and salary calculators which provide information on the cost of living in, as well as the cost of moving to, different communities.

If you are trying to determine the best place to live, you should start with the latest edition of Bert Sperling's and Peter Sander's *Cities Ranked and Rated* and David Savageau's *Places Rated Almanac* (John Wiley & Sons). These books rank cities by various indicators. Both *Money* magazine and *U.S. News & World Report* publish annual surveys of the best places to live in the U.S.

You should also consult several city job banks that will give you contact information on specific employers in major metropolitan communities. Adams Media regularly publishes *The National JobBank* as well as several annual job bank guides. Some of the most popular titles include:

- *Atlanta JobBank*
- *Austin/San Antonio JobBank*
- *Boston JobBank*
- *Carolina JobBank*
- *Colorado JobBank*
- *Connecticut JobBank*
- *Chicago JobBank*
- *Dallas/Fort Worth JobBank*
- *Houston JobBank*
- *Los Angeles JobBank*
- *New Jersey JobBank*
- *New York JobBank*
- *Ohio JobBank*
- *Philadelphia JobBank*
- *Phoenix JobBank*
- *San Francisco JobBank*
- *Seattle JobBank*
- *Virginia JobBank*
- *Washington D.C. JobBank*

After narrowing the number of communities that interest you, further research them in depth. Start by exploring community homepages on the Internet (search by community name). Then kick off community-based research. Ask your relatives, friends, and acquaintances for contacts in the particular community; they may know people whom you can write, telephone, or e-mail for information and referrals. Once you have decided to focus on one community, visit it in order to establish personal contacts with key reference points, such as the local Chamber of Commerce, real estate firms, schools, libraries, churches, 40-Plus Club (if appropriate), government agencies, business firms and associations, and support groups that work with ex-offenders. Begin developing personal networks based upon your research. Subscribe to the local newspaper and to any community magazines which help profile the community. Follow the help-wanted, society, financial, and real estate sections of the newspaper – especially the Sunday edition. Your overall research should focus on developing personal contacts which may assist you in both your job search and your move to the community.

Questions You Should Ask

The key to conducting useful research lies in the questions you ask. Once you narrow your focus to a few companies and organizations, you should focus on three key questions that will yield useful information for guiding your job search:

- **Who has the power to hire?** It's seldom the personnel office, which is charged with administrative duties. Hiring power usually lies in the operating units. This question leads to several other related questions: Who describes the positions? Who announces vacancies? Who receives applications? Who administers tests? Who selects eligible candidates? Who chooses whom to interview? Who conducts the interview? Who offers the job?

- **How does the company or organization operate?** Try to learn as much as possible about internal operations. Is this a good place to work? Are employees generally happy working here? What about advancement opportunities, working conditions, relationships among co-workers and supervisors, growth patterns, internal politics, management style, work values, and opportunities for taking initiative?

- **What do I need to do to get a job with this company or organization?** The best way to find how to get a job in a particular organization is to follow the advice in Chapter 10 on prospecting, networking, and informational interviewing. This question can only be answered by talking to people who know both the formal and informal hiring practices. Your networking activities also will help you answer the first two questions.

As you can answer these questions, you'll learn at great deal about a potential employer. You'll discover whether or not you are interested in working for the company, and you'll acquire valuable inside information that will give you an edge over the competition. You'll know who should get your resume, and you'll be able to ask good questions at the job interview.

9

Write Effective Applications, Resumes, and Letters

EMPLOYERS WANT TO SEE YOU on paper **before** they meet you in person. How you complete applications and write, produce, distribute, and follow up resumes and letters will largely determine whether or not you will be invited to a job interview and offered a job. As you will quickly discover, applications and resumes are **calling cards** for opening the doors of employers. Letters add sizzle to resumes as well as open more doors to getting a job.

Important Issues for You

You are well advised to pay particular attention to how you handle these critical written stages of your job search. In addition to observing the basic rules of effective applications, resumes, and letters, you need to deal with the issue of **disclosure** – revealing that you have a criminal record.

Let's look at the basic elements that go into this written phase of your job search as well as address the disclosure issue prior to facing it again in the job interview. In so doing, you should be better prepared to open the doors of employers despite red flags that might turn off some employers.

One word of advice before we proceed with this discussion. Many ex-offenders with low education, language, and skill levels have difficulty writing, especially in handling basic spelling and grammar. If you have serious writing problems – nouns, verbs, adverbs, sentence and paragraph structure – you will be rejected by many employers who value good communication skills. Most won't tell you to your face that you have significant communication problems; they simply won't hire you because you appear potentially illiterate and thus incompetent. Bad spelling and grammar are major **red flags** that will quickly knock you out of consideration and affect your employment future. Get help! It's **never** too late to improve your spelling and grammar as well as your overall communication skills. Start with a good communication improvement book, such as *Woe Is I*. Many of the groups and organizations we identified in Chapter 4 can assist you with this critical skill issue.

Application Tips

Many employers require applicants to fill out job applications. If, for example, you walk into a grocery store or retail business, you may be asked to go to a computer screen, or kiosk, to complete an online application, or you will be given a two- to four-paper application form to be completed by hand. Many companies routinely give anyone interested in a job a chance to fill out an application.

The following 20 tips should help you complete a job application to the expectations of employers and improve your chances of getting a job interview:

1. **Dress neatly.** Assume that you will be observed when you complete the application. The person taking your application may make a note about your appearance and communication skills. Since you may end up being interviewed on the spot, dress as if you were going to a job interview and observe all the rules for positive verbal and nonverbal behavior (see Chapter 11). First impressions are always important, be it on an application, over the telephone, or in person.

2. **Take two copies of the application form.** If you are picking up an application form to take with you, get two copies. Use the one copy to draft your answers and the other copy to submit as a neat, clean, and error-free application.

3. **Read the instructions carefully and follow them completely.** An application is your first screening test in more ways than you may think. Start by reading through the whole application to see exactly what information is required for completion. If you lack sufficient information, don't complete the application since you will be submitting an incomplete application, which is a negative. Return later with the information that you didn't have the first time. Follow the instructions. If it says print, then you print. If it says last name first, then write accordingly. If it asks for a phone number, provide one. If it ask for your supervisor's name, reason for leaving each job, and pay rates, supply this information. If it

says provide three references, then give the details on three references. Failure to complete an application according to instructions communicates a terrible message – you simply can't follow instructions, or you have something to hide! No one wants to hire such people. You've just wasted your time filling out an incomplete application.

4. **Use a black ink pen when writing.** Avoid using a pencil or an ink color other than black. In fact, many applications will ask you to use a black pen. An application completed in pencil looks unprofessional and one completed in a non-black ink may be difficult to read if the application is run through a copy machine.

5. **Answer each question.** It's important to respond to each question – no blanks left that could raise questions in the mind of the reviewer about your willingness to disclose. For example, if you don't have a permanent address or telephone number, use the address and number of a friend or relative who agrees to serve as your contact location. Do not appear homeless on an application – it raises all kinds of questions about transportation, stability, and work history. If a question does not relate to your situation, such as military service, type or write "N/A" which means "Not Applicable."

6. **Try to write as neatly as possible.** The neatness and style of your handwriting may be interpreted by the reader as an indication of your personality and work habits. If it looks sloppy, with letters or words crossed out, the reader may think you are confused, careless, or sloppy in your work habits.

7. **Be prepared to complete each section of the application.** If you know you will be applying for a job, take to the application center all information you may need to complete the application in full. You may want to complete a mock or draft application form, which you always take with you, that contains most information you are likely to be asked on an application. This would include a list of previous employers, addresses, telephone numbers, employment dates, information about your work, and documents (Social Security number and driver's license). You also want to have with you details on your educational background and references. Trying to recall this information by memory may lead to inaccurate statements or an incomplete application; you'll be demonstrating two negatives to the employer even before the job interview – you are unprepared and you're not serious about employment.

8. **Include all previous employers.** Reveal all of your previous employers, even if you were fired. Many people get fired and it's not held against them by other employers. You can always explain the situation, but you will have greater difficulty trying to explain a major employment gap. Many ex-offenders also include their prison work experience at a state or federal job, such as Custodian, State of Louisiana, or Machine Operator, State of Texas. If, indeed, you have janitorial duties and operated machines, such as those in the laundry room, these are truthful employment statements that do not prematurely raise a red flag that you served time in XYZ Penitentiary. You have work experience, you used skills, and you have someone who can serve as a reference. Most important of all, you filled in a potential time gap that might have indicated you were hiding something or you were unemployed for a long period of time. Hiding your record indicates you may be a con artist. No one wants to hire someone who is deceptive. If you can't be trusted with the truth at the application stage, why would anyone want to trust you on the job?

9. **If you lack work experience, be creative.** Each year millions of people first enter the job market without formal work experience or a job. However, that doesn't mean they lack work-related experience. If you did not hold a regular job but have volunteer or other life experiences related to skills found in the workplace, include these in the work experience section. Did you assist a group (church, school, sports team, community organization), did you sell something? (Yes, even illegal street activities may demonstrate certain "transferable" skills to legitimate work settings and activities.)

10. **Appear educated, even if you lack formal credentials.** Let's face it. Few employers want to hire someone without a high school education. If you lack a high school education but have a GED, include the date you completed your GED. If you do not have a GED, get enrolled in a program **before** you fill out any applications and then state on your application that you are completing your GED in a specific month and year. If you've completed a training program or acquired specialized skills, include those on your application under Education. Make sure you appear educated and thoughtful – no misspelling, poor grammar, or stupid and smart aleck statements – in each section of your application.

11. **Handle sensitive questions with tact.** An application is not a place to confess all your sins, reveal red flags, or prematurely show your hand. Like a resume, an application becomes your calling card to be invited to

the interview. In your case, the most sensitive question will be *"Have you ever been convicted of a crime? If yes, please explain."* Most applicants believe they have three choices in responding to this question: Lie, tell the truth, or leave it blank. All three choices may have negative consequences for getting the job interview or keeping the job. In addition, the law may require you to disclose your criminal record to employers, and you must sign the applications, indicating your answers are truthful. However, there is a fourth choice in answering this question which leaves the door open: simply write *"Please discuss with me"* or *"Will discuss at the interview."* These statements indicate you have a conviction, you're not hiding it, and you are prepared to discuss it at the appropriate time. If you must include some details, keep them short and focused on the future, such as *"Will complete parole or probation in 20__."* Depending on the nature of your crime, you cannot adequately explain your record in one or two sentences. Indeed, most short statements raise more negative questions than they answer. This question is best dealt with in a face-to-face meeting where you will have a chance to explain and demonstrate six things – (1) you made a serious mistake, (2) you took responsibility, (3) you've done several things to change your life, (4) you're not a risk, (5) you want a chance to prove yourself, and (6) you are positive, enthusiastic, energetic, and ready to perform beyond the employer's expectations. A similar response should be given to another sensitive question: *"Have you ever been fired?"* Respond by writing *"Please see me"* or *"Will discuss at the interview."*

12. **Avoid abbreviations.** Not all readers share the same knowledge of abbreviations. You can abbreviate the obvious, such as Street (St.), Avenue (Ave.), or Boulevard (Blvd.), but spell out the not-so-obvious. If, for example, you lived or worked in Los Angeles, your application should say Los Angeles rather than L.A.

13. **Avoid vague statements.** If you state that you can operate a computer, indicate at what level and with which programs. If you are a driver, indicate what type of vehicle or equipment you work with. The more details you give, the more impressive will be your application.

14. **Avoid revealing salary information.** If the application asks for your salary expectations (pay or salary desired), state *"Open"* or *"Will discuss at the interview."* Always keep this question to the very end of the interview – **after** you have been offered the job. The old poker saying that *"He who reveals his hand is at a disadvantage"* is very true in the job

search. Get the employer to first reveal his hand before you talk about your salary expectations. We'll have more to say on this subject in Chapter 12.

15. **Include interests and hobbies relevant to the job.** If asked about any interests and hobbies, try to select examples relevant to the job. If, for example, you are applying for an outdoor job that requires physical stamina, outdoor sports interests would be supportive of such a job.

16. **Include additional comments if appropriate.** Some applications will have a section for additional comments. This is the place you want to indicate your goals, state your interests, and make a pitch for the job. Get yourself set up for the job interview by stating something to this effect:

> "I'm especially interested in this job, because I love working with inventory management software and streamlining operations that save companies both time and money. I would appreciate an opportunity to discuss how my experience can best meet your needs."

17. **Remember to sign the application.** The very last thing you need to do is sign and date your application. Failure to do so may invalidate your application and raise questions about your ability to follow instructions.

18. **Read and re-read your answers.** Make sure you proofread your application for any errors, omissions, or misspellings. Like the perfect resume, you want an error-proof application.

19. **Attach your resume to the application form.** At least for employers, applications are a necessary evil in the screening and hiring processes. Most applications follow a similar and rather dull format that yields little information about who you really are and what you have done, can do, and will do in the future. Few applications allow the flexibility to state your goals, skills, and accomplishments. If you write an achievement-oriented resume, as we will shortly discuss, submit it along with your application. With a resume, you structure the reader's thinking around your major strengths rather than allow the reader to control information about you, which is exactly what an application does for the employer. With a well written resume, you may quickly grab the attention of the employer who will want to invite you to a job interview. Your resume, not your application, becomes the central focus of the job interview.

20. **Be sure to follow up.** When you submit the application, ask when you might expect to hear from the employer on the status of your application. If they say within two weeks, be sure to call and ask about your candidacy in two weeks. In some cases, the follow-up telephone call will result in a job interview. After all, the employer may still be reviewing applications, and your call may force him or her to take a second look at your application (and attached resume). Most important of all, your call indicates that you are still interested in the job.

Why a Resume?

Resumes used to be required for most white-collar or professional positions. They were seen as necessary documents for well educated and skilled individuals. However, today many employers expect to see a resume for more and more blue-collar and entry-level positions.

There are two basic reasons you need to write a resume rather than just rely on completing applications:

1. **Employers want to see you on paper in the form of a resume.** More and more employers require resumes as part of the pre-employment screening process. They expect candidates to present their qualifications in this form. Many employers include employment sections on their websites which require prospective candidates to complete an online application or questionnaire, submit an electronic resume, or complete a "profile," which is essentially a mini-resume.

2. **You need to organize yourself around a resume.** As you will quickly discover, a resume is a powerful device for organizing you and your job search. A relatively simple one-page resume requires you to develop an objective, identify your key skills and accomplishments, and document your education and work history. Most important of all, it gives you and others a snapshot of who you really are in terms of your goals and accomplishments. For many job seekers, a well-crafted resume that showcases their major strengths significantly improves their self-esteem (*"Wow . . . this is who I really am!"*) as well as transforms the way they see and approach the world of work.

Resume Rules

Resumes play a central role in a job search. Employers normally want to see a resume **before** interviewing a candidate. From the perspective of the employer, a resume should be a concise summary of your qualifications. It should tell an employer what you have done, can do, and are likely to do in the future. Employers use resumes to screen candidates for interviews. During the interview, the information on the resume may be the subject of several questions about a candidate's background, accomplishments, and future goals.

From the perspective of job seekers, a resume is an **advertisement** for a job. Within the space of one or two pages, it should give just enough information to persuade the reader to interview the writer. As such, the resume becomes a calling card for a job interview.

Common Writing, Production, Distribution, and Follow-Up Errors

Unfortunately, many job seekers produce poorly designed resumes that neither grab the attention of employers nor satisfy their need to know what the candidate has done, can do, and will do in the future. Many misunderstand the purpose of resumes and lose focus on what it is the resume should do – convince the reader to take action. Worst of all, many resumes are "dead upon arrival," because the writer makes numerous writing, production, distribution, and follow-up mistakes that quickly turn off employers. Whatever you do, make sure your resume does not include these **writing errors**:

1. Unrelated to the position in question.
2. Too long or too short.
3. Unattractive with a poorly designed format, small type style, and crowded copy.
4. Misspellings, poor grammar, wordiness, and repetition.
5. Punctuation errors.
6. Lengthy phrases, long sentences, and awkward paragraphs.
7. Slick, amateurish, or "gimmicky" – appears over-produced.
8. Boastful, egocentric, and aggressive.
9. Dishonest, untrustworthy, or suspicious information.
10. Missing critical categories, such as experience, skills, and education.
11. Difficult to interpret because of poor organization and lack of focus – uncertain what the person has done or can do.
12. Unexplained time gaps between jobs.
13. Too many jobs in a short period of time – a job hopper with little evidence of career advancement.
14. No evidence of past accomplishments or a pattern of performance from which to predict future performance; primarily focuses on formal duties and responsibilities that came with previous jobs.
15. Lacks credibility and content – includes much fluff and "canned" resume language.

16. States a strange, unclear, or vague objective.
17. Appears over-qualified or under-qualified for the position.
18. Includes distracting personal information that does not enhance the resume nor the candidate.
19. Fails to include critical contact information (telephone number and e-mail address) and uses an anonymous address (P.O. Box number).
20. Uses jargon and abbreviations unfamiliar to the reader.
21. Embellishes name with formal titles, middle names, and nicknames which make him or her appear odd or strange.
22. Repeatedly refers to "I" and appears self-centered.
23. Includes obvious self-serving references that raise credibility questions.
24. Sloppy, with handwritten corrections – crosses out "married" and writes "single"!
25. Includes red flag information such as being incarcerated, fired, lawsuits or claims, health or performance problems, or stating salary figures, including salary requirements, that may be too high or too low.

Employers also report encountering several of these **production, distribution, and follow-up errors**:

1. Poorly typed and reproduced – hard to read.
2. Produced on odd-sized paper.
3. Printed on poor quality paper or on extremely thin or thick paper.
4. Soiled with coffee stains, fingerprints, or ink marks.
5. Sent to the wrong person or department.
6. Mailed, faxed, or e-mailed to "To Whom It May Concern" or "Dear Sir."
7. E-mailed as an attachment which could have a virus if opened.
8. Enclosed in a tiny envelope that requires the resume to be unfolded and flattened several times.
9. Arrived without proper postage – the employer gets to pay the extra!
10. Sent the resume and letter by the slowest postage rate possible.
11. Envelope double-sealed with tape and is indestructible – nearly impossible to open by conventional means!
12. Back of envelope includes a handwritten note stating that something is missing on the resume, such as a telephone number, e-mail address, or new mailing address.
13. Resume taped to the inside of the envelope, an old European habit practiced by paranoid letter writers. Need to destroy the envelope and perhaps also the resume to get it out of the envelope.
14. Accompanied by extraneous or inappropriate enclosures which were not requested, such as copies of self-serving letters or recommendations, transcripts, or samples of work.

15. Arrives too late for consideration.
16. Comes without a cover letter.
17. Cover letter repeats what's on the resume – does not command attention nor move the reader to action.
18. Sent the same or different versions of the resume to the same person as a seemingly clever follow-up method.
19. Follow-up call made too soon – before the resume and letter arrive!
20. Follow-up call is too aggressive or the candidate appears too "hungry" for the position – appears needy or greedy.

Since the resume is so important to getting a job interview, make sure your resume is error free. Spend sufficient time crafting a resume that shouts loud and clear that you are someone who should be interviewed for a position.

Resumes and Resources for Ex-Offenders

Many ex-offenders face difficulties in writing, producing, and distributing resumes. Most of these difficulties center on some or all of the following:

1. Limited or unstable work history
2. Low levels of education and training
3. Unclear goals and lack of focus
4. Weak organization and writing skills
5. An "experience" time gap while incarcerated
6. Uncertainty about marketing oneself
7. Lack of equipment and money for production and distribution

In other words, ex-offenders are likely to make many of the mistakes we outlined above. If these difficulties characterize your situation, and you are not a talented writer, by all means seek assistance in writing a resume. Don't pretend you can write and distribute a resume on your own by just following our advice. It simply won't happen, or the product will be third-rate.

A career professional can give you much needed advice and assistance in putting together a resume that best represents you and is targeted toward the right people. Hopefully you will participate in a pre-release program that assisted you in writing a resume. If not, once you are released, contact a local support group, participate in a job readiness program, or contact personnel at your local One-Stop Career Center for assistance in writing a resume. You also can hire a professional resume writer to develop your resume. They will charge you from $200 to $600 for their services. If you can afford such a professional, they will probably produce an outstanding resume that will grab the attention of employers as well as help you focus your job search. You can contact professional resume writers through these organizations:

- **Professional Association of Resume**
  Writers and Career Coaches   www.parw.com

- **Professional Resume Writing and**
  Research Association   www.prwra.com

- **National Resume Writers'**
  Association   www.nrwa.com

You can see some terrific examples of their work by reviewing the following resume books written by professional resume writers, which are available in many libraries or through Impact Publications (www.impactpublications.com):

101 Best Resumes
101 More Best Resumes
202 Great Resumes
Best KeyWords for Resumes, Cover Letters, and Interviews
Best Resumes for People Without a Four-Year Degree
Blue Collar Resumes
The Damn Good Resume Guide
Expert Resumes for Computer and Web Jobs
Expert Resumes for Manufacturing Careers
Expert Resumes for People Returning to Work
Gallery of Best Resumes for People Without a Four-Year Degree
The Resume Catalog
Resume Magic
Resumes That Knock 'Em Dead

Indeed, you can learn a great deal about resumes for particular occupations by examining the many resume examples in these books.

For step-by-step instructions on how to produce each section of your resume as well as information on production, distribution, and follow-up, see three of our other books:

High Impact Resumes and Letters
Nail the Resume!
The Savvy Resume Writer

We also highly recommend Joyce Lain Kennedy's terrific book on resume writing:

Resumes for Dummies

Used together, these resume writing and example books will give you sufficient information to create your own winning resume.

Best Resume Practices

Whether you write your own resume or seek help from a professional, you should benefit from the following discussion on how to put together a winning resume.

Your resume should incorporate the characteristics of strong and effective resumes. It should:

- Clearly communicate your purpose and competencies in relation to employers' needs.
- Be concise and easy to read.
- Outline a pattern of success highlighted with examples of key accomplishments.
- Motivate the reader to read it in-depth.
- Tell employers that you are a responsible and purposeful individual – a doer who can quickly solve their problems.

Keep in mind that most employers are busy people who normally glance at a resume for only 20 to 30 seconds. Your resume, therefore, must sufficiently catch their attention to pass the 20- to 30-second evaluation test. Above all, it must motivate the reader to take action. When writing your resume, ask yourself the same question asked by employers: *"Why should I read this or contact this person for an interview?"* Your answer should result in an attractive, interesting, unique, and skills-based resume.

Types of Resumes

You have four basic types of resumes to choose from: chronological, functional, combination, or resume letter. Each form has various advantages and disadvantages, depending on your background and purpose. For example, someone first entering the job market or making a major career change should use a functional resume. We include examples of resumes at the end of this chapter.

The **chronological resume** is the standard resume used by most applicants who are not very savvy about job searching. It often comes in two forms: traditional and improved. The **traditional chronological resume** is also known as the "obituary resume," because it both "kills" your chances of getting a job and is a good source for writing your obituary. Summarizing your work history, this resume lists dates and names first and duties and responsibilities second; it includes extraneous information such as height, weight, age, marital status, gender, and hobbies. While relatively easy to write, this is the most ineffective resume you can produce. Its purpose at best is to inform people of what you have done in the past as well as where, when, and with whom. It tells employers little or nothing about what you want to do, can do, and will do for them.

The **improved chronological resume** better communicates to employers your purpose, past achievements, and probable future performance. This resume works best for individuals who have extensive experience directly related to a position. This resume should include a clear work objective. The work experience section should include the names and locations of former employers followed by a brief description of relevant accomplishments, skills, and responsibilities; inclusive employment dates should appear at the end. It should stress **accomplishments** and **skills** rather than formal duties and responsibilities – that you are a productive and responsible person who gets things done, a doer. While this resume performs better than the traditional chronological resume, it still has major limitations because of its chronological format. It simply doesn't highlight very well major accomplishments and a pattern of success. Also, since you have an employment gap because of your incarceration, a chronological resume will draw attention to that gap.

Functional resumes should be used by individuals making a significant career change, first entering the workforce, or re-entering the job market after a lengthy absence. This resume should stress your accomplishments and transferable skills regardless of previous work settings and job titles. This could include accomplishments as a volunteer worker or Sunday school teacher. Names of employers and dates of employment should not appear on this resume.

Functional resumes have certain weaknesses. While they are important bridges for the inexperienced and for those making a career change, some employers dislike these resumes. Since many employers still look for names, dates, and direct job experience, this resume does not meet their expectations. You should use a functional resume only if you have limited work experience or your past experience doesn't strengthen your objective when making a career change. For many ex-offenders, this resume helps them deal with such issues as limited work experience and obvious time gaps.

Combination resumes, also known as hybrid resumes, combine the best features of both chronological and functional resumes. Having more advantages than disadvantages, this resume best communicates accomplishments to employers. It's an ideal resume for experienced professionals who are advancing in their careers as well as for those making a career change.

Combination resumes have the potential to both **meet** and **raise** the expectations of employers. You should stress your accomplishments and skills as well as include your work history. Your work history should appear as a separate section immediately following your presentation of accomplishments and skills in the "Areas of Effectiveness," "Experience," or "Achievements" section. It is not necessary to include dates unless they enhance your resume. This is the perfect resume for someone with work experience who wishes to change to a job in a related career field.

Resume letters are substitutes for resumes. Appearing as a job inquiry or application letter, resume letters highlight various sections of your resume, such as work history, experience, areas of effectiveness, objective, or education, in relation to employers' needs. These letters are used when you prefer not sending your more general resume. Resume letters have one major weakness: they give employers insufficient information and thus may prematurely eliminate you from consideration.

Structuring Resume Content

After choosing an appropriate resume format, you should generate the necessary information for structuring each category of your resume. You developed much of this information when you identified your motivated abilities and skills and specified your objective in Chapter 7. Include the following information on separate sheets of paper:

Contact Information:	Name, street address, and telephone/fax numbers, e-mail address.
Work Objective:	Refer to the information in Chapter 7 on writing an objective.
Education:	Degrees, schools, dates, highlights, special training.
Work Experience:	Paid, unpaid, civilian, military, and part-time employment. Include job titles, employers, locations, dates, skills, accomplishments, duties, and responsibilities. Use the functional language outlined in Chapter 6.
Achievements:	Things you did that provided **benefits** to others, especially initiatives that resulted in outcomes for previous employers.
Other Experience:	Volunteer, civic, and professional memberships. Include your contributions, demonstrated skills, offices held, names, and dates.
Special Skills or Licenses/ Certificates:	Computer, Internet, foreign languages, teaching, paramedical, etc. relevant to your objective.

Other Information: References, expected salary, willingness
                              to relocate/travel, availability dates, and
                              other information supporting your objective.

Producing Drafts

Once you generate the basic data for constructing your resume, your next task is to
convert this data into draft resumes. If, for example, you write a combination resume,
the internal organization of the resume should be as follows:

- Contact information
- Work objective
- Qualifications/experience/achievements
- Work history or employment
- Education

Be careful in including any other type of information on your resume. Other information most often is extraneous or negative information. You should only include
information designed to strengthen your objective.

While your first draft may run more than two pages, try to get everything into
one or two pages for the final draft. Most employers lose interest after reading the
first page. If you produce a two-page resume, one of the best formats is to attach a
supplemental page to a self-contained one-page resume.

Your final draft should conform to the following rules:

Resume "Don'ts"

- **Don't** use abbreviations except for your middle name.
- **Don't** create a cramped and crowded look.
- **Don't** make statements you can't document.
- **Don't** use the passive voice.
- **Don't** change tense of verbs.
- **Don't** use lengthy sentences and descriptions.
- **Don't** refer to yourself as "I."
- **Don't** emphasize employment dates.
- **Don't** include negative information, such as your record.
- **Don't** include extraneous information.
- **Don't** include salary information or references.

Resume "Do's"

- **Do** include an employer-centered objective.
- **Do** focus on your major accomplishments as they relate to the needs
  of the employer.
- **Do** include nouns so your resume can be scanned for keywords.

- **Do** use action verbs and the active voice to emphasize your accomplishments and keywords desired by employers.
- **Do** be direct, succinct, and expressive with your language.
- **Do** appear neat, well organized, and professional.
- **Do** use ample spacing and highlights (all caps, underlining, bulleting) for different emphases (except if it's an electronic resume).
- **Do** maintain an eye-pleasing balance.
- **Do** check carefully your spelling, grammar, and punctuation.
- **Do** clearly communicate your purpose and value to employers.
- **Do** communicate your strongest points first.
- **Do** keep your resume to one page but never more than two pages.

Resume Distribution

The only good resumes are the ones that get read, remembered, referred, and result in a job interview. Therefore, after completing a first-rate resume, you must decide what to do with it. Are you planning to only respond to classified ads with a standard mailing piece consisting of your conventional or electronic resume and a formal cover letter? Do you prefer posting your resume online with resume databases or e-mailing it to potential employers? But wait a minute; classified ads and resume databases only represent one portion of the job market. What other creative distribution methods might you use, such as sending it to friends, relatives, and former employers; mailing it in a shoe box with a note (*"Now that I've got my foot in the door, how about an interview?"*); gift wrapping it; or having it delivered by a singing messenger? What's the best way to proceed?

Most of your writing activities should focus on the hidden job market where jobs are neither announced nor listed. At the same time, you should respond to job listings in newspapers, magazines, human resources offices, and on websites, as well as get your resume into online resume databases. While this is largely a numbers game, you can increase your odds by the way you respond to the listings.

You should be selective in your responses. Since you know what you want to do, you will be looking for only certain types of positions. Once you identify them, your response entails little expenditure of time and effort – a quick e-mail, fax, or a paper envelope, letter, stamp, resume, and some of your time. You have little to lose. While you have the potential to gain by sending a letter and resume in response to an ad, remember the odds are usually against you.

It is difficult to interpret job listings, regardless of whether they are in print or electronic format. Some employers place blind ads with P.O. Box numbers and e-mail addresses in order to collect resumes for future reference. Others wish to avoid aggressive applicants who telephone or "drop in" for interviews. Many employers work through professional recruiters who place these ads, or they post job listings on electronic bulletin boards. While you may try to second guess the rationale behind such ads, it's always best to respond to them as you would to ads with an employer's name, address, or telephone number. Assume there is a real job behind each ad.

Most ads request a copy of your resume. Employers increasingly specify that it be sent by e-mail or fax. You should respond with a cover letter and resume as soon as you see the ad. Depending on how much information about the position is revealed in the ad, your letter should be tailored to emphasize your qualifications as they relate to the ad. Examine the ad carefully. Underline any words or phrases which relate to your qualifications. In your cover letter, you should use similar terminology in emphasizing your qualifications. The most powerful cover letter you can send is the classic "T" letter (see page 57) which literally matches your skills and accomplishments with each of the employer's requirements. Keep the letter brief and to the point.

You may be able to increase your odds by sending a second copy of your letter and resume two or three weeks after your initial response. Most applicants normally reply to an ad during the seven-day period immediately after it appears in print. Since employers often are swamped with responses, your letter and resume may get lost in the crowd. If you send a second copy of your resume two or three weeks later, the employer will have more time to give you special attention. By then, he or she also will have a better basis on which to compare you to the others. However, if the employer electronically scans resumes, sending a second copy of your resume and letter will not affect the outcome.

Keep in mind that your cover letter and resume may be screened among 400 other resumes and letters. Thus, you want your cover letter to be eye-catching and easy to read. Keep it brief and concise, and highlight your qualifications as stated in the employer's ad. If you know your resume will be electronically scanned, make sure it includes lots of keywords and is formatted properly for scanners. Don't spend a great deal of time responding to an ad or waiting anxiously at your mailbox, telephone, or computer for a reply. Keep moving on to other job search activities.

Your letters and resumes can be distributed and managed in various ways. Many people broadcast or "shotgun" hundreds of cover letters and resumes to prospective employers. This is a form of gambling where the odds are always against you. For every 100 people you contact in this manner, expect one or two who might be interested in you. After all, successful direct-mail experts at best expect only a 2 percent return on their mass mailings!

If you choose to use the broadcast method, you can increase your odds by using the **telephone**. Call the employer within a week after he or she receives your letter. This technique will probably increase your effectiveness rate from 1 to 5 percent.

However, many people are broadcasting their resumes today, and more and more employers are using automated resume management systems. As more resumes and letters descend on employers, the effectiveness rates may be even lower. This also can be an expensive marketing method. You would be much better off posting an electronic version of your resume on various online employment sites where your exposure rate will be much higher and more targeted to the needs of specific employers. Start by surveying job listings and posting your resume on these top sites:

- www.directemployers.com
- www.monster.com
- www.careerbuilder.com
- www.careerjournal.com
- www.jobs.com
- http://hotjobs.yahoo.com
- www.nationjob.com
- www.flipdog.com
- www.careerflex.com
- www.employment911.com

This electronic form of broadcasting is also the cheapest way to go – it's usually free to job seekers.

Your best distribution strategy will be your own modification of the following procedure:

- Selectively identify for whom you are interested in working.
- Send an approach letter.
- Follow up with a telephone call requesting an informational interview.

In more than 50 percent of the cases, you will get an interview. It is best not to include a copy of your resume with the approach letter. If you include a resume, you communicate the **wrong** message – that you want a job rather than information and advice. Keep your resume for the very **end** of the interview. Chapter 10 outlines procedures for conducting this informational interview.

The Internet has quickly become the best friend of both employers and headhunters, who can recruit personnel much faster and cheaper than through more traditional recruitment channels. Even small companies, with fewer than 10 employees, now use the Internet to advertise jobs and search resume databases for qualified candidates. At the same time, the Internet offers job seekers an important tool to add to their job search arsenal. Make sure you include the Internet in your job search by posting your resume on numerous sites, conducting research, and networking for information, advice, and referrals. Start with the 10 major sites listed above. While you may not get your next job through the Internet, at least you will acquire lots of useful information over the Internet.

For more information on the use of electronic resume databases and online recruiting, we recommend the following resources:

Adams Internet Job Search Almanac (Michelle Roy Kelly, ed.)
America's Top Internet Job Sites (Ron and Caryl Krannich)
Career Exploration on the Internet (Laura R. Gabler)
Cyberspace Job Search Kit (Fred E. Jandt and Mary B. Nemnich)
Electronic Resumes and Online Networking (Rebecca Smith)

e-Resumes (Susan Britton Whitcomb and Pat Kendall)
The Everything Online Job Search Book (Steve Graber)
The Guide to Internet Job Searching (Margaret Riley Dikel)
Job-Hunting on the Internet (Richard Nelson Bolles)

Letter Power

Regardless of how you send your resume, it should be accompanied by a cover letter. Indeed, certain types of cover letters – especially powerful "T" letters – are often more important than resumes. After interviewing for information or a position, you should send a thank-you letter. Other occasions will arise when it is both proper and necessary for you to write different types of job search letters. Numerous examples of job search letters are presented in our *High Impact Resumes and Letters, Nail the Cover Letter*, and *201 Dynamite Job Search Letters*. For a unique set of powerful "T" letters, see *Haldane's Best Cover Letters for Professionals*. All of these resources are published by Impact Publications.

Your letter writing should follow the principles of good resume and business writing. Job hunting letters are like resumes – they advertise you for interviews. Like good advertisements, these letters should follow four basic principles for effectiveness:

1. Catch the reader's attention.
2. Persuade the reader of your benefits or value.
3. Convince the reader with evidence.
4. Move the reader to acquire the product – you!

In addition, the content of your letters should be the basis for conducting screening interviews as well as face-to-face interviews.

Basic Preparation Rules

Before you begin writing a job search letter, ask yourself several questions to clarify the content of your letter:

- What is the **purpose** of the letter?
- What are the **needs** of my audience?
- What **benefits** will my audience gain from me?
- What is a good opening sentence or paragraph for grabbing the **attention** of my audience?
- How can I maintain the **interest** of my audience?
- How can I best end the letter so that the audience will be **persuaded** to contact me?
- If sent with a resume, how can my letter best **advertise the resume**?

- Have I spent enough time **revising** and **proofreading** the letter?
- Does the letter represent my **best professional effort?**

Since your letters are a form of business communication, they should conform to the rules of good business correspondence:

- Organize what you will say by outlining the content of your letter.
- Know your purpose and structure your letter accordingly.
- Communicate your message in a logical and sequential manner.
- State your purpose immediately in the first sentence and paragraph.
- End by stating what your reader can expect next from you.
- Use short paragraphs and sentences; avoid complex sentences.
- Punctuate properly and use correct grammar and spelling.
- Use simple and straightforward language; avoid jargon or slang.
- Communicate your message as directly and briefly as possible.

The rules stress how to both **organize and communicate** your message with impact. At the same time, you should always have a specific purpose in mind as well as know the needs of your audience.

Types of Letters

Cover letters provide cover for your resume. You should avoid overwhelming a one-page resume with a two-page letter or repeating the contents of the resume in the letter. A short and succinct one-page letter which highlights one or two points in your resume is sufficient. Three paragraphs will suffice. The first paragraph should state your interests and purposes for writing. The second paragraph should highlight your possible value to the employer. The third paragraph should state that you will call the individual at a particular time to schedule an interview.

However, do not expect great results from cover letters. Many professional job search firms use computers and mailing lists to flood the job market with thousands of unsolicited resumes and cover letters each day. Other job seekers use "canned" job search letters produced by computer software programs, such as *WinWay Resumes*, designed to generate model job search letters. As a result, employers are increasingly suspicious of the authenticity of such letters. To cope with the sheer volume of communications, many employers use resume management software to scan, store, and retrieve such communications – or they throw away most of the unsolicited resumes and letters they receive.

Approach letters are written for the purpose of developing job contacts, leads, or information as well as for organizing networks and getting interviews – the subjects of Chapter 10. Your primary purpose should be to get employers to engage in the 5R's of informational interviewing:

- **Reveal** useful information and advice.
- **Refer** you to others.
- **Read** your resume.
- **Revise** your resume.
- **Remember** you for future reference.

These letters help you gain access to the hidden job market by making important networking contacts that lead to those all-important informational interviews.

Approach letters can be sent to many places to uncover job leads, or they can target particular individuals or organizations. It is best to target these letters since they have maximum impact when personalized in reference to a position.

The structure of approach letters is similar to that of other letters. The first paragraph states your purpose. In so doing, you may want to use a personal statement for openers, such as *"John Taylor recommended that I write to you..."* or *"I am familiar with your..."* State your purpose, but do not suggest that you are asking for a job – only career advice or information. In your final paragraph, request a meeting and indicate you will call to schedule such a meeting at a mutually convenient time.

Thank-you letters may well become your most effective job search letters. They especially communicate your thoughtfulness. These letters come in different forms and are written for various occasions. The most common thank-you letter is written after receiving assistance, such as job search information and advice or a critique of your resume. Other occasions include:

- **Immediately after an interview:** Thank the interviewer for the opportunity to interview for the position. Repeat your interest in the position.

- **Receive a job offer:** Thank the employer for his or her faith in you and express your appreciation of the offer.

- **Rejected for a job:** Thank the employer for the opportunity to interview for the job. Ask to be remembered for future reference.

- **Terminate employment:** Thank the employer for the experience and ask to be remembered for future reference.

- **Begin a new job:** Thank the employer for giving you this new opportunity and express your confidence in doing the good work he is expecting.

The goal of the thank-you letter to be **remembered** by potential employers in a **positive** light. In a job search, being remembered by employers is the closest thing to being invited to an interview and offered a job!

Functional Resume
(Limited Relevant Experience)

Gerald Walters

2713 Calder Avenue
Gary, Indiana 44432

Tel. 333-444-2222

Objective

An **entry-level warehouse position** with a small business that requires an energetic worker and values hard working, responsible, and loyal employees who are focused on getting the job done right and on time.

Summary of Qualifications

- Experienced in lifting heavy boxes and equipment
- Enjoy solving inventory problems and keeping a well organized work area
- Work well with supervisors, co-workers, and clients in getting jobs done
- Reputation for being a hard worker, quick learner, and adaptable

Experience

Heavy Lifting: Regularly handle heavy boxes and equipment weighing over 100 pounds. Experienced in operating a forklift, packaging equipment, and computers.

Organization: Maintain a well-organized work area, keep good records, stock shelves, and load trucks. Cited by supervisor as one who is exceptionally dependable, well organized, and takes initiative in solving problems.

Customer Service: Experienced in handling customer orders and solving customer problems.

Work History

State of Pennsylvania: Education and training programs centered on developing new workplace skills. Framington, Pennsylvania. 2004 to present.

Graysorn Construction Company: Varied maintenance jobs involving commercial construction and warehousing functions. Pittsburgh, Pennsylvania, 2002-2003.

Subway: Ordered supplies, maintained inventory, and provided good customer service. Pittsburgh, Pennsylvania, 2001.

Education/Training

- Currently completing GED
- Completed a basic workplace skills computer training course

Combination Resume
(Relevant Experience)

Victor Taylor
471 16ᵗʰ Street
Altanta, GA 33333
Tel. 222-333-4444

OBJECTIVE: A position as an **architectural drafter** with a firm specializing in commercial construction where technical knowledge and practical experience will enhance construction design and improve building operations.

EXPERIENCE: <u>Draftsman</u>: A.C.T. Construction Company, Atlanta, GA. Helped develop construction plans for $15 million of residential and commercial construction. 2002-2004

<u>Cabinet Maker</u>: Garner-Williams Company, Birmingham, AL. Designed and constructed kitchen counter tops and cabinets; installed the material in homes; cut and laid linoleum flooring in apartment complexes. 1999-2001

<u>Carpenter's Assistant</u>: Thompson Associates, Atlanta, GA. Assisted carpenter in the reconstruction of a restaurant and in building of forms for pouring concrete. 1997-1998

<u>Materials Control Auditor</u>: Battles Machine and Foundry, Alanta, GA. Collected data on the amount of material being utilized daily in the operation of the foundry. Evaluated the information to determine the amount of materials being wasted. Submitted reports to production supervisor on the analysis of weekly and monthly production. 1993-1996

TRAINING: <u>Drafting School, Atlanta Vocational and Technical Center</u>, 2001. Completed 15 months of training in drafting night school.

EDUCATION: <u>Atlanta Community High School</u>, Atlanta, GA. Graduated in 1992.

PERSONAL: Single...willing to relocate...prefer working both indoors and outdoors...strive for perfection...hard worker...enjoy photography, landscaping, furniture design, and construction.

REFERENCES: Available upon request.

"T" Letter
(Alternative to a Resume)

September 21, 20 __

Jack Tillman
ACE Electrical Solutions
2781 Washington Avenue
Baltimore, MD 17233

Dear Mr. Tillman:

I'm responding to your ad that appears in today's Baltimore Sun for an electrician. I believe I am an excellent candidate for this position. Given my interests, training, and experience as an electrician, I would bring to this position the following qualifications:

Your Requirements	My Qualifications
One year commercial experience	Completed one-year apprenticeship and served two years as an electrician's helper on complex commercial projects
Responsible	Praised by previous employer and co-workers as being a quick starter who takes initiative, is responsible, and gets the job done well and on time.
Trouble-shooter	Skilled in solving complex wiring problems that have saved customers additional costs.
Good customer relations	Received several letters from repeat customers expressing satisfaction for quickly solving problems and proposing cost-effective solutions to lighting issues.

In addition, I know the importance of building strong long-term customer relations as part of building a small business. I enjoy taking on new challenges and working with teams to achieve company goals.

I believe there is a strong match between your needs and my qualifications. Could we meet soon to discuss how we might best work together? I'll call your office on Wednesday at 11am to see if your schedule might permit such a meeting.

I appreciate your consideration and look forward to speaking with you on Wednesday.

Sincerely,

Aaron Easton

Aaron Easton
eastonar@hotmail.com

Thank-You Letter
(Post Job Interview)

981 River Drive
Los Angeles, CA 13344

December 2, 20____

Tom Peterson
Circulation Department
Los Angeles Gazette
2150 Waterfront Drive
Los Angeles, CA 13347

Dear Mr. Peterson:

I really appreciated having the opportunity to interview with you today for the position of Dispatcher. I remain extremely interested in this position since it is a perfect fit for my interests, skills, and experience. I am especially interested because it is an evening job. Since I am used to working an evening schedule, this would be a perfect schedule for me.

If I have not heard from you by next Friday, I will check back with you to see how your selection process is progressing. I look forward to hearing from you and hope I will have the opportunity to work with you.

Sincerely,

Steven Chase

Steven Chase
chasestev@yahoo.com

Cover Letter
(Parts Manager)

7813 Peoria Avenue
Chicago, IL 60030

July 23, 20____

Emily Southern
Atlas Auto Supply
153 West 19th Street
Chicago, IL 60033

Dear Ms. Southern:

Please accept the enclosed resume as my application in response to your ad in today's *Chicago Tribune* for a Parts Manager. You stated you needed an experienced manager who has worked with large equipment and who is familiar with ordering inventory and managing personnel.

I believe I have the necessary experience and skills to do this job well. During the past 10 years I have worked at all levels and in a variety of positions in the parts business. I began in receiving, moved on to manage a stockroom, took customer orders, and managed a parts warehouse with 11 employees. I'm experienced in operating computerized inventory systems. In my last job I decreased warehouse labor costs by 35% by installing a new inventory system.

I would appreciate the opportunity to interview for this position. Please expect a phone call from me on Thursday afternoon. I'll be calling for more information about the position as well as to answer any questions you may have about my candidacy.

Sincerely,

Terry Wilder

Terry Wilder
wildert@hotmail.com

10

Network for Information, Advice, and Referrals

YOU SHOULD USE SEVERAL job search approaches simultaneously, as we noted earlier. However, you also should devote the greatest amount of your time to networking. This is the single most effective approach to finding the best jobs. With networking, you rely on family, friends, and acquaintances for information, advice, and referrals for locating jobs on the hidden job market as well as for dealing with many other issues related to your reentry. You develop, expand, and maintain (build and nurture) your network for achieving success. Here's the really good news for you, which also applies to other job seekers, regardless of their backgrounds: Ex-offenders who quickly find jobs and advance their careers tend to do so through **networking** rather than by responding to classified job ads or relying on job placement services. Remember that fact every day you get up and start looking for a job. If you don't network, you will decrease your chances of getting a good job.

You Must Take Action and Do It Now!

If you learn only one thing from this book, make sure it's networking. This is a key interpersonal and communication skill that will serve you well while looking for a job as well as advancing on the job and changing jobs and careers. It's a powerful tool you must learn to use throughout your work life.

Unfortunately, many people talk about networking and acknowledge understanding its importance and how it works. But few people actually develop an active networking campaign that produces desired results. Rather than make 10 contacts a day, for example, they sit back and do nothing except complain about their failure in finding a job. This should not happen to you.

If you do nothing to advance your job search, don't expect to get anything in return. You simply **must** take action, which means **networking** your way to a new job through a very well organized, targeted, and active networking campaign.

It's All About Getting Interviews and Job Offers

Everything you do up to this point in your job search should be aimed at **getting a job interview**. The skills you identified and the goals you set in Chapter 7, the information you gathered in Chapter 8, and the resume and letters you wrote in Chapter 9 are carefully related to one another so you can clearly communicate your best qualifications to employers who, in turn, will decide to invite you to a job interview.

> *The informational interview also helps you deal with the "criminal record" issue as you develop and refine an effective story for overcoming objections to hiring someone with your background.*

But there are secrets to getting a job interview you should know about before continuing further with your job search. The most important secret is the **informational interview** – a type of interview that yields useful job search information, advice, and referrals leading to job interviews and offers. Based on prospecting and networking techniques, these interviews minimize rejections and competition as well as quickly open the doors to organizations and employers you would not normally know about. For ex-offenders, the informational interview is an ideal way to deal with the "criminal record" issue as you develop and refine an effective story for overcoming objections to hiring someone with your background.

If you want to quickly generate several interviews, you first need to understand the informational interview and how to initiate and use it for maximum impact. In so doing, you'll be exploring the **hidden job market** of unadvertised vacancies. You'll begin locating opportunities that are best suited for your particular motivated abilities and skills.

Learn to Effectively Prospect and Network

What do you do after you complete your resume? Most people send cover letters and resumes in response to job listings and walk into companies to complete application forms; they then wait to be called for a job interview. Viewing the job search as basically a direct-mail and paper-generation operation, many job seekers are disappointed in discovering the reality of such approaches: a 2 percent response rate is considered successful!

Successful job seekers are **people-oriented and proactive**. They develop face-to-face strategies in which the resume plays a **supportive** rather than central role in their job search. They first present themselves to employers; the resume appears only at the end of a face-to-face conversation.

Throughout the job search you should acquire useful names and contact information as well as meet people who will assist you in contacting potential employers. Such information and contacts become key building blocks for generating job interviews and offers.

Since the most and best jobs are found on the hidden job market, you must use methods appropriate for this job market. Indeed, research and experience clearly show the most effective means of communication are face-to-face and word-of-mouth. The informal, interpersonal system of communication is the central nervous system of the hidden job market. Your goal should be to penetrate this job market with proven methods for success. Appropriate methods for making important job contacts are **prospecting and networking**. The best methods for getting these contacts to provide you with useful job information are **informational and referral interviews**.

> *The most effective means of communication are face-to-face and word-of-mouth.*

Focus on Communicating Your Qualifications

Taken together, these interpersonal methods help you clearly **communicate your qualifications to employers** Although many job seekers may be reluctant to use this informal communication system, they greatly limit their potential for success if they do not.

Put yourself in the position of the employer for a moment, especially one who is not fully staffed nor automated to handle hundreds of resumes and phone, fax, and e-mail inquiries. You have a job vacancy to fill. Even under the best of circumstances, hiring is a challenging process filled with all types of potential problems. Not only is it time consuming, the outcome is often uncertain. Worst of all, you may spend a great deal of time and money and still hire the wrong person for the position! You know if you advertise the position, you may be bombarded with hundreds of resumes, applications, phone calls, faxes, e-mails, and walk-ins. While you do want to hire the best qualified individual for the job, you simply don't have time nor patience to review scores of applications. Even if you use a P.O. Box number, the paperwork may quickly overwhelm you. Furthermore, with limited information from application forms, cover letters, and resumes, you find it hard to identify the best qualified individuals to invite for an interview; many candidates look the same on paper.

So what do you do? You might hire a job placement firm or use the services of a temporary employment agency to take on this additional work. Or you may decide to recruit on the Internet by doing keyword searches of various online resume databases or post a job announcement on your homepage. You may even try your luck by spending a few hundred dollars to use a several major commercial recruitment sites, such as www.monster.com or www.careerbuilder.com.

On the other hand, you may want to better control the hiring process, especially since it appears to be filled with uncertainty and headaches. You want to minimize your risks and time so you can get back to what you do best – accomplishing the goals of the organization. So you decide to "put the word out" by doing a little word-of-mouth recruiting. Like many other employers, you begin by calling your friends, acquaintances, and business associates and ask if they or someone else might know of any good candidates for the position. If they can't help, you ask them to give you a call should they learn of anyone qualified for your vacancy. You, in effect, create your own hidden job market – an informal information network for locating desirable candidates. Best of all, your trusted contacts initially **screen** the candidates in the process of **referring** them to you. This both saves you a great deal of time and minimizes your risks in hiring a stranger. Individuals in your network begin sending you names of people they feel would be ideal for your position. After all, they have either worked with these people or know well their ability to work with others and do the job. There's nothing like a personal reference from someone whose judgment an employer trusts.

> *There's nothing like a personal reference from someone whose judgment an employer trusts.*

Even if you are fully staffed and technically capable of handling the recruitment process, you still may use an informal, interpersonal, and parallel recruitment approach to minimize your risks. Indeed, many large companies encourage **employee referrals** for recruiting personnel. While they may post a vacancy on their website or use a commercial recruitment site to find candidates, they also encourage and reward their employees to refer candidates. The reward may be a nice bonus for anyone whose referral results in a new hire. These employee referral systems encourage networking within the hidden job market.

Let's shift our attention – from the employer to the job seeker. Since you now know how the employer thinks and operates, what should you, the job seeker, do to improve your chances of getting an interview and job offer? Networking for information, advice, and referrals should play a central role in your overall job search. Remember, employers need to solve personnel problems. By conducting **informational interviews and networking,** you help employers identify their needs, limit their alternatives, and thus make decisions and save money. Especially for ex-offenders, such interviews and networking activities help relieve employers' anxiety about hiring what they might consider to be "risky" individuals.

At the same time, you gain several advantages by conducting these interviews:

- You are less likely to encounter rejections since you are not asking for a job – only information, advice, referrals, and to be remembered.

- You encounter little competition.

- You go directly to the people who have the power to hire.

- You are likely to be invited to job interviews based upon the referrals you receive.

Most employers want more information on candidates than just "paper qualifications" represented in application forms, resumes, and letters. Studies show that employers, in general, seek candidates who have these skills: communication, problem solving, analytical, assessment, and planning. Surprising to many job seekers, technical expertise ranks third or fourth on employers' lists of most desired skills. These findings support a frequent observation made by employers: the major problems with employees relate to communication, problem solving, and analysis; most individuals get fired because of political and interpersonal conflicts rather than for technical incompetence.

Employers want to hire people they **like** both personally and professionally. Therefore, communicating your qualifications to employers involves more than just informing them of your technical competence. You must communicate that you have the necessary personal **and** professional skills to perform the job. Prospecting, networking, and informational interviewing activities are the best methods for communicating such "qualifications" to employers.

Develop Networks

Networking is the process of purposefully developing relations with others. Networking in the job search involves connecting with other people who can help you find a job. Your network consists of you interacting with these other individuals. The more you develop, maintain, and expand your networks, the more successful should be your job search.

Your network is your interpersonal environment. While you know and interact with hundreds of people, on a day-to-day basis, you may encounter no more than 20 people. You frequently contact these people in face-to-face situations. Some people are more **important** to you than others. You **like** some more than others. And some will be more **helpful** to you in your job search than others. Your basic network may include the following individuals and groups: friends, acquaintances, immediate family, distant relatives, spouse, supervisor, P.O., fellow workers, delivery service people, and local businesspeople and professionals, such as your banker, lawyer, doctor, minister, and insurance agent. You should contact many of these individuals for advice relating to your job search.

You need to **identify everyone in your network** who might help you with your job search. You first need to expand your basic network to include individuals you know and have interacted with over the past 10 or more years. Make a list of 100 or more people you know, such as:

- Relatives
- Your P.O.
- Former supervisors
- Teachers/instructors
- Ministers/clergy
- Church members
- Support group members
- Friends/pen pals
- Neighbors
- Former employers
- Social acquaintances
- Classmates
- Anyone you do business with:
  - store personnel
  - bank personnel
  - doctors
  - dentists
  - opticians
  - lawyers
  - real estate agents
  - insurance agents
  - travel agents
  - direct-sales personnel
- People you meet on the Internet
- Speakers at meetings you attend
- Delivery service personnel (Postal Service, UPS, Federal Express)
- Local leaders
- Politicians, including your local representative

You can probably think of many other people to put on your list. Try to identify those who have legitimate jobs and who are successful. In other words, you want to **run with real winners** who have good job-oriented contacts. Pretty soon you should have a long list of people to whom you can direct your networking activities.

After developing your comprehensive list of contacts, classify the names into different categories of individuals:

- Those in influential positions or who have hiring authority
- Those with job leads
- Those most likely to refer you to others
- Those with long-distance contacts

Select at least 25 names from your list for initiating your first round of contacts. You are now ready to begin an active prospecting and networking campaign which should lead to informational interviews, formal job interviews, and job offers.

After identifying your extended network, you should try to **link your network to the networks** of others. The figure on page 152 illustrates this linkage principle. Individuals in these other networks also have job information and contacts. Ask people in your basic network for referrals to individuals in **their** networks. This approach should greatly enlarge your basic job search network.

What do you do if individuals in your immediate and extended network cannot provide you with certain job information and contacts? While it is much easier and more effective to meet new people through personal contacts, on occasion you may need to **approach strangers without prior contacts**. In this situation, try the "cold turkey" approach. Write a letter to someone you feel may be useful to your job search. Research this individual so you are acquainted with their background and accomplishments. In the letter, refer to their accomplishments, mention your need for job information, and specify a date and time you will call to schedule a meeting. Another approach is to introduce yourself to someone by telephone or e-mail and request a meeting and/or job information. While you may experience rejections in using these approaches, you also will experience successes. And those successes should lead to further expansion of your job search network.

Develop a Prospecting Campaign for Information

The key to successful networking is an active and routine **prospecting campaign**. Salespersons in insurance, real estate, Amway, Shaklee, and other direct-sales businesses understand the importance of prospecting; indeed, many have turned the art of prospecting into a science as well as billion-dollar global businesses! The basic operating principle is **probability**: the number of sales you make is a direct function of the amount of effort you put into developing new contacts and following through. Expect no more than a 10 percent acceptance rate: for every 10 people you meet, nine will reject you and one will accept you. Therefore, the more people you contact, the more acceptances you will receive. If you want to be successful, you must collect many more "no's" than "yeses." In a 10 percent probability situation, you need to contact 100 people for 10 successes.

These prospecting principles are extremely useful for conducting a job search or making a career change. Like sales situations, the job search is a highly ego-involved activity often characterized by numerous rejections accompanied by a few acceptances. While no one wants to be rejected, few people are willing and able to handle more than a few rejections. They take a "no" as a sign of personal failure – and quit prematurely. In fact, the typical job search looks something like this:

No, No, No, No, No, No, Maybe, No, No, No, Yes, No, No, No, No, No, No, No, Maybe, No, Maybe, Yes, No, No, No, No, Yes, Yes

Linking Your Networks to Others

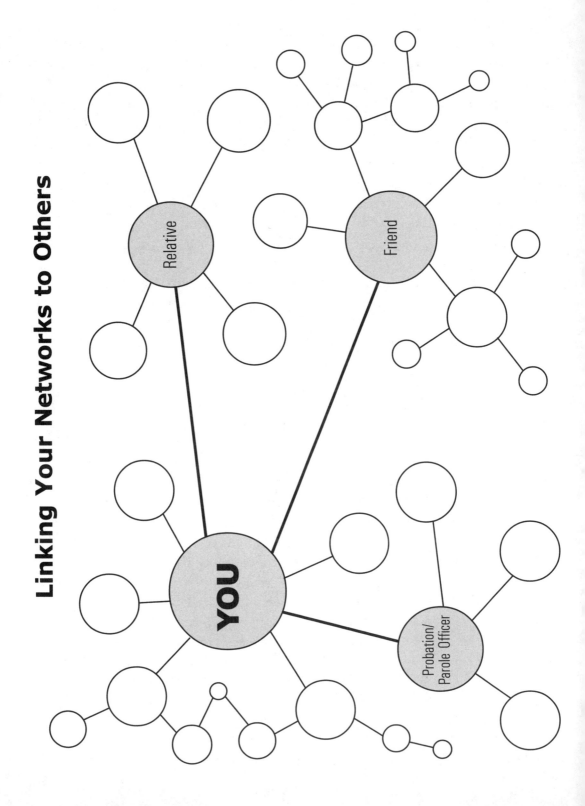

If you get disillusioned and quit after receiving four rejections, you will prematurely fail. While it may be initially hard to do, you need to continue making calls and writing letters in the process of "collecting" more rejections in order to get an acceptance. In fact, we often recommend that individuals get up in the morning with the idea of collecting at least 20 rejections! You will eventually get acceptances, but you must first deal with many rejections on the road to success. **Persistence does pay off in the long run**.

You also can minimize rejections by focusing your prospecting activities on gathering information rather than making sales. Therefore, you are well advised to do the following:

- Develop a well organized and active prospecting campaign for uncovering quality job leads.

- Be positive by accepting rejections as part of the game that leads to acceptances.

- Link prospecting to informational interviewing.

- Keep prospecting for more information and "yeses" which will eventually translate into job interviews and offers.

A good prospecting pace as you start your search is to make two new contacts each day. Start by contacting people in your immediate network. Let them know you are conducting a job search, but emphasize that you are only doing research (see Chapter 8). Ask for a few moments of their time to talk about what you are doing. You are only seeking **information and advice** at this time – not a job.

It should take you about 20 minutes to make a contact by letter or telephone. If you make two contacts each day, by the end of the first week you will have 10 new contacts for a total investment of less than seven hours. By the second week you may want to increase your prospecting pace to four new contacts each day or 20 each week. The more contacts you make, the more useful information, advice, and job leads you will receive. If your job search bogs down, you probably need to increase your prospecting activities.

Expect each contact to refer you to two or three others, who will also refer you to others. Your contacts should multiply considerably within only a few weeks.

Learn to Handle and Minimize Rejections

These prospecting and networking methods are effective, and they can have a major impact on your job search – and your life. While they are responsible for building, maintaining, and expanding multi-million dollar businesses, they work extremely well for job hunters. But they only work for those who have a positive attitude and who are patient and persist. **The key to networking success is to focus on gathering information while also learning to handle rejections.** Learn from rejections, forget them, and go on to more productive networking activities. The major reason direct-sales people fail is because they don't persist. The reason they don't persist is because they either can't take, or they get tired of taking, rejections. This should not happen to you. **Always welcome rejections: they will eventually lead to acceptances.**

Rejections are no fun, especially in such an ego-involved activity as a job search. But you will encounter rejections as you travel on the road toward job search success. This road is littered with individuals who quit prematurely because they were rejected four or five times. Don't be one of them!

> *The job search is a highly ego-involved activity often characterized by numerous rejections accompanied by a few acceptances.*

Our prospecting and networking techniques differ from sales approaches in one major respect: we have special techniques for minimizing the number of rejections. If handled properly, at least 50 percent – maybe as many as 90 percent – of your prospects will turn into "yeses" rather than "nos." The reason for this unusually high acceptance rate is how you introduce and handle yourself as you contact your prospects. Many insurance agents and direct distributors expect a 90 percent rejection rate, because they are trying to sell specific products potential clients may or may not need. Most people don't like to be put on the spot – especially when it is in their own home or office – to make a decision to buy a product.

Be Honest and Sincere

The principles of selling yourself in the job market are similar. People don't want to be put on the spot. They feel uncomfortable if they think you expect them to give you a job. Thus, you should never introduce yourself to a prospect by asking them for a job or a job lead. You should do just the opposite: relieve their anxiety by mentioning that you are not looking for a job from them – only job information and advice. You must be honest and sincere in communicating these intentions to your contact. The biggest turn-off for individuals targeted for informational interviews is insincere job seekers who try to use this as a mechanism to get a job.

Your approach to prospects must be subtle, honest, and professional. You are seeking **information, advice, and referrals** relating to several subjects: job opportunities, your job search approach, your resume, and contacts who may have similar information, advice, and referrals. Most people gladly volunteer such informa tion. They generally like to talk about themselves, their careers, and others. Similar to advice columnists, they like to give advice. This approach flatters individuals by placing them in the role of the expert-advisor. Who doesn't want to be recognized as an expert-advisor, especially on such a critical topic as one's employment?

This approach should yield a great deal of information, advice, and referrals from your prospects. One other important outcome should result from using this approach: people will **remember** you as the person who made them feel at ease and who received their valuable advice. If they hear of job opportunities for someone with your qualifications, chances are they will pass the information on to you. After contacting 100 prospects, you will have created 100 sets of eyes and ears to help you in your job search!

Practice the 5R's of Informational Interviewing

The guiding principle behind prospecting, networking, and informational interviews is this: **The best way to get a job is to ask for job information, advice, and referrals; never ask for a job**. Remember, you want your prospects to engage in the 5R's of informational interviewing:

- **Reveal** useful information and advice.
- **Refer** you to others.
- **Read** your resume.
- **Revise** your resume.
- **Remember** you for future reference.

The best way to get a job is to ask for job information, advice, and referrals; never ask for a job.

If you network according to this principle, you should join the ranks of thousands of successful job seekers who have experienced the 5R's of informational interviewing. Largely avoiding the advertised job market, you may find your perfect job through such powerful networking activities.

Approach Key People

Whom should you contact within an organization for an informational interview? Contact people who are **busy**, who have the **power to hire**, and who are **knowledgeable** about the organization. The least likely candidate will be someone in the human resources department. Most often the heads of operating units are the most busy, powerful, and knowledgeable individuals in the organization. However, getting access to such individuals may be difficult. Some people at the top may appear to be informed and powerful, but they may lack information on the day-to-day personnel changes or their influence is limited in the hiring process. It is difficult to give one best answer to this question.

Therefore, we recommend contacting several types of people. Aim for the busy, powerful, and informed, but be prepared to settle for less. Secretaries, receptionists, and the person you want to meet may refer you to others. From a practical standpoint, you may have to take whomever you can schedule an appointment with. Sometimes people who are less powerful can be helpful. Talk to a secretary or receptionist sometime about their boss or working in the organization. You may be surprised by what you learn!

Nonetheless, you will conduct informational interviews with different types of people. Some will be friends, relatives, or acquaintances. Others will be referrals or new contacts. You will gain the easiest access to people you already know. This can usually be done informally by telephone. You might meet at their home or office or at a restaurant.

You should use a more formal approach to gain access to referrals and new contacts. The best way to initiate a contact with a prospective employer is to **send an approach letter** and follow it up with a phone call. This letter should include the following elements:

OPENERS   If you have a referral, tell the individual you are considering a career in _____. His or her name was given to you by _____who suggested he or she might be a good person to give you useful information about careers in _____. Should you lack a referral to the individual and thus must use a "cold turkey" approach to making this contact, you might begin your letter by stating that you are aware he or she has been at the forefront of _____ business – or whatever is both truthful and appropriate for the situation. Try to make a personal connection to this person. A subtle, but honest, form of flattery will be helpful at this stage.

REQUEST   Demonstrate your thoughtfulness and courtesy rather than aggressiveness by mentioning that you know he or she is busy. You hope to schedule a mutually convenient time for a brief meeting to discuss your questions and career plans. Most people will be flattered by such a request and happy to talk with you about their work – if they have time and are interested in you.

CLOSINGS   In closing the letter, mention that you will call the person to see if an appointment can be arranged. Be specific by stating the time and day you will call – for example, Thursday at 2pm. You must take initiative to follow up the letter with a definite contact time. If you don't, you cannot expect to hear from the person. It is **your** responsibility to make the telephone call to schedule a meeting.

ENCLOSURE   Do **not** enclose your resume with this approach letter. Take your resume to the interview and present it as a topic of discussion near the end of your meeting. If you send it with the approach letter, you communicate a mixed and contradictory message. Remember your purpose for this interview: to gather information and advice. You are not – and never should be – asking for a job. A resume accompanying a letter appears to be an application or a job request.

Many people will meet with you, assuming you are sincere in your approach. On the other hand, many people also are very busy and simply don't have the time to meet with you. If the person puts you off when you telephone for an appointment, clearly state your purpose and emphasize that you are not looking for a job with this person – only information and advice. If the person insists on putting you off, make the best of the situation: try to conduct the informational interview over the telephone. Alternatively, write a nice thank-you letter in which you again state your intended purpose; mention your disappointment in not being able to learn from the person's experience; and ask to be remembered for future reference. Enclose your resume with this letter.

While you are ostensibly seeking information and advice, treat this meeting as an important preliminary interview. You need to communicate your qualifications – that you are competent, intelligent, honest, and likable. These are the same qualities you should communicate in a formal job interview. Hence, follow the same advice given for conducting a formal interview and dressing appropriately for a face-to-face meeting (Chapter 11).

Conduct the Interview, Including the "CR" Question

An informational interview will be relatively unstructured compared to a formal job interview. Since you want the individual to advise you, make sure you ask questions that will give you useful information. You, in effect, become the interviewer. You should structure this interview with a particular sequence of questions. Most questions should be open-ended, requiring the individual to give specific answers based upon his or her experience.

The structure and dialogue for the informational interview might go something like this. You plan to take no more than 45 minutes for this interview. The first three to five minutes will be devoted to small talk – the weather, traffic, the office, mutual acquaintances, or an interesting or humorous observation. Since these are the most critical moments in the interview, be especially careful how you communicate nonverbally. Begin your interview by stating your appreciation for the individual's time. Use your own words, but follow the "gist" of the statement below:

"I want to thank you again for scheduling this meeting with me. I know you're busy. I appreciate the special arrangements you made to see me on a subject which is very important to my future."

Your next comment should reiterate your purpose as stated in your letter:

"As you know, I am exploring job and career alternatives. I know what I do well and what I want to do. But before I commit myself to a new job, I need to know more about various career options. I thought you would be able to provide me with some insights into career opportunities, job requirements, and possible problems or promising directions in the field of _____."

A statement of this type normally will get a positive reaction from the individual who may want to know more about what it is you want to do. Be sure to clearly communicate your job objective. If you can't, you may indicate that you are lost, indecisive, or uncertain about yourself. The person may feel you are wasting his or her time.

Your next line of questioning should focus on "how" and "what" questions centering on (1) specific jobs and (2) the job search process. Begin by asking about various aspects of specific jobs:

- Duties and responsibilities
- Knowledge, skills, and abilities required
- Work environment relating to employees, work, deadlines, stress
- Advantages and disadvantages
- Advancement opportunities and outlook
- Salary ranges

Your informer will probably take a great deal of time talking about his or her experience in each area. Be a good listener, but make sure you move along with the questions.

Your next line of questioning should focus on your job search activities. You need as much information as possible on how to:

- Acquire the necessary skills
- Best find a job in this field
- Overcome any objections employers may have to you
- Uncover job vacancies which may be advertised
- Develop job leads
- Approach prospective employers

Your next line of questioning should raise the "CR" question – your criminal record. This is a good time to disclose what may be a red flag for many employers. The question might be something like this, but it must honestly reflect your situation in the most positive way:

"I have a potential problem that I would appreciate your advice on. I'm currently on parole. A few years ago, when I was running with the wrong crowd, I did some very stupid things related to drugs. As a result, I spent two years in Paris State Prison. I lost everything – family, friends, and my self-esteem. While I hit bottom, I swore I would turn my life around. In fact, being incarcerated was the best thing to happen to me at that stage in my life. It was a real wake-up call. I got my GED, took a couple of college courses, participated in vocational training programs, and have excellent references from my supervisor, caseworker, and parole officer. I now know what I want to do with my life. However, when employers learn about my criminal record, they may automatically reject me. If you were in my situation, how would you handle the criminal record issue with employers?"

The advice you get in response to this question may be some of the most important advice you get as you network. Indeed, you may discover many people in your network may try to bend over backwards to help you reenter the workforce despite your criminal record. This is an excellent time to fully disclose your key red flag issue. Again, you're not interviewing for a job – just getting valuable information and advice. The advice will help you overcome any reluctance to reveal your background to employers with whom you will be interviewing for an actual job.

Your final line of questioning should focus on your resume. Do not show your resume until you pose this last set of questions. The purposes of these questions are to: (1) get the individual to read your resume in-depth, (2) acquire useful advice on how to strengthen it, (3) be referred to prospective employers, and (4) be remembered. With the resume in front of you and the other person, ask the following questions:

- Is this an appropriate type of resume for the jobs I have outlined?

- If an employer received this resume in the mail, how do you think he or she would react to it?

- Do you see possible weaknesses or areas that need to be improved?

- What about the length, paper quality and color, layout, and type style/size? Are they appropriate?

- What should I do with this resume? Broadcast it to hundreds of employers with a cover letter? Use a "T" letter instead?

- How might I best improve the form and content of my resume?

- Who might be most interested in receiving this resume?

You should obtain useful advice on how to strengthen both the content and use of your resume. Most important, these questions force the individual to **read** your resume, which, in turn, may be **remembered** for future reference.

Your last question is especially important in this interview. You want to be both **remembered** and **referred**. Some variation of the following question should help:

> *"I really appreciate all this advice. It is very helpful and it should improve my job search considerably. Could I ask you one more favor? Do you know two or three other people who might be willing to assist me with these same questions? I want to conduct as much research as possible, and their advice might be helpful also."*

Before you leave, mention one more important item:

> *"During the next few months, if you hear of any job opportunities for someone with my interests and qualifications, I would appreciate being kept in mind. And please feel free to pass my name on to others."*

Send a nice thank-you letter – preferably by mail – within 48 hours of completing this informational interview. Express your genuine gratitude for the individual's time and advice. Restate your interests, and ask to be remembered and referred.

Be sure to follow up on any useful advice you receive, particularly referrals. Approach referrals in the same manner you approached the person who gave you the referral. Write a letter requesting a meeting. Begin the letter by mentioning:

> *"Mr./Ms. _____ suggested that I contact you concerning my research on careers in _____."*

If you continue prospecting, networking, and conducting informational interviews, soon you will be busy conducting interviews and receiving job offers. While 100 informational interviews over a two-month period should lead to several formal job interviews and offers, the pay-offs are uncertain because job vacancies are unpredictable. We know cases where the first referral turned into a formal interview and job offer. More typical cases require constant prospecting, networking, and informational interviewing activities. The telephone call or letter inviting you to a job interview can come at any time. While the timing may be unpredictable, your persistent job search activities will be largely responsible for the final outcome.

Telephone for Job Leads

Telephone communication should play an important role in prospecting, networking, and informational interviews. However, controversy centers around how and when to use the telephone for generating job leads and scheduling interviews. Some people recommend writing a letter and waiting for a written or telephone reply. Others suggest writing a letter and following it with a telephone call. Still others argue you should use the telephone exclusively rather than write letters.

How you use the telephone will indicate what type of job search you are conducting. Exclusive reliance on the telephone is a technique used by highly formalized job clubs that operate phone banks for generating job leads. Using the Yellow Pages or Internet phone directories as the guide to employers, a job club member may call as many as 50 employers a day to schedule job interviews. A rather aggressive yet typical telephone dialogue goes something like this:

"Hello, my name is Bill Webber. I would like to speak to the head of the sales depart-ment. By the way, what is the name of the sales director?"

"You want to talk to Ms. Carson. Her number is 777-222-1111, or I can connect you directly."

"Hello, Ms. Carson. My name is Bill Webber. I am very interested in your new line of paper products for small businesses. I would like to meet with you to discuss a possible sales position for someone with my qualifications. Would it be possible to see you on Friday at 2pm?"

Not surprisingly, this telephone approach generates many "no's." If you have a hard time handling rejections, this telephone approach will help you confront your anxieties. The principle behind this approach is **probability**: for every 25 telephone "no" you receive, you will probably get one or two "yeses." Success is just 25 telephone calls away! If you start calling prospective employers at 9am and finish your 25 calls by 12 noon, you should generate at least one or two interviews. That's not bad for three hours of job search work. It beats a direct-mail approach.

While the telephone is more efficient than writing letters, its effectiveness is questionable. When you use the telephone in this manner, you are basically pitching for a job. You are asking the employer: *"Do you have a job for me?"* There is nothing subtle about this approach. Luck pays an important role – you place a phone call at the right time when a job vacancy is available, often before it gets advertised. If you need a job – any job – in a hurry, which is the situation for most ex-offenders, this is one of the most efficient ways of finding employment. However, if you are more concerned with finding a job that is right for you – a job you do well and enjoy doing, one that is fit for you – this telephone approach may not be appropriate.

You must use your own judgment in determining when and how to use the telephone in your job search. There are appropriate times and methods for using the telephone, and these should relate to your job search goals and needs. We prefer the networking approach we previously outlined – writing a letter requesting an informational interview and following up with a telephone call. While you take the initiative in scheduling an appointment, you do not put the individual on the spot by asking for a job. You are only **seeking information and advice**. This low-keyed approach results in numerous acceptances and has a higher probability of paying off with interviews than the aggressive telephone request. You should be trying to uncover jobs that are right for you rather than any job that happens to pop up from a telephoning blitz.

Join a Job Club or Support Group

The techniques outlined thus far are designed for individuals conducting a self-directed job search. Job clubs and support groups are two important alternatives to these techniques.

Job clubs are designed to provide a group structure and support system to individuals seeking employment. These groups consist of about 12 individuals who are led by a trained counselor and supported with telephones, copying machines, and a resource center.

Formal job clubs, such as the 40-Plus Club, organize job search activities for both the advertised and hidden job markets. Job club activities may include:

- Signing commitment agreements to achieve specific job search targets.
- Contacting friends, relatives, and acquaintances for job leads.
- Completing activity forms.
- Using telephones, computers, photocopy machines, postage, and other equipment and supplies.
- Meeting with fellow participants to discuss job search progress.
- Meeting with career counselors or other career specialists.
- Attending job fairs and hiring conferences.
- Telephoning to uncover job leads.
- Using the Internet to research the job market and contact potential employers.
- Researching newspapers, telephone books, and directories.
- Developing research, telephone, interview, and social skills.
- Writing letters and resumes.
- Responding to want ads.
- Completing employment applications.
- Assessing weekly progress and sharing information with fellow group members.

In other words, the job club formalizes many of the prospecting, networking, and informational interviewing activities within a group context and interjects the role of the telephone as the key communication device for developing and expanding networks.

Many job clubs place excessive reliance on using the telephone and Internet for uncovering job leads. Members call prospective employers and ask about job openings. The Yellow Pages and the Internet become the job hunter's best friends. During a two-week period, a job club member might spend most of his or her mornings telephoning for job leads and scheduling interviews. Afternoons are normally devoted to job interviewing.

Many job club methods are designed for individuals who need a job – any job – quickly. Since individuals try to fit into available vacancies, their specific objectives and skills are of secondary concern. Other job club methods are more consistent with the focus and methods outlined in this book, especially those used by 40-Plus Clubs (www.40plus.org/chapters) and Five O'Clock Clubs (www.fiveoclockclub.com).

Instead of participating in such clubs, you may want to form a support group that adapts some job club methods around our central concept of finding a job fit for you – one appropriate to your objective and in line with your particular mix of skills, abilities, and interests. Support groups are a useful alternative to job clubs. They have one major advantage to conducting a job search on your own: they may cut your job search time in half because they provide an important structure for achieving goals. Forming or joining one of these groups can help direct as well as enhance your individual job search activities. Several of the ex-offender support groups identified in Chapter 5 may be good candidates for forming such job-oriented groups.

Your support group should consist of three or more individuals who are job hunting. Try to schedule regular meetings with specific purposes in mind. While the group may be highly social, especially if it involves close friends, it also should be task-oriented. Meet at least once a week and include your spouse. At each meeting set **performance goals** for the week. For example, your goal can be to make 20 new contacts and conduct five informational interviews. The contacts can be made by telephone, e-mail, letter, or in person. Share your experiences and job information with each other. **Critique** each other's progress, make suggestions for improving the job search, and develop new strategies together. By doing this, you will be gaining valuable information and feedback which is normally difficult to gain on one's own. This group should provide important psychological supports to help you through your job search. After all, job hunting can be a lonely, frustrating, and exasperating experience. By sharing your experiences with others, you will find you are not alone. You will quickly learn that rejections are part of the game. The group will encourage you, and you will feel good about helping others achieve their goals. Try developing small incentives, such as the individual who receives the most job interviews for the month will be treated to dinner by other members of the group.

Explore Online Networks and Networking

Networking is increasingly taking on new communication forms in today's high-tech world. Job seekers can take advantage of several websites and electronic databases for conducting a job search, from gathering information on the job market to disseminating resumes to employers. The Internet also allows job seekers to network for information, advice, and job leads. If you belong to one of the major Internet service providers, such as America Online, or have direct access to the Internet's World Wide Web, you can use mailing lists, news groups, bulletin boards, blogs, chat groups, message boards, and e-mail to gather job information and make contacts with potential employers. Using e-mail, you can make personal contacts which give you job leads for further networking via computer or through the more traditional networking methods outlined in this chapter.

Several websites will help you develop networking skills as well as put you in contact with important employment-related networks. These sites include a wealth of information on the networking process:

- **WetFeet**   www.wetfeet.com/advice/networking.asp
- **Monster.com**   http://network.monster.com
- **Quintessential Careers**   www.quintcareers.com/networking.html
- **Riley Guide**   www.rileyguide.com/netintv.html
- **WinningTheJob**   www.winningthejob.com

Once you begin the process of developing your networks, you may want to use the following websites to locate long-lost friends, classmates, and others who might be helpful in your networking campaign:

- **AnyWho**   www.anywho.com
- **Classmates**   www.classmates.com
- **InfoSpace**   www.infospace.com
- **Reunion** (high school)   www.reunion.com
- **Switchboard**   www.switchboard.com
- **Yahoo! People Search**   http://people.yahoo.com

If you have military experience and wish to locate some of your former military buddies, be sure to explore these people finders for locating military personnel:

- **GI Search.com**   www.gisearch.com
- **Military.com**   www.military.com
- **Military Connections**   www.militaryconnections.com

If you've lost contact with your former classmates, try these websites for locating alumni groups:

- **Alumni.net**   www.alumni.net
- **Curious Cat Alumni**
  Connections   www.curiouscat.net/alumni

Many of the large Internet employment sites maintain message boards. Two of the largest message board operations, which offer opportunities to network for information and advice, are found at these websites:

- **Monster.com**   http://network.monster.com
- **Vault.com**   www.vault.com/community/mb/
                                          mb_home.jsp

The latest trend or fad in online networking is based upon the "six degrees of separation theory" – everyone is connected to everyone else in the world by only six other people. A somewhat dubious theory, nonetheless, these networks have been responsible for a great deal of news media hype since 2003 on how to expand one's network of connections for personal and professional purposes. Building electronic communities, these networks are designed to put users into contact with thousands of other people for all types of purposes – from dating to making friends to finding a job to recruiting to developing sales forces to closing business deals. The ultimate soft approach to cold calling, these electronic networks tend to be of questionable value to job seekers who have actually used them. After all, they formalize what is essentially an informal, personal process that works best in one degree removed face-to-face situations. Even so, these new electronic networks offer some interesting online networking opportunities for those who have the time and dedication to make them work. They probably are most effective for those who need to prospect for new business and potential sales contacts, which is the direction many of the more entrepreneurial such networks now take. The following websites are devoted to promoting this type of networking activity:

- **LinkedIn**   www.linkedin.com
- **Friendster**   www.friendster.com
- **Ryze Business Networking**   http://new.ryze.com
- **Spoke**   www.spoke.com
- **EntreMate**   www.entremate.com

The first website, www.linkedin.com, tends to be used by more job seekers and recruiters than the other networking sites. If you want to try your luck with this type of online networking in your job search, we recommend starting with LinkedIn.

The Internet can significantly enhance your job search. It offers new networking possibilities for individuals who are literate in today's digital technology. If you have access to the Internet, we recommend getting your resume into various employment websites. (See page 137.) Explore their job vacancies, resources, chat groups, and message boards. Within just a few minutes of electronic networking, you may pick up important job information, advice, and leads that could turn into a real job.

11

Develop Winning Job
Interview Skills

T HE JOB INTERVIEW IS the single most important step in the whole job search process – no interview, no job offer, no salary, no benefits. If you've followed our advice in previous chapters, you should now have a strong foundation for handling the job interview. Nonetheless, job interviews can be stressful, especially for ex-offenders with red flags in their backgrounds.

Throughout the job interview your major purpose should be to sell yourself to the employer. At the same time, you want to get as much information about the job and the employer in order to decide whether or not the job is right for you.

Let's examine various aspects of the job interview. In so doing, we'll prepare you for different phases of a job interview. We want you to leave the interview with the confidence that you made the very best impression on the interviewer.

Hire Slow, Fire Fast

Within the past few years, the job interview – as well as the whole hiring process – has changed in several important ways. These changes require both interviewees and interviewers to better prepare for the job interview. Indeed, **preparation is the key to interview success**. Most changes reflect the need of employers to better define their hiring needs and then make more intelligent and cost-effective hiring decisions.

While employers used to hire fast and fire slow, today more employers see the wisdom of doing just the opposite – hire slow and fire fast. This means more extensive screening of candidates and focusing on **patterns of accomplishments** in order to better **predict** employee behavior. Employers want a perfect "fit." This also means conducting a different style of interviewing. Rather than call a candidate in for one interview, an employer may interview a single candidate three to five times before making a job offer. So, how do you handle your fifth interview? Not surprisingly, many candidates have difficulty remaining upbeat after the third interview! Those who prepared canned answers to interview questions may have difficulty staying on message after responding to dozens of questions that require them to demonstrate their personality, likability, competence, and ability to make thoughtful decisions.

At the same time, employers are taking more time to screen candidates for red flags with everything from drug, aptitude, psychological, and polygraph tests to in-depth background checks on criminal records, work history, and even credit history. Within the interview itself, more and more employers are asking **behavior-based questions** to identify a candidate's ability to make decisions and solve problems relevant to the job. Consequently, candidates who prepare for interviews with memorized or canned answers to anticipated interview questions do not do well in such interviews; they appear coached or rehearsed and thus lack authenticity and credibility. Going beyond behavior-based questions, many employers also seek better indicators of a candidate's decision-making style and pattern of performance by conducting **situational interviews**. Giving interviewees hypothetical or real-work problems to solve, interviewers want to see how a candidate actually behaves, rather than what they say, within the context of the company. Accordingly, employers want to know more about your motivated abilities and skills (Chapter 7) and whether or not your MAS is a good fit for their organization by actually observing you in action.

> *While employers used to hire fast and fire slow, many see the wisdom of doing just the opposite – hire slow and fire fast.*

The overall trend is simple: No more hiring surprises due to poor hiring skills! Employers want to better predict individual performance within their organizations. They can't afford to make costly hiring mistakes.

Prepare for Stressful Interviews

Nearly 95 percent of all organizations require job interviews prior to hiring employees. In fact, employers consider an effective interview to be the most important hiring criterion – outranking education, related work experience, resumes, letters, and recommendations.

While the job interview is the most important job search activity, it also is the most stressful job search experience. Your application, resume, and letters may get you to the interview, but you must perform well in person in order to get a job offer. Knowing the stakes are high, most people face interviews with dry throats and sweaty palms; it is a time of great stress. You will be on stage, and you are expected to put on your best performance.

How do you prepare for the interview? First, you need to understand the nature and purpose of the interview. Second, you must prepare to respond to different interview situations and interviewers. Make sure whoever assists you in preparing for the interview evaluates your performance. Practice the whole interviewing scenario, from the time you enter the door until you leave. Sharpen communication skills as you prepare to give positive answers to questions as well as ask intelligent questions. The more you practice, the better prepared you will be for the real job interview.

A Two-Way Communication Exchange

An interview is a two-way communication exchange between an interviewer and interviewee. It involves both verbal and nonverbal communication. While we tend to concentrate on the content of what we say, research shows that approximately 65 percent of all communication is **nonverbal**. Furthermore, we tend to give more **credibility** to nonverbal than to verbal messages. Regardless of what you say, how you dress, sit, stand, use your hands, move your head and eyes, and listen communicates both positive and negative messages.

Job interviews can occur in many different settings and under various circumstances. You may write job interview letters, schedule interviews by telephone, be interviewed over the phone, and encounter one-on-one as well as panel, group, series, behavioral, and situational interviews. Each situation requires a different set of communication behaviors. For example, while telephone communication is efficient, it may be ineffective for interview purposes. Only certain types of information can be effectively communicated over the telephone because this medium is primarily verbal. Honesty, intelligence, and likability – three of the most important values you want to communicate to employers – are primarily communicated nonverbally. Therefore, you should be very careful of telephone interviews – whether giving or receiving them.

Job interviews have different purposes and can be negative in many ways. From your perspective, the purpose of an initial job interview is to get a second interview or a job offer, and the purpose of the second interview is to get more interviews until a job offer is forthcoming. However, for many employers, the purpose of the interview is to eliminate you from additional interviews or a job offer. The interviewer wants to know why he or she should **not** hire you. The interviewer tries to do this by identifying your weaknesses. These differing purposes can create an adversarial relationship and contribute to the overall interviewing stress experienced by both the applicant and the interviewer.

Since the interviewer has certain expectations about required personalities and performance in candidates, he or she wants to **identify your weaknesses**. You must counter by **communicating your strengths** to lessen the interviewer's fears of hiring you. Recognizing that you are an unknown quantity to the employer, you must raise the interviewer's expectations of you.

Avoid 42 Common Interview Errors

Employers report encountering many job seekers who make a variety of interview errors that quickly knock them out of competition. Make sure you don't make any of these mistakes, which constitute a handy list of interview "don'ts":

1. Arrives late to the interview.
2. Comes to the interview with a friend, relative, or child.
3. Makes a bad impression – rude and obnoxious – in the waiting area.
4. Dresses inappropriately and looks sloppy and unkempt.
5. Wears sunglasses, blue jeans, and heavy-duty boots.
6. Presents a poor appearance and negative image.
7. Expresses negative attitudes, often saying *"can't"* or *"didn't."*
8. Offers lots of excuses and blames others for weaknesses.
9. Engages in inappropriate behavior – shows off tattoos and leg injury.
10. Appears somewhat incoherent and unfocused.
11. Uses poor grammar and seems inarticulate.
12. Gives short and incomplete answers to questions.
13. Lacks a sense of direction or purpose.
14. Appears ill or has a possible undisclosed medical condition.
15. Volunteers personal information that would be illegal to ask.
16. Emits bad body odors.
17. Shows little enthusiasm, drive, or initiative.
18. Lacks confidence and self-esteem.
19. Appears too eager and hungry for the job.
20. Communicates dishonesty or deception.
21. Seems too smooth and superficial.
22. Appears evasive when asked about possible red flags.
23. Speaks negatively of previous employers and co-workers.
24. Maintains poor eye contact and fidgets a lot.
25. Offers a limp or overly firm handshake.
26. Shows little interest in the company.
27. Talks about salary and benefits early in the interview.
28. Is discourteous, ill-mannered, and disrespectful – argues a lot.

29. Tries to look cool and speaks an inappropriate street language.
30. Tells inappropriate jokes and laughs a lot.
31. Talks too much – a real motor-mouth.
32. Drops names to impress the interviewer.
33. Appears needy and greedy.
34. Fails to talk about accomplishments.
35. Does not ask questions about the job or employer.
36. Appears self-centered rather than employer-centered.
37. Demonstrates poor listening skills.
38. Seems not too bright for the job.
39. Fails to know his/her worth when talking about compensation.
40. Forgets to bring appropriate documents, including a list of references.
41. Closes the interview by just getting up and leaving.
42. Never follows up.

Observe 43 Interview "Do's"

There are certain things you need to know and do before, during, and after the job interview. Each phase of the interview has its own separate set of "do's":

Preparing for the Interview

1. **DO** prepare your wardrobe, questions, and answers before the day of the interview.
2. **DO** research the company/organization, the job, and comparable salaries and benefits (see Chapter 8).
3. **DO** plan to sell yourself throughout the interview, from the moment you enter the door to 24 hours after the interview.
4. **DO** ask a friend or relative to help you prepare for the interview by role playing the interviewer and interviewee.
5. **DO** practice giving positive employer-centered answers to possible interview questions, but never memorize answers that will make you sound rehearsed, appear insincere, and contribute to nervousness, especially when you forget your "lines."
6. **DO** prepare to address some really tough questions about your background, especially why the interviewer should hire someone with a criminal record, your work and educational achievements, your goals, and whether or not you are bonded.
7. **DO** look at yourself in the mirror and listen to what you say and how you say it, and then grade yourself and your performance from 1 to 10. Keep doing this until you become a "10." If you can't grade yourself, find someone who is a tough and objective grader.

8. **DO** outline a 30-second pitch of why you should be hired that you can occasionally repeat in different ways during the interview.

9. **DO** develop five one- to two-minute stories giving good examples of your major strengths and accomplishments that support your job objective.

10. **DO** learn how long it will take to get to the interview location, plan your transportation, and then plan to arrive at least 20 minutes early.

11. **DO** gather any documents you need to take to the interview, such as a list of references, a mock application form, your resume, drivers license, Social Security number, examples of your work, and any letters of recommendation or commendations.

12. **DO** ask people you plan to use as references if you may use them as references in your job search

13. **DO** lower your stress level and nervousness by preparing well, taking deep breaths, and focusing on the interviewer rather than yourself.

14. **DO** write down any questions you need to ask the interviewer.

15. **DO** tell yourself that this is going to be the best day for starting your new life.

16. **DO** check the weather before you leave, just in case you need an umbrella or coat.

17. **DO** get a good night's sleep, avoid alcohol, and eat lightly the day before the interview.

18. **DO** practice good personal hygiene, from bathing and brushing teeth to washing hair, shaving, and cleaning hands and fingernails.

Arriving At the Interview Site

19. **DO** arrive on time.

20. **DO** come alone – no friends, relatives, or children should enter the building with you.

21. **DO** remove your coat before sitting down in the waiting area.

22. **DO** observe the surroundings and visit the restroom.

23. **DO** be courteous, professional, sincere, open, and honest at all times and with everyone you meet, especially those in the waiting area before the actual interview; everyone you meet may be "interviewing" you and thus could be important to the final hiring decision.

24. **DO** behave yourself properly in the waiting room by being seen doing something relevant to the job or company, such a reading a company brochure, or asking thoughtful company-related questions (not salary and benefits).

Greeting the Interviewer

25. **DO** stand up and greet the interviewer by looking him or her in the eye, extending your hand, giving a firm handshake, and stating your first and last name: *"Hi, I'm John Strong."*

26. **DO** address the interviewer by his or her proper title and last name: Mr./Mrs./Miss/Dr. _____. No first names unless asked to do so by the interviewer or people you meet.

27. **DO** wait to be seated before sitting down in the interviewer's office.

28. **DO** engage in some small talk, perhaps about the weather, something interesting you see in the office (painting, book, sculpture, diploma).

Conducting the Formal Interview

29. **DO** bring a pen and notebook to take notes during the interview.

30. **DO** sit up straight with a slightly forward lean, relax, keep your hands to your side or on your lap, listen carefully, project yourself, focus on the interviewer rather than on yourself, and look alive and happy.

31. **DO** appear friendly, enthusiastic, energetic, interested, and alert through-out the interview.

32. **DO** control your emotions, avoid being defensive, keep your cool, and go on to do your best, even if the interviewer asks you an illegal or insulting question

33. **DO** recover quickly from any errors you make. If you stumble or knock something over, or know you gave a bad answer to a question, keep on moving. Excuse yourself, go on to the next question, and focus on other more important things rather than try to keep recovering from a mistake. How you recover may be more important to the interviewer than the error you made.

34. **DO** speak well of others and situations, even though you may have had problems in the past. Always think of something good to say about other people and situations you have been in. How you talk about them is a good indicator of your attitudes, motivations, and behavior. Take, for example, how you might respond to questions concerning your incarcera-tion or being fired. Put a positive spin on such experiences.

35. **DO** give complete 30-second to two-minute answers to questions that constantly focus on your goals and strengths.

36. **DO** ask thoughtful questions about the job, company, employer, and competition, which you should have listed and written on a card or in your notebook. Refer to your notes to make sure you ask the right questions and impress upon the interviewer that you are prepared and interested in the company.

37. **DO** let the interviewer finish his or her questions or comments before responding.
38. **DO** delay any discussion of salary and benefits until the very end of the interview and after you have received a job offer. Prematurely talking about salary and benefits can quickly kill your candidacy as well as put you at a disadvantage.

Closing the Interview

39. **DO** let the interviewer initiate the close of the interview by indicating it's time to move on.
40. **DO** ask for a business card so you can follow up with a nice thank-you letter.
41. **DO** close the interview properly by (1) summarizing what you understand to be the responsibilities of the job, (2) stating why you believe this job would be an excellent fit for both you and the employer, (3) expressing your gratitude for the opportunity to interview for the position, (4) asking when the interviewer plans to make the hiring decision and when you might hear again from the interviewer, and (5) asking if it would be okay if you called the interviewer to check on the status of your candidacy.

Following Up the Interview

42. **DO** follow up with a nice thank-you letter within 24 hours.
43. **DO** make the follow-up call you indicated you would make.

Interview Sequence

Our lists of interview errors and "do's" are appropriate for several phases of the job interview. Most job interviews follow this basic sequence, which may take from 30 minutes to more than one hour to complete:

1. Greeting
2. Establishing common ground/icebreakers/small talk
3. Indicating purpose of interview
4. Drawing out information through the exchange of questions, answers, observations, and analysis:
   1. General and specific questions
   2. Brief and drawn out answers
   3. Conversations to clarify questions, explain answers, and reach mutual understanding

5. Summarizing information and understanding
6. Indicating next steps to be taken
7. Closing

Prepare to Answer Questions

Hopefully your prospecting, networking, informational interviewing, and resume and letter writing activities result in several invitations to interview for jobs appropriate to your objective. Once you receive an invitation to interview, you should prepare for the interview as if it were a $1,000,000+ prize. After all, that may be what you earn during your employment.

The invitation to interview will most likely come by telephone. In some cases, a preliminary interview will be conducted by telephone. The employer may want to shorten the list of eligible candidates from, for example, ten to three. By calling each individual, the employer can quickly eliminate marginal candidates as well as update the job status of each individual. When you get such a telephone call, you have no time to prepare. You may be dripping wet as you step from the shower or you may have a splitting headache as you pick up the phone. Telephone interviews always seem to occur at bad times.

You should prepare for the interview as if it were a $1,000,000+ prize.

Whatever your situation, put your best foot forward based upon your thorough preparation for an interview. You should keep a copy of your resume and a list of answering strategies and questions you would like to ask near the telephone just in case you receive such a call.

Telephone interviews often result in a face-to-face interview at the employer's office. Once you confirm an interview time and place, you should do as much research on the organization and employer as possible, as well as learn to lessen your anxiety and stress levels by practicing the interview situation. **Preparation and practice** are the keys to doing your best.

During the interview, you want to impress upon the interviewer your knowledge of the company by asking insightful questions and giving intelligent answers. Your library, Internet, and networking research should yield useful information on the organization and employer. Be sure you know something about the organization. Interviewers are normally impressed by interviewees who demonstrate knowledge and interest in their company.

You should practice the actual interview by mentally addressing questions interviewers are likely to ask. Most of these questions will relate to your educational background, work experience, career goals, personality, and related concerns. Frequently asked questions include:

Education

- Describe your educational background.
- Why did you drop out of school?
- What was your grade point average?
- Why were your grades so low? So high?
- What subjects did you enjoy the most? The least? Why?
- What leadership positions did you hold?
- Did you do the best you could in school? If not, why not?
- What educational programs did you participate in while in prison?
- Are you planning to go to college?
- What will you major in?
- If you could, what would you change about your education?
- What type of specialized training have you received?

Work Experience

- What were your major achievements in each of your past jobs?
- Why did you change jobs before?
- What is your typical workday like?
- What did you like about your boss? Dislike?
- If I called your last supervisor and asked about you, what might he tell me concerning your work habits and accomplishments?
- Which job did you enjoy the most? Why? Which job did you enjoy the least? Why?
- Have you ever been fired? Why?
- What did you especially like about your last job?
- Do you think you have enough experience for this job?

Career Goals

- Why do you want to join our company?
- Why do you think you are qualified for this position?
- Why are you looking for a job?
- What ideally would you like to do?
- Why should we hire you?
- How would you improve our operations?
- What do you want to be doing five years from now?
- How much do you expect to be making five years from now?
- What are your short-range and long-range career goals?
- If you were free to choose your job and employer, where would you go?
- What other types of jobs are you considering? Companies?

- When will you be ready to begin work?
- How do you feel about relocating, traveling, working overtime, working shifts, and working on weekends?
- What attracted you to us?

Personality and Other Concerns

- Tell me about yourself.
- What are your major weaknesses? Your major strengths?
- What causes you to lose your temper?
- What do you do in your spare time? Any hobbies?
- What types of books do you read?
- What role does your family play in your career?
- How well do you work under pressure? In meeting deadlines?
- How much initiative do you take?
- What types of people do you prefer working with?
- How _____ (creative, analytical, tactful, etc.) are you?
- If you could change your life, what would you do differently?

While different employers will ask different combinations of questions, we recommend spending extra time preparing for these seven most frequently asked questions:

- Tell me about yourself.
- Why should I hire you?
- What are your major weaknesses?
- Tell me about your plans for the future.
- How do your most recent jobs relate to this position?
- How would your previous employers characterize you?
- What are your salary requirements?

Handle Objections and Negatives With Ease

Interviewers must have a healthy skepticism of job candidates. They expect people to exaggerate their competencies and overstate what they will do for the employer. They sometimes encounter dishonest applicants, and some people they hire fail to meet their expectations. Being realists who have made poor hiring decisions before, they want to know why they should **not** hire you. Although they do not always ask you these questions, they think about them nonetheless:

- Why should I hire an ex-offender?
- What do you really want?

- What can you really do for me?
- What are your weaknesses?
- What problems will I have with you?

Underlying these questions are specific employers' fears or objections to hiring you:

- You're not as good as you say you are; you probably hyped your resume or lied about yourself. You may be incompetent and need lots of start-up time to get up and running.
- You just want a paycheck, benefits, and security. It may be hard to keep you motivated and enthusiastic about your work.
- You may talk and complain a lot, blame others, avoid responsibilities, and talk about salary and benefits all the time.
- You have weaknesses like the rest of us. Is it alcohol, sex, drugs, finances, shiftlessness, stealing, lying, cheating, petty politics?
- You may be lazy, come to work late, leave early, or not show up at all.
- You may drive your co-workers crazy with your annoying behavior.
- You won't stay long with us. You'll probably quit in a few months or violate your parole and get arrested again.

Employers raise such suspicions and objections, because it is difficult to trust strangers in the employment game, and they may have been "burned" before. Indeed, there is an alarming rise in the number of individuals lying on their resumes or falsifying their credentials.

How can you best handle employers' objections? You must first recognize their biases and then **raise** their expectations. You do this by stressing your strengths and avoiding your weaknesses. You must be impeccably honest in doing so.

Your answers to employers' questions should be positive and emphasize your **strengths**. Remember, the interviewer wants to know what's wrong with you – your **weaknesses**. When answering questions, both the **substance** and **form** of your answers should be positive. For example, such words as "couldn't," "can't," "won't," and "don't" may create a negative tone and distract from the positive and enthusiastic image you are trying to create. While you cannot eliminate all negative words, at least recognize that the type of words you use makes a difference; try to better manage your word choice. Compare your reactions to the following answers:

QUESTION: **Why do you want to work here?**

ANSWER 1:   *I just got out of prison and need a job. I don't know if you'll give me the job since I haven't worked in a few years. But I won't give you any trouble. I think I'll like working here. The people seem nice. I hope you won't hold my record against me.*

ANSWER 2: *I've always wanted to work for this company. You have a great reputation for being a leader in commercial moving and having the most professional movers in the business. My experience as a truck driver, my recent training in customer service, and my strong organization and communication skills are ideally suited for this position. I'm really excited about joining your team and making sure that you continue being the very best in this business. I also have some ideas on how we might be able to save money on two of the regular delivery routes. I am ready to take on more responsibilities and hope to work closely with you.*

Which one has the greatest impact in terms of projecting positives and strengths? The first answer communicates too many negatives and makes the interviewee sound like a beggar. The second answer is positive and upbeat in its emphasis on skills, accomplishments, and the future.

In addition to choosing positive words, select **content information** which is positive and **adds** to the interviewer's knowledge about you. Avoid simplistic "yes/no" answers; they say nothing about you. Instead, provide information which explains your reasons and motivations behind specific events or activities. For example, how do you react to these two factual answers?

QUESTION: **I see you recently completed your GED. Did you drop out of high school?**

ANSWER 1: *Yes, I did.*

ANSWER 2: *Yes. I did very poorly in high school – bad grades along with a poor attitude and attendance. I flunked two grades and was often suspended for bad behavior. I even attended an alternative school and got into more trouble, ending up in the juvenile detention center for two years. There I meet a wonderful teacher, Mrs. Taylor, who took a personal interest in me. She urged me to study for my GED. I really hadn't read until I met her. With her encouragement, I studied real hard and scored a 60 on the GED. Getting my GED really got me focused on planning my future, which now centers on more education and training. I know I can do whatever I set my mind to do. I really love working with numbers. As you can see from my resume, I've taken a couple of accounting courses at T. L. Johnson Junior College. I'm planning to complete my A.A degree within the next three years. I'm hoping this bookkeeping position will eventually lead to an accounting position within your company. I'm really excited about this position and have enjoyed meeting your staff and learning about your work.*

Let's try another question reflecting possible objections to hiring you:

QUESTION: **Your background bothers me. Why should I hire someone with a criminal record?**

ANSWER 1: *I can understand that.*

ANSWER 2: *I understand your hesitation in hiring someone with my background. I would, too, if I were you. Yes, many people who get out of prison go back to their old ways and soon return to prison. But I'm not like others who may play games to get the job and then disappoint you. I've been there and learned more than you can imagine. I was young, foolish, and made a terrible mistake. But I decided to turn my attitude and life around. Prison was actually good for me. I took advantage of every educational, vocational training, and work opportunity available while I was incarcerated. I now have clear goals, which include working for someone like you. I also have excellent character, education, and work references from several people I've worked with over the past two years, including my parole officer who knows my case very well. If you have any doubts about my character and ability to do this job, I would urge you to put me on a lengthy probationary period during which time you can be assured that you made the best hiring decision. Frankly, I plan to become your star performer within the first three months.*

The first answer is incomplete. It misses an important opportunity to give evidence that you have resolved this issue in a positive manner, which is clearly reflected in the second response.

> **Exercise:** On eight separate sheets of paper, write answers to these eight questions (one question per sheet):
>
>   1. Why should I hire you?
>   2. Why should I hire someone with a criminal record?
>   3. Tell me about yourself.
>   4. What are your weaknesses?
>   5. Tell me about your plans for the future.
>   6. How do your most recent jobs relate to this position?
>   7. How would your previous employers characterize you?
>   8. What are your salary requirements?

All of these examples stress the basic point about effective interviewing. Your single best strategy for managing the interview is to **emphasize your strengths and positives and be enthusiastic about the job**. Questions come in several forms. Anticipate these questions, especially the negative ones, and practice positive responses in order to project your best self in an interview situation.

Deal With the Incarceration Question

The question you probably dread most relates to your incarceration. How do you respond to it in the most positive manner? How should you handle it? Should you raise the issue if the employer does not? Questions about your criminal record are on the employer's mind whether they are spoken or unspoken. Are you going to repeat your negative behavior? Have you really changed, or are your problems likely to recur and affect your work on your next job? If he hires you, will he inherit your past?

Even if the employer does not ask about your incarceration, you may decide to bring it up yourself either because you are required to do so, or because you don't want to worry about someone else telling him in the future. You want to explain the situation honestly, but in the most positive way that you can. It is important that you address each of the red flags in your background as honestly **and** in as positive a light as possible. Making excuses or blaming others for your problems will not reassure the employer that he will not inherit similar problems with your behavior if he hires you! You could respond to the incarceration question **or** you might bring it up yourself with something like the following:

You know about my incarceration. I would like to explain the situation and the changes I have made in my life to make sure it never happens again.

You immediately want to stress two important points:

1. You accept that your behavior was wrong. You are aware of the negative consequences of the behavior that got you into trouble.

2. You take responsibility for the past inappropriate behavior and don't put the blame on others.

Don't talk too much about these first two points. Many ex-offenders talk too long and in too much detail about their past crime(s). Accept responsibility, but don't dwell on it! Move on. You want to talk more about the next two areas – those that deal with the changes you have made for your future:

3. Mention the changes you have made in your life so this will not happen again. The situation that supported the past negative behavior no longer exists. For example, if part of the problem in the past was that you got in with the wrong crowd and their activities influenced your behavior, demonstrate that your present situation is different. You no longer hang out with that crowd. You now associate with a different group of people who do not get into trouble.

4. As you have changed your situation, you have made it easier for you to change your behavior. You have overcome the negative cycle.

5. It was a difficult learning experience you had to go through. But you have "done your time" and are ready to get on with a more positive life. You want the chance to demonstrate to the employer that with your skills and your attitude you will make a positive contribution to the company.

Anticipate Behavior-Based Questions

More and more employers are conducting "behavior-based interviews." These interviews are specific and challenge candidates to provide concrete examples of their achievements. Such interviews are designed to uncover **clear patterns of behavior** which are good predictors of future performance. Behavior-based questions are likely to begin with some variation of:

- *Give me an example of a time when you . . .*
- *Give me an example of how you . . .*
- *Tell me about how you . . .*

Depending on the position in question, you may or may not encounter these types of questions. Behavior-based questions especially arise during interviews for positions involving decisions of responsibility. If you are asked such questions, give examples of your relevant accomplishments. Briefly describe the situation, enthusiastically explain what you did (adding information as to why if you think this would not be evident), and indicate the outcome. For example, if the interviewer asks,

"Tell me about a time when you anticipated a potential problem."

The applicant might respond,

"When I was working at McDonald's, I noticed the children's playground was unprotected from the parking area. I told my supervisor that this could be a dangerous situation if someone accidentally jumped the curb and plowed into a crowd of kids. He took a look at the area and agreed that heavy-duty guard rails needed to be installed in front of the curb. It was a good thing he did this. Three weeks after they were installed, a lady got into her car, mistakenly put it in drive, and slammed into the guard rail. It really scared a group of 30 kids and parents who were there for a birthday party. Had we not installed the guard rail, I'm afraid several of the kids would have been injured or even killed. I really felt good about doing this. I also was glad someone at work listened to me and took appropriate action. My supervisor promoted me after that incident."

Obviously you want to select examples that promote your skills and have a positive outcome. Even if the interviewer asks about a time when something negative happened, try to select an example where you were able to turn the situation around and something positive came out of it. For example, if asked, *"Tell me about a time you made a bad decision,"* try to identify an occasion where:

- Even though it wasn't the best decision, you were able to pull something positive out of the situation.

- Though it was a poor decision, you learned from it, and in the next similar situation you made a good decision or know how you will handle it differently the next time a similar situation arises.

- It was a bad decision but the negative outcome had only minor impact.

In other words, try to pull something positive – either that you did or that you learned – out of even a negative experience you are asked to relate. As you prepare for your interview, consider situations where you:

- demonstrated leadership	- handled changing events
- solved a problem	- handled criticism
- increased company profits	- met a deadline/missed a deadline
- made a good/poor decision	- worked as part of a team

Add to this list other behavioral questions you think of that pertain to the job for which you are applying.

You may encounter hypothetical questions in which you are asked not what you did, but what you would do if something occurred. With hypothetical questions, the interviewer is less interested in your actual answer – often there is no correct or incorrect response – than in your thought process. He wants to know how you would solve a problem or respond to a particular type of situation.

Develop Strong Storytelling Skills

Individuals who do well in behavior-based interviews are those who have a rich background of accomplishments as well as are good storytellers. Indeed, **storytelling** is one of the key skills involved in conducting effective interviews. If you want to do well in this type of interview, be sure to **anticipate questions** you might be asked so you can prepare a well thought-out response – a set of revealing stories about your performance – prior to the interview. It is far easier to formulate positive responses to questions in a relaxed setting than in a stressful job interview setting.

Face Situational Interviews

More and more employers also are conducting situational interviews, which enable them to observe the actual behavior of candidates in particular situations. Again, you may or may not encounter such interviews. While candidates can prepare for

---

Exercise: On seven separate sheets of paper, write stories that relate to these seven behavior-based questions (one question/story per sheet):

1. Tell me about a time in which you failed to meet a deadline.
2. Give me an example of how you took initiative in solving a problem.
3. Tell me how you took responsibility for a problem you created.
4. Give me examples of your three most satisfying accomplishments in your last job.
5. Tell me about a time in which you were fired from a job.
6. Give me an example of how you worked effectively under pressure.
7. Tell me how you saved your boss money.

---

behavior-based interviews by focusing on their accomplishments and telling stories about their past performance, such interviews are still primarily verbal exchanges.

Situational interviews rely less on analyzing verbal cues and more on analyzing actual observed behavior or performance in key work-related situations. The popular television program *The Apprentice* is a good example of situational interviews. Employers especially like conducting these interviews, because they know candidates can't prepare well for the situations in which they may be asked to perform. These interviews give employers a chance to observe a candidate's decision-making skills in the process of solving work-related problems. Many of these interviews involve mock scenarios in which a candidate is asked to role play. For example, someone interviewing for a customer service position may be asked to play the role of a customer service representative by handling telephone calls from an irate customer. In this scenario the interviewer has a chance to observe the candidate in action. Does he or she talk down, get angry, or resolve the problem to the satisfaction of the customer? The behavior of a competent customer service representative can be readily observed in such a role playing scenario. Other examples of situational interviews may involve mock negotiation sessions, selling a product, constructing something, or repairing a product.

> *Employers like to conduct situational interviews because they know candidates can't prepare well for the situations in which they may be asked to perform.*

Encounter Illegal Questions

Many questions are illegal, but some employers ask them nonetheless. Consider how you would respond to these questions:

- Are you married, divorced, separated, or single?
- How old are you?
- Do you go to church regularly?
- Do you have many debts?
- Do you own or rent your home?
- What social and political organizations do you belong to?
- What does your spouse think about your career?
- Are you living with anyone?
- Are you practicing birth control?
- How much insurance do you have?
- How much do you weigh?
- How tall are you?

Don't get upset and say *"That's an illegal question...I refuse to answer it!"* While you may be perfectly right in saying so, this response lacks tact, which may be what the employer is looking for. Some employers may ask such questions just to see how you answer or react under stress. Others may do so out of ignorance of the law. Whatever the case, be prepared to handle these questions with tact.

Ask Thoughtful Questions

Interviewers expect candidates to ask intelligent questions concerning the organization and the nature of the work. In fact, many employers indicate that it's often the quality of the questions asked by the candidate that is instrumental in offering them the job. Moreover, you need information and should indicate your interest in the employer by asking questions. Consider asking some of these questions if they haven't been answered early in the interview:

- Tell me about the duties and responsibilities of this job.
- What's the most important thing I should know about your company?
- How does this position relate to other positions within this company?
- How long has this position been in the organization?
- What would be the ideal type of person for this position? Skills? Personality? Working style? Background?
- Can you tell me about the people who have been in this position before? Backgrounds? Promotions? Terminations?
- Whom would I be working with in this position?
- Tell me something about these people. Their strengths? Their weaknesses? Their performance expectations?
- What am I expected to accomplish during the first year?
- How will I be evaluated?

- Are promotions and raises tied to performance criteria?
- Tell me how this operates?
- What is the normal salary range for such a position?
- Based on your experience, what type of problems would someone new in this position likely encounter?
- I'm interested in your career with this organization. When did you start? What are your plans for the future?
- How do people get promoted and advance in this company?
- What does the future look like for this company?
- Could I meet with the person who will be my supervisor?

You may want to write your questions on a 3x5 card and take them with you to the interview. While it is best to recall these questions, you may need to refer to your list when the interviewer asks you if you have any questions. You might do this by saying: *"Yes, I jotted down a few questions which I want to make sure I ask you before leaving."*

Appropriate Dress, Appearance, and Grooming

Dress, appearance, and grooming are the first things you communicate to others. Before you have a chance to speak, others notice how you look and accordingly draw certain conclusions about your personality and competence. Indeed, research shows that appearance makes the greatest difference when an evaluator has little information about the other person. This is precisely the situation you find yourself in at the start of the interview.

Many people object to having their capabilities evaluated on the basis of their appearance and manner of dress. *"But that is not fair,"* they argue. *"People should be hired on the basis of their ability to do the job – not on how they look."* But debating the lack of merit or complaining about the unfairness of such behavior does not alter reality. Like it or not, many people do make initial judgments about others based on their appearance. Since you cannot alter this fact and bemoaning it will get you nowhere, it is better to learn to use it to your advantage. If you learn to effectively manage your image, you can convey marvelous messages regarding your authority, credibility, and competence.

Some estimates indicate that as much as 65 percent of the hiring decision may be based on the nonverbal aspects of the interview! Employers sometimes refer to this phenomenon with such terms as "chemistry," "body warmth," or that "gut feeling" the individual is right for the job. This correlates with findings of communication studies that approximately 65 percent of a message is communicated nonverbally.

So how should you dress and groom for the job interview? The general rule is to be conservative in your dress and appearance and neat and clean in your grooming. The following tips should help you develop a proper appearance for the job interview.

1. **Dress one step above the position for which you are interviewing.** If you don't know what that is, check with people in your support group, someone who works with that company or a similar company, or visit the company to observe the people at work.

2. **Wear clothes that fit well and look neat, clean, and appropriate for the setting.** No blue jeans, shorts, baggy or low-riding pants, sleeveless blouses, or baseball caps. In general, women should wear a conservative blouse and skirt, dress, slacks, and/or suit jacket. Men should wear a light-colored shirt, dark tie, a jacket, and/or dark trousers. For laborer positions, neat and clean work clothes will be sufficient.

3. **Choose clothes with coordinated patterns and colors.** Avoid wearing different plaids together, clashing colors, and unusual combination of fabrics.

4. **Select conservative colors,** such as cream or white, navy blue, and dark brown. Reds, oranges, bright greens, and yellows do not test well in job interviews.

5. **Avoid wearing excessive or gaudy jewelry.** You want the interviewer to focus on you rather than your dangling jewelry. Excessive jewelry is a distraction and raises questions about your choice of body adornments.

6. **Minimize the number of obvious body piercings.** Like excessive jewelry, body piercings are distractions and raise questions about your decisions and lifestyle. Avoid showing off any facial piercings.

7. **Avoid excessive fragrances.** One of the first things an interviewer notices is your scent. Be very careful wearing heavy perfume or cologne. You may love their scent, but they could be irritating to an interviewer, who may think you smell terrible.

8. **Hide tattoos as much as possible.** If you have tattoos running up and down your arms, cover them with a long-sleeve shirt. Consider having some tattoos removed since they may hinder your employability.

9. **Make sure you have clean and trimmed nails and cover any obvious sores or injuries.** Look like you can take care of yourself.

10. **Shower and use deodorant on the day of the interview.** Bad body odors will quickly turn off most people.

11. **Wear shoes that are in good condition and are clean and shined.** Employers do look at your shoes as a sign of personal care.

12. **Keep you hair clean, trimmed, neatly combed, and in a conservative style.** Avoid unusual or trendy hairstyles and colors. Green or orange hair will not enhance your candidacy. Men should avoid excessive facial hair.

13. **Women should avoid heavy makeup,** over-sized jewelry, large handbags, excessively high heels, or showing a bare midriff or too much skin in any area.

14. **Avoid accentuating any weight problems** with tight-fitting clothes. In addition to fitting well, your clothes should downplay weight issues.

15. **Brush your teeth and use mouthwash** just before the interview to avoid bad breath.

16. **Excuse yourself if you have a cold or look ill on the day of the interview (sneezing, coughing, sniffling, watery eyes).** Point this fact out at the beginning of the interview. Otherwise, the interviewer may think you have some type of permanent illness, or will come to work sick or may miss work because of health problems.

17. **Avoid chewing gum or smoking during the interview.** You just don't do these things in interviews.

18. **Always wear a smile.** Employers like to hire happy and joyful people.

If you are female and don't have or can't afford a wardrobe appropriate for job interviews and the workplace, you may want to contact these organizations that work with ex-offenders and other disadvantaged groups in need of interview clothes:

- **Dress for Success**   www.dressforsuccess.org
- **Connections to Success**   www.connectionstosuccess.org
- **The Women's Alliance**   www.thewomensalliance.org

The Dress for Success site also includes several useful job interview tips. Men may want to contact some local chapters of The Women's Alliance, which also provide wardrobe assistance to men. In Contra Costa and Alameda Counties in California, for example, the local branch of The Women's Alliance is called Wardrobe for Opportunity and includes a men's section (www.wardrobe.org/mensprogram.html). Connections to Success also operates a Wheels for Success program, which provides automobiles for disadvantaged individuals in need of personal transportation.

Several communities have their own programs designed to help low-income and disadvantaged men and women dress properly for job interviews. If you are living in a half-way house or shelter, personnel there will know about such programs. Also check the used clothing sections of your local Goodwill Industries and Salvation Army for inexpensive clothes appropriate for a job interview. Visit the stores nearest affluent communities since they offer better quality used clothes. Personnel in these stores also may be able to tell you who operates a local wardrobe program for low income job seekers. As you will quickly discover, several community-based resources are available to make sure you dress for success and thus make the best impression when interviewing for a job.

Appear Likable to Employers

Remember, most people invited to a job interview have already been "screened in." They supposedly possess the basic qualifications for the job, such as education and work experience. At this point employers will look for several qualities in the candidates, such as honesty, credibility, intelligence, competence, enthusiasm, spontaneity, friendliness, and likability. You communicate many of these qualities through your clothing as well as through other nonverbal behaviors.

In the end, employers hire people they **like** and who will get along well with others on the job. Therefore, you should communicate that you are a likable candidate who can get along well with others. You can communicate these messages by engaging in several nonverbal behaviors. Four of the most important ones include:

1. **Sit with a very slight forward lean toward the interviewer.** It should be so slight as to be almost imperceptible. If not overdone, it communicates your interest in what the interviewer is saying.

2. **Make eye contact frequently, but don't overdo it.** Good eye contact establishes rapport with the interviewer. You will be perceived as more trustworthy if you will look at the interviewer as you ask and answer questions. To say someone has "shifty eyes" or cannot "look us in the eye" is to imply they may not be completely honest. To have a direct, though moderate eye gaze conveys interest, as well as trustworthiness.

3. **A moderate amount of smiling will also help reinforce your positive image.** You should smile enough to convey your positive attitude, but not so much that you will not be taken seriously. Some people naturally smile often and others hardly ever smile. Monitor your behavior or ask a friend to give you frank feedback.

4. **Try to convey interest and enthusiasm through your vocal inflections.**
    Your tone of voice can say a lot about you and how interested you are in
    the interviewer and organization.

Close the Interview

Be prepared to end the interview. Many people don't know when or how to close
interviews. They go on and on until someone breaks an uneasy moment of silence
with an indication that it is time to go.

Interviewers normally will initiate the close by standing, shaking hands, and
thanking you for coming to the interview. Don't end by saying *"Goodbye and thank
you."* As this stage, you should summarize the interview in terms of your interests,
strengths, and goals. Briefly restate your qualifications and continuing interest in
working with the employer. At this point it is proper to ask the interviewer about
selection plans:

"When do you anticipate making your final decision?"

Follow this question with your last one:

*"May I call you next week (or whatever is appropriate in response to your question
about timing of the final decision) to inquire about my status?"*

By taking the initiative in this manner, the employer will be prompted to clarify your
status soon, and you will have an opportunity to talk to him or her further.

Many interviewers will ask you for a list of references. Be sure to prepare such a
list **prior to** the interview. Include the names, addresses, and phone numbers of four
individuals who will give you positive professional and personal recommendations.
If asked for references, you will appear well prepared by presenting a list in this
manner. If you fail to prepare this information ahead of time, you may appear at best
disorganized and at worst lacking good references. Always anticipate being asked for
specific names, addresses, and phone numbers of your references.

Remember to Follow Up

Once you have been interviewed, be sure to follow through to get nearer to the job
offer. One of the best follow-up methods is the thank you letter; you will find
examples of these letters at the end of Chapter 9. After talking to the employer over
the telephone or in a face-to-face interview, send a thank you letter by e-mail and/or
mail. If mailed, which we prefer, this letter should be typed – not handwritten – on
good quality paper. In this letter express your gratitude for the opportunity to inter-

view. Re-state your interest in the position and highlight any particularly noteworthy points made in your conversation or anything you wish to further clarify. Close the letter by mentioning that you will call in a few days to inquire about the employer's decision. When you do this, the employer should **remember** you as a thoughtful person.

If you call and the employer has not yet made a decision, follow through with another phone call in a few days. Send any additional information to the employer which may enhance your application. You might also want to ask one of your references to call the employer to further recommend you for the position. However, don't engage in overkill by making a pest of yourself. You want to tactfully communicate two things to the employer at this point: (1) you are interested in the job, and (2) you will do a good job.

Useful Interview Resources

For more information on developing interviewing skills, including follow-up and thank-you letters, look for our *Job Interview Tips for People With Not-So-Hot Backgrounds, Interview for Success, Nail the Job Interview!, Savvy Interviewing, High Impact Resumes and Letters*, and *201 Dynamite Job Search Letters*; Richard Fein's *101 Dynamite Questions to Ask At Your Job Interview*; Wendy Enelow's *KeyWords to Nail Your Job Interview*; and Bernard Haldane Associates's *Haldane's Best Answers to Tough Interview Questions* (all published by Impact Publications and included in the order form at the end of this book). You also should check out the following websites, which include tips on interviewing:

▪ Monster.com	www.interview.monster.com
▪ InterviewPro	www.interviewpro.com
▪ JobInterview.net	www.job-interview.net
▪ Interview Coach	www.interviewcoach.com
▪ Quintessential Careers	www.quintcareers.com/intvres.html
▪ Wetfeet.com	www.wetfeet.com/advice/ interviewing.asp
▪ The Riley Guide	www.rileyguide.com/interview.html
▪ CareerJournal	www.careerjournal.com
▪ JobWeb.com	www.jobweb.com/Resumes_Interviews
▪ Vault.com	www.vault.com
▪ WinningTheJob	www.winningthejob.com

Most sites offer free interview tips and services, including Monster.com's "virtual interview." A few sites, such as InterviewCoach.com, charge consulting fees for assisting individuals in preparing for the job interview.

12

Negotiate Salary and Benefits Like a Pro

S UCCESSFUL JOB INTERVIEWS LEAD to job offers and a compensation package consisting of salary and benefits. If you are interviewing for a job as a laborer or for an entry-level position, chances are salary and benefits will be set and you'll have little room to negotiate. However, you may be able to negotiate the hours you work, including any overtime, but only if you have skills the employer very much needs. For other level jobs, salary is seldom totally predetermined. Most employers have some flexibility to negotiate salary and benefits.

Depending on the level of the position and the type of job you seek, the following discussion may or may not be useful to you. But hopefully it will become useful as you move ahead in your career and acquire jobs that have salary flexibility and offer numerous benefits which you can negotiate. The general compensation principle is this: **The greater the job responsibilities, the more flexibility you and the employer have to negotiate salary and benefits** (see the comprehensive checklist at the end of this chapter). Consider this section to be a "sneak preview" of possible compensation options in your future work life.

Raising the Money Question

The question of wages/salary may be raised anytime during the job search. Employers may want you to state a salary expectation figure on an application form, in a cover letter, or over the telephone. Most frequently, however, employers will ask about salary during the employment interview.

If at all possible, keep the wage/salary question **open** until the very last. Revealing your hand early in the interview will not be to your advantage. Even with application forms, cover letters, and telephone screening interviews, try to delay the discussion of money by stating "open" or "negotiable." After all, the ultimate purpose of your job search activities is to demonstrate your **value** to employers. You should not attempt to translate your value into dollar figures until you have had a chance to convince the employer of your worth. This is best done near the end of the job interview, preferably after you have received a job offer.

Although employers will have a salary figure or range in mind when they interview you, they still want to know your salary expectations. How much will you cost them? Will it be more or less than the job is worth? Employers prefer hiring individuals for the least amount possible.

You, on the other hand, want to be hired for as much as possible. Obviously, there is room for disagreement and unhappiness as well as negotiation, compromise, and agreement.

One easy way employers screen you in or out of consideration is to raise the salary question early in the interview. A standard question is: *"What are your salary requirements?"* For entry-level or blue collar jobs, wages are often stated as an hourly rate. For professional positions, salary is stated as a yearly figure. When asked, don't answer with a specific dollar figure. You should aim at establishing your value in the eyes of the employer prior to talking about a figure. If you give the employer a salary figure at this stage, you are likely to lock yourself into it, regardless of how much you impress the employer or what you find out about the duties and responsibilities of the job. Therefore, **salary should be the last major item you discuss with the employer**.

You should never ask about money prior to being offered the job, even though it is one of your major concerns. Try to let the employer initiate the salary question. And when he or she does, take your time. Don't appear too anxious. While you may know – based on your previous research – approximately what the employer will offer, try to get the employer to state a figure first. If you do this, you will be in a stronger negotiating position.

Reach Common Ground and Agreement

After finding out what the employer is prepared to offer, you have several choices. First, you can indicate that his or her figure is acceptable to you and thus conclude your final interview. Second, you can haggle for more money in the hope of reaching a compromise. Third, you can delay final action by asking for more time to consider the figure. Finally, you can tell the employer the figure is unacceptable and leave.

The first and the last options indicate you are either too eager or playing hard-to-get. We recommend the second and third options. If you decide to reach agreement on salary in this interview, negotiate in a professional manner. You can do this best by establishing a **salary range** from which to bargain in relation to the employer's salary range. For example, if the employer indicates that he or she is prepared to offer $35,000 to $40,000 (or $9.50 to $10.50 per hour), you should establish common ground for negotiation by placing your salary or wage range into the employer's range. Your response to the employer's stated range might be:

"Yes, that does come near what I was expecting. I was thinking more in terms of $40,000 to $45,000 (or $10.50 to $11.50 per hour)."

You, in effect, place the top of the employer's range into the bottom of your range. At this point you should be able to negotiate a salary of $40,000 to $45,000 (or a wage rate of $10.50 to $11.50 per hour), depending on how much flexibility the employer has with money. Many employers have more flexibility than they are willing to admit.

Once you have placed your expectations at the top of the employer's salary range, you need to emphasize your value with **supports,** such as examples, illustrations, descriptions, definitions, statistics, comparisons, or testimonials. It is not enough to simply state you were "thinking" in a certain range; you must state why you believe you are worth the salary you want. Using statistics and comparisons as your supports, you might say, for example:

"The salary surveys I have read indicate that for the position of _____ in this industry and region the salary is between $40,000 and $45,000. Since, as we have discussed, I have extensive experience in all the areas you outlined, I would not need training in the job duties themselves – just a brief orientation to the operating procedures you use here at _____. I'm sure I could be up and running in this job within a week or two. Taking everything into consideration – especially my skills and experience and what I see as my future contributions here – I really believe a salary of $45,000 is fair compensation. Is this possible here at _____?"

How you negotiate your salary will affect your future relations with the employer.

Another option is to ask the employer for time to think about the salary offer. You want to consider it for a day or two. A common professional courtesy is to give you at least 48 hours to consider an offer. During this time, you may want to carefully examine the job. Is it worth what you are being offered? Can you do better? What are other employers offering for comparable positions? If one or two other employers are considering you for a job, let this employer know his or her job is not the only one under consideration. Let the employer know you may be in demand elsewhere. This should give you a better bargaining position. Contact the other employers and let them know you have a job offer and that you would like to have your application status with them clarified before you make any decisions with the other employer. Depending on how much flexibility an employer may have to accelerate a hiring decision, you may be able to go back to the first employer with another job offer. With a second job offer in hand, you should greatly enhance your bargaining position.

In both recommended options, you need to keep in mind that you should always negotiate from a position of knowledge and strength – not because of need or greed. Learn about salaries for your occupation, establish your value, discover what the employer is willing to pay, and negotiate in a professional manner. For how you negotiate your salary will affect your future relations with the employer. In general, applicants who negotiate well will be treated well on the job.

Carefully Examine Benefits

Many employers will try to impress candidates with the benefits offered by the company. These might include retirement, bonuses, stock options, medical and life insurance, and cost of living adjustments. If the employer includes these benefits in the salary negotiations, do not be overly impressed. Most benefits are standard – they come with the job. When negotiating salary, it is best to talk about specific dollar figures. But don't neglect to both calculate and negotiate benefits according to the lengthy checklist of benefit options we outline on pages 197-200. Benefits can translate into a significant portion of one's compensation. In fact, the U.S. Department of Labor estimates that benefits now constitute 43 percent of total compensation for the average worker. For example, a $40,000 offer with Company X may translate into a compensation package worth $50,000; but a $40,000 offer with Company Y may actually be worth more than $60,000 when you examine their different benefits.

If the salary offered by the employer does not meet your expectations, but you still want the job, you might try to negotiate for some benefits which are not considered standard, such as longer paid vacations, some flextime, or profit sharing.

Take Time Before Accepting

You should accept an offer only after reaching a salary agreement. If you jump at an offer, you may appear needy. Take time to consider your options. Remember, you are committing your time and effort in exchange for money and status. Is this the job you really want? Take some time to think about the offer before giving the employer a definite answer. But don't play hard-to-get and thereby create ill-will with your boss.

While considering the offer, ask yourself several of the same questions you asked at the beginning of your job search:

- What do I want to be doing five years from now?

- How will this job affect my personal life?

- Do I know enough about the employer and the future of this organization?

- How have other people in this position fared? Why did they leave?

- Are there other job opportunities that would better meet my goals?

Accepting a job is serious business. If you make a mistake, you could be locked into a very unhappy situation for a long time.

If you receive one job offer while considering another, you will be able to compare relative advantages and disadvantages. You also will have some leverage for negotiating salary and benefits. While you should not play games, let the employer know you have alternative job offers. This communicates that you are in demand, others also know your value, and the employer's price is not the only one in town. Use this leverage to negotiate your salary, benefits, and job responsibilities.

If you get a job offer but you are considering other employers, let the others know you have a job offer. Telephone them to inquire about your status as well as inform them of the job offer. Sometimes this will prompt employers to make a hiring decision sooner than anticipated. In addition you will be informing them that you are in demand; they should seriously consider you before you get away!

Some job seekers play a bluffing game by telling employers they have alternative job offers even though they don't. Some candidates do this and get away with it. We don't recommend this approach. Not only is it dishonest, it will work to your disadvantage if the employer learns that you were lying. But more important, you should be selling yourself on the basis of your strengths rather than your deceit and greed. If you can't sell yourself honestly, don't expect to get along well on the job. When you compromise your integrity, you lower your value to others and yourself.

Your job search is not over with the job offer and acceptance. You need to set the stage. Be thoughtful by sending your new employer a nice thank-you letter. As we noted in Chapter 9, this is one of the most effective letters to write for getting your new job off on the right foot. The employer will remember you as a thoughtful individual whom he looks forward to working with.

The whole point of our job search methods is to clearly communicate to employers that you are competent and worthy of being paid top dollar. If you follow our advice, you should do very well with employers in interviews and negotiating your salary as well as working on the job.

Useful Salary Negotiation Resources

For more information on salary negotiations for both job seekers and employees, see our *Salary Negotiation Tips for Professionals, Dynamite Salary Negotiations*, and *Get a Raise in 7 Days* (Impact Publications). These books outline various steps for calculating your worth and conducting face-to-face negotiations, including numerous sample dialogues. For online assistance with salary information and negotiations, be sure to visit these websites:

■ Salary.com	www.salary.com
■ JobStar	www.jobstar.org
■ Monster.com	http://salary.monster.com
■ SalaryExpert	www.salaryexpert.com
■ SalarySource	www.salarysource.com
■ WageWeb	www.wageweb.com
■ Abbott-Langer	www.abbott-langer. com
■ Quintessential Careers	www.quintcareers.com/salary_ negotiation.html
■ Riley Guide	www.rileyguide.com/netintv.html
■ Robert Half International	www.rhii.com

Checklist of Compensation Options

When it's time to talk about compensation with an employer, it's always a good idea to prepare a written statement of your current, or previous, compensation package. This statement should summarize the various elements included in your compensation package as well as the value of each. Some elements, such as an office with a window, may not have a dollar value but they may be important to you.

One of the easiest ways to survey your compensation options and assign value to your ideal compensation package is to use the checklist of compensation options on pages 198-200. Consider each item and then value it by assigning a dollar amount. When finished, add up the total dollars assigned to get a complete picture of the value of your present or past compensation package. You can later compare this to future offers.

Element	Value

Basic Compensation Issues

- Base salary — $ _____
- Commissions — $ _____
- Corporate profit sharing — $ _____
- Personal performance bonuses/incentives — $ _____
- Cost of living adjustment — $ _____
- Overtime — $ _____
- Signing bonus — $ _____
- Cash in lieu of certain benefits — $ _____

Health Benefits

- Medical insurance — $ _____
- Dental insurance — $ _____
- Vision insurance — $ _____
- Prescription package — $ _____
- Life insurance — $ _____
- Accidental death and disability insurance — $ _____
- Evacuation insurance (international travel) — $ _____

Vacation and Time Issues

- Vacation time — $ _____
- Sick days — $ _____
- Personal time — $ _____
- Holidays — $ _____
- Flextime — $ _____
- Compensatory time — $ _____
- Paternity/maternity leave — $ _____
- Family leave — $ _____

Retirement-Oriented Benefits

- Defined-benefit plan — $ _____
- 401(k) plan — $ _____
- Deferred compensation — $ _____
- Savings plans — $ _____
- Stock-purchase plans — $ _____
- Stock bonus — $ _____
- Stock options — $ _____
- Ownership/equity — $ _____

Education

- Professional continuing education — $ _____
- Tuition reimbursement for you or family members — $ _____

Military

- Compensatory pay during active duty $ _____
- National Guard $ _____

Perquisites

- Cellular phone $ _____
- Company car or vehicle/mileage allowance $ _____
- Expense accounts $ _____
- Liberalization of business-related expenses $ _____
- Child care $ _____
- Cafeteria privileges $ _____
- Executive dining room privileges $ _____
- First-class hotels $ _____
- First-class air travel $ _____
- Upgrade business travel $ _____
- Personal use of frequent-flyer awards $ _____
- Convention participation: professionally related $ _____
- Parking $ _____
- Paid travel for spouse $ _____
- Professional association memberships $ _____
- Athletic club memberships $ _____
- Social club memberships $ _____
- Use of company-owned facilities $ _____
- Executive office $ _____
- Office with a window $ _____
- Laptop computers $ _____
- Private secretary $ _____
- Portable fax $ _____
- Employee discounts $ _____
- Incentive trips $ _____
- Sabbaticals $ _____
- Discounted buying club memberships $ _____
- Free drinks and meals $ _____

Relocation Expenses

- Direct moving expenses $ _____
- Moving costs for unusual property $ _____
- Trips to find suitable housing $ _____
- Loss on sale of present home
  or lease termination $ _____
- Company handling sale of present home $ _____
- Housing cost differential between cities $ _____
- Mortgage rate differential $ _____
- Mortgage fees and closing costs $ _____
- Temporary dual housing $ _____
- Trips home during dual residency $ _____

- Real estate fees $ _____
- Utilities hookup $ _____
- Drapes/carpets $ _____
- Appliance installation $ _____
- Auto/pet shipping $ _____
- Signing bonus for incidental expenses $ _____
- Additional meals expense account $ _____
- Bridge loan while owning two homes $ _____
- Outplacement assistance for spouse $ _____

Home Office Options

- Personal computer $ _____
- Internet access $ _____
- Copier $ _____
- Printer $ _____
- Financial planning assistance $ _____
- Separate phone line $ _____
- Separate fax line $ _____
- CPA/tax assistance $ _____
- Incidental/support office functions $ _____
- Office supplies $ _____
- Furniture and accessories $ _____

Severance Packages (Parachutes)

- Base salary $ _____
- Bonuses/incentives $ _____
- Non-compete clause $ _____
- Stock/equity $ _____
- Outplacement assistance $ _____
- Voicemail access $ _____
- Statement (letter) explaining why you left $ _____
- Vacation reimbursement $ _____
- Health benefits or COBRA reimbursements $ _____
- 401(k) contributions $ _____

TOTAL $

13

Starting Right, Surviving, and Advancing Your Career

CONGRATULATIONS! NOW THAT you've gotten the job, you need to do several things in order to (1) set the stage for starting the job, (2) develop good initial relationships, (3) keep your job, (4) advance on the job, and (5) move ahead in your career. Surviving and thriving on the job is all about having good work habits, maintaining good relationships, and focusing on accomplishing the goals of the company or organization.

After negotiating the job offer, shaking hands, and feeling great for having succeeded in getting a job that is right for you, what's next? How do you get started on the right foot and continue to advance your career? In this chapter we recommend several steps for best handling your job and career future after congratulating yourself on a job search well done.

Become a Thoughtful Professional

If you managed your interviews and salary negotiations in a professional manner, your new employer should view you in a positive light. Once you've completed the interview, negotiated the salary, and accepted the offer, you should do two things:

1. **Send your new employer a nice thank-you letter.**

   Never underestimate the power of a simple thank-you letter. It may be the single most important action you take. Mention your appreciation for the professional manner in which you were hired and how pleased you are to be joining the company. Reaffirm your goals and your commitment to producing results. This letter should be much appreciated by the employer. After all, employers seldom receive such thoughtful letters, and your reaffirmation helps ease the employer's fears of hiring an untested quantity.

2. **Send thank-you letters to those individuals who assisted you with your job search, especially those with whom you conducted informational and referral interviews recommended in Chapter 10.**

Tell them of your new position, thank them for their assistance, and offer your assistance in the future. Not only is this a nice and thoughtful thing to do, it also is a wise thing to do for your future.

In both cases, put your best professional foot forward by sending a traditional paper letter by mail. Such a letter means more and will more likely be read than a quick and easy e-mail note.

Always remember your network discussed in Chapter 10 (pages 150-152). You work with people who can help you in many ways. Take good care of your network by sending thank-you letters and keeping in contact. In a few years you may be looking for another position. In addition, people in your network may later want to hire you away from your present employer. Since they know what you can do and they like you, they may want to keep you informed of new opportunities. While you will be developing new contacts and expanding your network in your new job, your former contacts should be remembered for future reference. An occasional letter, holiday card, or telephone call are thoughtful things to do.

Treat Your Boss As a Client

In today's highly competitive and fast-paced work environments, the skills required for the job you have today may change tomorrow. Indeed, the job you have today may disappear because of outsourcing, off-shoring, or just bad economic times. The job you were initially hired to do may also expand and result in a substantial raise or promotion; be open to such changes.

Always make sure your on-the-job skills are up-to-date and that you are doing more than what you consider to be "your job." This may mean acquiring new skills and redefining your job. Take initiative and demonstrate your entrepreneurial skills. Treat your boss as if he or she were your client by **exceeding most expectations** related to performing your job.

Your continuing employment depends on satisfying the needs of your client. Individuals who unexpectedly get laid off are often ones who did a particular job well but suddenly discover they have the wrong set of skills for an organization undergoing important changes. Never assume the skills and experience you have today will be sufficient for the job tomorrow. Always define what you are doing today in reference to the larger needs of the company. Ask yourself, for example, *am I a continuing asset to what may be a rapidly changing company? Will I be needed as much tomorrow as I am today?*

Avoid the Pitfalls of Politics

After three months on the job, you should know who's who, who has clout, whom to avoid, and how to get things done in spite of people, their positions, and their personal agendas. In other words, you will become part of the informal structure of the organization. You should become aware of it, and use it to your advantage.

While it goes without saying that you should demonstrate excellent work habits and perform well in your job, you need more than just habits and performance. You also should understand the informal organization, develop new networks, and use them to advance your career. This means conducting an internal career advancement campaign as well as an annual career check-up.

> *Treat your boss as if he or she were your client by exceeding performance expectations.*

Don't expect to advance by sitting around and doing your job, however good you may be. Learn about different personalities as well as who has the real power in your organization and learn to play positive politics. After a while many organizations appear to be similar in terms of politics and personalities. Intensely interpersonal jobs are the most politically and personality charged. Indeed, people usually get fired because of politics and personal conflicts – not gross incompetence. What do you do, for example, if you find yourself working for a tyrannical or incompetent boss, or a jealous co-worker is out to get you? Some companies can be unhealthy for your career development and your mental health.

Conduct an Annual Career Check-Up

We recommend an annual career check-up. Take out your resume and review it. Ask yourself several questions about your current job and your goals:

- Am I achieving my goals and purpose in life?
- Has my objective changed?
- Is this job meeting my expectations?
- Am I doing what I'm good at and enjoy doing?
- Are my skills up-to-date for this job and organization?

- Am I fully using my skills as well as acquiring new skills?
- Does this company fully value my contributions?
- Is this job worth keeping?
- How can I best achieve career satisfaction either in this job or in another job or career?
- What other opportunities elsewhere might be better than this job?

Perhaps changing jobs is not the best alternative for you. If you encounter difficulties with your job, you should first understand the problem. Perhaps the problem can be resolved by working with your present employer. Many employers prefer this approach. They know that increased job satisfaction translates into less job stress and absenteeism as well as more profits for the company. Happy workers become more productive employees.

Alternatively, you may want play a "just in case" scenario by entering your resume into various online resume databases where you can literally keep yourself in the job market 24 hours a day, 365 days a year. Whether you are actively looking for a job or just keeping in touch with potential opportunities, putting your resume online may be a good way to conduct a career check-up on a regular basis. Many Internet recruitment sites offer a new approach to the job search: no longer will you need to start a job search campaign only when you lose your job or decide to change jobs. Putting your resume online with such websites as Monster.com, HotJobs.com Yahoo.com, DirectEmployers.com, and CareerBuilder.com allows you to remain constantly active in the job market. In so doing, new and unexpected job opportunities may come your way even though you are perfectly happy with your current job. In other words, participation in such resume databases may result in employers coming to you rather than you seeking out employers by using the job search strategies and techniques outlined in this book.

25 Job-Keeping Skills and Personal Qualities

Assuming you enjoy your work, how can you best ensure keeping your job as well as advancing your career in the future? How can you best avoid becoming a victim of cutbacks, politics, and terminations?

Most employers want their employees to perform according to certain expectations. As we noted earlier, employers want truthfulness, honesty, and value in their employees. They expect their workers to:

1. Be on time consistently.
2. Follow directions.
3. Be honest and truthful.
4. Be dependable in everything they do.

5. Get the job done quickly, starting with things they least like to do.
6. Do the job well and with a positive attitude.
7. Take initiative rather than wait to be given directions.
8. Be accurate and show competence.
9. Dress and groom appropriately, being both conservative and professional in their appearance.
10. Maintain good health and cleanliness.
11. Be professional and respectful.
12. Be enthusiastic and energetic.
13. Be a loyal employee who looks out for the company and boss.
14. Avoid doing personal business (phone calls, e-mail, Internet surfing) on company time.
15. Solve problems skillfully.
16. Be pleasant to work with and to be around.
17. Avoid conflicts and arguments with others.
18. Help out when needed, even if doing so is not part of their normal responsibilities.
19. Be unselfish and give credit to others, especially the boss (always make him/her look good), even though the credit should go to the employee.
20. Persevere in spite of unusual challenges and difficulties – never give up!
21. Take responsibility for their job and everything they do.
22. Make useful suggestions and find creative ways to solve the employer's problems.
23. Earn the respect of their fellow workers.
24. Become a good team player.

While using these skills and personal qualities will not ensure job security, they will most likely enhance your security and potential for advancement. Most of them will make an employee indispensable to a company and a special asset to an employer or boss. When an employer asks himself who he can most rely upon to do a job, do it well, and do it enthusiastically, make sure it's **you** he thinks about.

A final job-keeping skill – (#25) manage your political environment – is one employers don't like to talk about. It may well be more important than all the other job-keeping skills. Many people who get fired are victims of political assassination rather than failures at meeting the boss's job performance expectations or scoring well on the annual performance appraisal.

You must become savvy at the game of office politics in order to survive in many jobs. For example, what might happen if the boss you have a good working relationship with today is replaced tomorrow by someone you don't know or by someone you know but don't like? Through no fault of your own – except having been associated with a particular mentor or patron – you may become a victim of the new boss's housecleaning. Accordingly, you get a two-hour notice to clean out your desk and get out. Such political assassinations are common occurrences in the publishing, advertising, media, and other businesses.

10 Job Survival Strategies

The following 10 survival strategies can be used to minimize the uncertainty and instability surrounding many jobs today:

1. **Learn to read the signs of coming changes.** Know when to leave and when to stay by reading the signs of possible cutbacks, layoffs, and firings before they occur. How is employee morale? Are you communicating as well with others as before? Are others being terminated? Adjust to the danger signals by securing your job or by looking for another job.

2. **Document your achievements.** Keep a record of what you accomplish – problems you solve, contributions you make to improving productivity and profits. Most employers look for two major outcomes – saving money or making money. How do you contribute to these two?

3. **Toot your horn for promotion.** Talk about your accomplishments with co-workers and supervisors – but don't boast. Keep them informed about your work; let them know you are available for promotion. If they don't know what you are accomplishing, they may think you are not contributing much to their operations.

4. **Expand your horizons.** Become more aware of other areas in the company and acquire skills for performing other jobs. The more skills you have, the more valuable you should be to the company.

5. **Prepare for your next job.** Most people will have three to five different careers and 15 or more jobs throughout their lives. The job you have today will most likely not be the job you have five or 10 years from now. Therefore, you need to plan ahead by acquiring more skills for your future jobs. Seek more training through:

   - apprenticeships
   - community colleges
   - weekend colleges
   - private, trade, or technical schools
   - Internet and correspondence courses

- industrial training programs
- government training programs
- military training
- cooperative education
- four-year college or university

6. **Find a good mentor.** Attach yourself to someone in a position of influence and power whom you admire and who can help you acquire more responsibilities, skills, and advancement. Avoid currying favor.

7. **Continue networking.** Educate yourself as well as expand your interpersonal network of job contacts by regularly talking to people about their jobs and careers. Networking will be your ticket to job and career advancement.

8. **Use your motivated abilities and skills**. Success tends to attract more success. Regularly use the abilities and skills you enjoy in different everyday settings.

9. **Think like an entrepreneur.** You are responsible for your own employment fate. No one owes you a job. Like any business, you receive money in exchange for services rendered. Your boss is your most important client. Make sure you're offering good quality services to this client. If not, the boss may want to hire someone else to provide the necessary services.

10. **Keep a positive attitude.** Attitude is everything when it comes to getting ahead. Try to keep a positive attitude in everything you say and do. People like working with and promoting enthusiastic and positive people.

Make Changes When Necessary

We are not proposing disloyalty to employers or regular job-hopping. Instead, we believe in the great American principle of "self-interest rightly understood"; your first obligation is to yourself. No one owes you a job, and nor should you feel you owe someone your career and life. Jobs and careers should not be life sentences. Periodically assess your career health and feel free to make changes when necessary. You owe it to yourself and others around you to be your very best self.

> *Jobs and careers should not be life sentences. Periodically assess your career health and feel free to make changes when necessary.*

Since many jobs change for the worse, it may not be worth staying around for headaches and ulcers. Indeed, many people stay around too long; they fail to read signs that say it's time to go. If the organization does not meet your career expectations, use the same job search methods that got you into the organization. Be prepared to bail out for greener pastures by doing your job research and conducting informational and referral interviews. While the grass may not always be greener on the other side, many times it is; you will know by conducting another job search.

Revitalize and Transform Your Job

Assuming you know how to survive on your job, what do you do if you experience burnout and high levels of job stress, or are just plain bored with your job? A job change, rather than resolving these problems, may lead to a repetition of the same patterns elsewhere. Techniques for changing the nature of your present job may prove to be your best option.

Most people will sometimes experience what Marilyn Moats Kennedy (*Career Knockouts*, Follett) calls the "Killer B's": blockage, boredom, and burnout. What can individuals do to make their jobs less stressful, more interesting, and more rewarding? One answer is found in techniques collectively referred to as "job revitalization."

Job revitalization involves changing work patterns. It requires you to take risks. Again, you need to evaluate your present situation, outline your career and life goals, and develop and implement a plan of action. A job revitalization campaign may include meeting with your boss to develop an on-the-job career development plan. Set goals with your boss and discuss with him or her how you can best meet these goals on the job. If your boss is not familiar with career development and job revitalization alternatives, suggest some of these options:

- Rotating jobs
- Redesigning your job
- Creating a new position
- Promotions
- Enlarging your job duties and responsibilities

- Part-time work
- Sabbatical or leave of absence
- Flextime scheduling
- Job sharing
- Retraining or educational program
- Internship

Perhaps your supervisor can think of other options which would be acceptable to company policy as well as productive for both you and the organization.

More and more companies recognize the value of introducing career development programs, and they encourage job revitalization among their employees. They know it is more cost-effective to retain good employees by offering them new job options for career growth within the organization than to see them go. They are especially protective of their star employees, trying to find new ways to keep them happy and productive! Such programs and policies support the productivity and profit goals of organizations. They are good management practices. As organizations in the coming decade stress greater productivity, hiring right, and retaining star performers, they will place more emphasis on career development and job revitalization. For extensive treatments of these subjects within the context of today's workplace, see Dr. Beverly Kaye and Sharon Jordan-Evans, *Love 'Em or Lose 'Em: Getting Good People to Stay* (Barrett-Koehler); Dr. Jim Harris and Joan Brannick, *Finding and Keeping Great Employees* (AMACOM); and Robert E. Kelley, *How to Be a Star At Work* (Time Books).

From Ex-Offender to Excellent Employee

You should prepare yourself for today's new job realities. This means avoiding organizations, careers, and jobs that are declining as well as knowing what you do well and enjoy doing. It also means regularly acquiring the necessary training and retraining to remain marketable. And it means using the many support services and job search skills outlined in this book to find better jobs and manage your career. If you do this, you should be well prepared to find a good job and advance your career despite some temporary red flags in your background. Best of all, you'll transform yourself from an ex-offender to an indispensable employee who has a reputation for excellence in the workplace!

Index

The Authors

FOR MORE THAN TWO DECADES Ron and Caryl Krannich, Ph.Ds, have pursued a passion – assisting hundreds of thousands of individuals, from students, the unemployed, and ex-offenders to military personnel, international job seekers, and CEOs, in making critical job and career transitions. Focusing on key job search skills, career changes, and employment fields, their impressive body of work has helped shape career thinking and behavior both in the United States and abroad.

Ron and Caryl are two of America's leading career and travel writers who have authored more than 70 books. A former Peace Corps Volunteer and Fulbright Scholar, Ron received his Ph.D. in Political Science from Northern Illinois University. Caryl received her Ph.D. in Speech Communication from Penn State University. Together they operate Development Concepts Incorporated, a training, consulting, and publishing firm.

The Krannichs are both former university professors, high school teachers, management trainers, and consultants. Their career books focus on key job search skills, military and civilian career transitions, government and international careers, travel jobs, communication skills, and nonprofit organizations, and include such classics as *High Impact Resumes and Letters*, *Interview for Success*, *101 Secrets of Highly Effective Speakers*, and *Change Your Job, Change Your Life*. Their books represent one of today's most comprehensive collections of career writing. With nearly 3 million copies in print, their publications (see www.impactpublications.com and www.winningthejob.com) are widely available in bookstores, libraries, and career centers.

Ron and Caryl live a double life with travel being their best kept *"do what you love"* career secret. Authors of over 20 travel-shopping guidebooks on various destinations around the world, they continue to pursue their international and travel interests through their innovative *Treasures and Pleasures of . . . Best of the Best* travel-shopping series (www.ishoparoundtheworld.com and www.travel-smarter.com) as well as follow the career advice they give to others: *"Pursue a passion that enables you to do what you really love to do."*

As both career and travel experts, the Krannichs' work is frequently featured in major newspapers, magazines, and newsletters as well as on radio, television, and the Internet. Available for interviews, consultation, and presentations, they can be contacted through the publisher: info@impactpublications.com.

Career Resources

THE FOLLOWING CAREER RESOURCES are available directly from Impact Publications. Full descriptions of each title, as well as several downloadable catalogs and specialty flyers, can be found on two websites: www.impactpublications. com and www.exoffenderreentry.com. All titles in **bold** are by the authors, Ron and Caryl Krannich. Complete the following form or list the titles, include shipping (see formula at the end), enclose payment, and send your order to:

IMPACT PUBLICATIONS
9104 Manassas Drive, Suite N
Manassas Park, VA 20111-5211 USA
1-800-361-1055 (orders only)
Tel. 703-361-7300 or Fax 703-335-9486
E-mail address: query@impactpublications.com
Quick & easy online ordering: www.impactpublications.com

Orders from individuals must be prepaid by check, money order, or major credit card. We accept telephone, fax, and email orders.

Qty.	TITLES	Price	TOTAL

Ex-Offender Job Finding Guides

____	9 to 5 Beats Ten to Life	$15.00	____
____	**Best Resumes and Letters for Ex-Offender's**	$19.95	____
____	**Ex-Offender's Job Hunting Guide**	$17.95	____
____	**Ex-Offender's Quick Job Hunting Guide**	$9.95	____
____	Man, I Need a Job	$7.95	____
____	Putting the Bars Behind You (6 books)	$57.95	____

Addiction and Recovery

____	The Addiction Workbook	$18.95	____
____	Denial Is Not a River In Egypt	$12.95	____
____	How to Quit Drugs for Good!	$16.95	____
____	The Recovery Book	$15.95	____

Anger, Rage, and Conflict

____	Angry Men	$14.95	____
____	Angry Women	$15.95	____
____	Beyond Anger: A Guide for Men	$14.95	____
____	Cage Your Rage Workbook	$15.00	____

Testing and Assessment

____	Career Tests	$12.95	____
____	Discover the Best Jobs for You	$15.95	____

____	Do What You Are	$18.95 ____
____	Finding Your Perfect Work	$16.95 ____
____	I Could Do Anything If Only I Knew What It Was	$16.00 ____
____	I Don't Know What I Want, But I Know It's Not This	$14.00 ____
____	**I Want to Do Something Else, But I Don't Know What It Is**	$15.95 ____
____	What Should I Do With My Life?	$14.95 ____
____	What Type Am I?	$14.95 ____
____	What's Your Type of Career?	$17.95 ____

Attitudes, Motivation, and Goals

____	100 Ways to Motivate Yourself	$14.99 ____
____	Attitude Is Everything	$14.95 ____
____	Change Your Attitude	$15.99 ____
____	Changing for Good	$12.95 ____
____	Finding Your Own North Star	$14.95 ____
____	Goals	$14.95 ____
____	How to Find Your Mission in Life	$7.95 ____
____	The Purpose-Driven Life	$19.99 ____
____	Reinventing Yourself	$18.99 ____
____	Success Principles	$24.95 ____

Inspiration and Empowerment

____	7 Habits of Highly Effective People (2nd Edition)	$15.00 ____
____	12 Bad Habits That Hold Good People Back	$15.95 ____
____	17 Lies That Are Holding You Back and the Truth That Will Set You Free	$15.95 ____
____	101 Secrets of Highly Effective Speakers	$15.95 ____
____	Awaken the Giant Within	$15.00 ____
____	Change Your Thinking, Change Your Life	$24.95 ____
____	Change Your Attitude	$15.99 ____
____	Create Your Own Future	$16.95 ____
____	Do What You Love for the Rest of Your Life	$24.95 ____
____	Don't Throw Away Tomorrow	$21.95 ____
____	Dream It, Do It	$16.95 ____
____	Finding Your Own North Star	$14.95 ____
____	Forgiveness	$13.95 ____
____	Life Strategies	$13.95 ____
____	Maximum Achievement	$14.00 ____
____	Power of Positive Thinking	$12.95 ____
____	Power of Purpose	$20.00 ____
____	Self Matters	$14.00 ____
____	Your Best Life Now	$19.99 ____
____	Who Moved My Cheese?	$19.95 ____

Career Exploration and Job Strategies

____	25 Jobs That Have It All	$12.95 ____
____	50 Cutting Edge Jobs	$15.95 ____
____	95 Mistakes Job Seekers Make & How to Avoid Them	$13.95 ____
____	100 Great Jobs and How to Get Them	$17.95 ____
____	300 Best Jobs Without a Four-Year Degree	$16.95 ____
____	**America's Top 100 Jobs for People Re-Entering the Workforce**	$19.95 ____
____	**America's Top 100 Jobs for People Without a Four-Year Degree**	$19.95 ____
____	**Change Your Job, Change Your Life**	$21.95 ____
____	Cool Careers for Dummies	$19.99 ____
____	Five Secrets to Finding a Job	$12.95 ____
____	How to Get a Job and Keep It	$16.95 ____
____	How to Get Interviews From Classified Job Ads	$14.95 ____
____	How to Succeed Without a Career Path	$13.95 ____
____	**The Job Hunting Guide: Transitioning From College to Career**	$14.95 ____
____	**Job Hunting Tips for People With Hot and Not-So-Hot Backgrounds**	$17.95 ____
____	Job Search Handbook for People With Disabilities	$17.95 ____
____	Me, Myself, and I, Inc.	$17.95 ____
____	**No One Will Hire Me!**	$13.95 ____
____	Occupational Outlook Handbook	$16.90 ____
____	O*NET Dictionary of Occupational Titles	$39.95 ____
____	What Color Is Your Parachute?	$17.95 ____

Internet Job Search

____	America's Top Internet Job Sites	$19.95 ____
____	Guide to Internet Job Searching	$14.95 ____

Resumes and Letters

____	101 Great Tips for a Dynamite Resume	$13.95 ____
____	201 Dynamite Job Search Letters	$19.95 ____
____	Best KeyWords for Resumes, Cover Letters, & Interviews	$17.95 ____
____	Best Resumes for People Without a Four-Year Degree	$19.95 ____
____	Blue Collar Resumes	$11.99 ____
____	Cover Letters for Dummies	$16.99 ____
____	Cover Letters That Knock 'Em Dead	$12.95 ____
____	Expert Resumes for People Returning to Work	$16.95 ____
____	Haldane's Best Cover Letters for Professionals	$15.95 ____
____	Haldane's Best Resumes for Professionals	$15.95 ____
____	High Impact Resumes and Letters	$19.95 ____
____	Military Resumes and Cover Letters	$21.95 ____
____	Nail the Cover Letter	$17.95 ____
____	Nail the Resume	$17.95 ____
____	Resumes for Dummies	$16.99 ____
____	The Savvy Resume Writer	$12.95 ____

Networking

____	A Foot in the Door	$14.95 ____
____	How to Work a Room	$14.00 ____
____	Masters of Networking	$16.95 ____
____	Networking for Job Search and Career Success	$16.95 ____
____	The Savvy Networker	$13.95 ____

Dress, Image, and Etiquette

____	Dressing Smart for Men	$16.95 ____
____	Dressing Smart for Women	$16.95 ____
____	Power Etiquette	$14.95 ____

Interviews

____	101 Dynamite Questions to Ask At Your Job Interview	$13.95 ____
____	Haldane's Best Answers to Tough Interview Questions	$15.95 ____
____	Interview for Success	$15.95 ____
____	Job Interview Tips for People With Not-So-Hot Backgrounds	$14.95 ____
____	Job Interviews for Dummies	$16.99 ____
____	KeyWords to Nail Your Job Interview	$17.95 ____
____	Nail the Job Interview!	$13.95 ____
____	The Savvy Interviewer	$10.95 ____

Salary Negotiations

____	Dynamite Salary Negotiations	$15.95 ____
____	Get a Raise in 7 Days	$14.95 ____
____	Salary Negotiation Tips for Professionals	$16.95 ____

VIDEOS
Ex-Offenders in Transition

____	9 to 5 Beats Ten to Life	$95.00 ____
____	After Prison	$129.00 ____
____	Back in the World	$330.00 ____
____	Best 10¼ Tips for People With a Not-So-Hot Past	$125.00 ____
____	Cage Your Rage Video Program	$460.00 ____
____	Ex-Offender's Guide to Job Fair Success	$99.00 ____
____	Finding a Job When Your Past Is Not So Hot	$125.00 ____
____	Finding Employment: The Ex-Offender's Guide	$129.00 ____
____	Making It On the Outside	$119.00 ____
____	Out for Good	$95.00 ____

____	Post Prison Blues	$129.00 ____
____	Putting the Bars Behind You	$149.00 ____
____	Re-Entry: Life on the Outside	$125.00 ____
____	Tough Questions, Straight Answers	$95.00 ____

Interview, Networking, and Salary Videos

____	Build a Network for Work and Life	$99.00 ____
____	Common Mistakes People Make in Interviews	$79.95 ____
____	Make a First Good Impression	$129.00 ____
____	Mastering the Interview	$98.00 ____
____	Seizing the Job Interview	$79.00 ____
____	Why Should I Hire You?	$99.00 ____

Resumes, Applications, and Cover Letter Videos

____	The Complete Job Application	$99.00 ____
____	The Ideal Resume	$79.95 ____
____	Quick Resume Video	$149.00 ____
____	Resumes, Cover Letters, and Portfolios	$98.00 ____

Attitude, Motivation, and Empowerment Videos

____	Down But Not Out	$129.00 ____
____	Gumby Attitude	$69.00 ____
____	Looking for Work With Attitude Plus	$129.00 ____

SUBTOTAL _____

Virginia residents add 5% sales tax _____

POSTAGE/HANDLING ($5 for first
product and 8% of SUBTOTAL) _$5.00_

8% of SUBTOTAL -- _____

TOTAL ENCLOSED -- _____

SHIP TO:

NAME _____

ADDRESS: _____

_____

_____

PAYMENT METHOD:

❑ I enclose check/money order for $ _____ made payable to
IMPACT PUBLICATIONS.

❑ Please charge $ _____ to my credit card:

❑ Visa ❑ MasterCard ❑ American Express ❑ Discover

Card # _____ Expiration date: ____/____

Signature _____

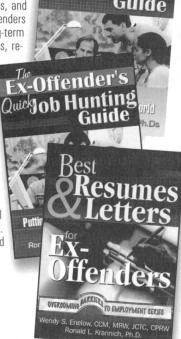